In Search of Answers

A Memoir

In Search of Answers

A Memoir

K. SARADAMONI

Tulika Books

Published in 2023 by

Tulika Books

44 (first floor), Shahpur Jat, New Delhi 110 049, India
www.tulikabooks.in

First edition (hardback) 2023

ISBN: 978-81-958394-0-7

Printed at Chaman Enterprises, New Delhi

Contents

For more information on the
life and work of Dr K. Saradamoni,
please scan this QR code:

Foreword

My mother started writing her autobiography some ten years ago. She used to rush to the computer and sit and type away in the middle of her other chores. She called it 'My Life', and even today, it is filed under that name on the computer. Strangely enough, she chose to write in English even though she wrote prolifically in Malayalam too.

The first draft was done by early 2015. I then started attending the Book Fair in Delhi to see if we could find a publisher. This was much more difficult than we ever imagined. For some, her life story was something that would be of relevance to only her family and immediate circle of friends, and not a wider audience. For others, she needed to fit into a 'women's studies' slot for easier marketing. So they wanted her to rewrite the entire book! I couldn't but help wonder if the same would have happened had she still been based in Delhi.

In the early hours of 11 January 2016, Amma suffered a heart attack while we were holidaying with Australian friends Ian and Josie in Kollam. Luckily, timely medical intervention saved her life. But life would never be the same again. She needed help in many areas and there were many constraints. With an excellent cardiologist, Dr Girija, and a very good home nurse, Girija Mani, we were able to continue keeping her in good health and cheer, and, most importantly, mentally alert. She continued to work on this book and other articles, and attended select seminars and protest rallies. We celebrated her 90th birthday with great gusto, hoping that we would be able to do the same five years later.

Then the pandemic struck. The world around us changed. No more doctor's visits, no more home nurses; life became tied to the four walls of home. We kept hearing of Covid deaths of near and dear ones. Collette, who is mentioned in this book, died of Covid in France in March 2021. Roscotte Krishna Pillai too passed away in October

2020 in Trivandrum of this deadly disease. The publishing industry shut down and Amma began to despair that this book would never get published. I then promised her that no matter what, I would see to it that it did.

In the early hours of 26 May 2021, Amma discarded her body and moved to another plane. After the first few months of grief and shock, I slowly started to try to put all her papers in order, and foremost in my mind was this book. Here, I would like to express my gratitude to Professor Narayani Gupta who introduced me to Indu Chandrasekhar of Tulika Books. When Indu agreed to publish the book, a weight lifted from my shoulders.

I had started looking for the photographs in our collection many years ago. In a life that was as well photo-documented as hers was, this was no easy task. If there are people whose images have not found their way into this book, it is only because of space constraints. I also found certain letters, articles, a diary entry and telex messages from the Nairobi conference in 1985. We decided to use them here in the appendix.

Amma was always amazed that a life which started in a very ordinary household like hers could actually develop in a way that took her around the world. For her, Economics was not a number-crunching and model-making exercise but a means to change the world for the most deprived populations who live in it. The last demonstration she took part in, sitting on our front porch one month before her death, was one for 'free vaccines for all'. After her passing, we found a handwritten article in Malayalam, 'Whither Kerala?' Till the end, she was an activist and an academic – a 'concerned social scientist' as she liked to term herself.

Trivandrum
July 2023

G. Asha

Acknowledgements

I cannot forget Devi, an editor with Orient BlackSwan, who encouraged me to write this book. I am sad that she is no longer with us. Another person who always encouraged me to complete the book is Uday Kumar, Professor of English in JNU. Meera, a young student of English, found the time to read the chapters and help edit them. I express my gratitude to her. I thank Baiju Chandran of Doordarshan, Trivandrum, for his encouragement during the writing of this book. I am grateful to Dr Girija, my cardiologist, who has been taking care of my health for over twenty-five years now. More than a doctor, she is like a daughter to me. My daughters show interest in my writing about my life and times. Asha, who lives with me, spent a lot of time going through the manuscript and encouraging me to finish it even when my health was not in good shape. Above all, I thank my parents, especially my father, who was a great lover of books. Last, but not the least, I owe much in my life to the love, friendship and support given to me by my husband and comrade, Gopi.

❖

Prologue

I cannot remember when the thought of writing the story of my life crossed my mind. Neither do I know whether I should call this my autobiography. 'My Life' is what I chose to call these chapters when I was composing them on my computer.

I have read many biographies and autobiographies just for the pleasure of it. For my research, too, I have read many of them. I enjoyed reading them even as a child because they took me to places I had not seen – across land, river or sea. Sometimes, the children in those books played the same games as we did. In some books, there was happiness and joy; in some, poverty, misery, deprivation and struggles. Even as an adult, I often found myself identifying with the life experiences narrated in biographies and autobiographies. When I read about someone who lost a parent at a young age, I felt a closeness to that character.

Though I cannot see how or when this idea got into my head, at some point, I began to think that everybody had a story to tell. My children and some young friends began telling me that I should tell the world mine. I finally decided to start writing the story of my life.

I believe that we should have a sense of history. In a sense, an autobiography is history. It has in it traces of geography as well. Each new place, the sights they offer, the people we meet and the moments we spend with them do not leave us that easily or completely. They influence our thoughts and actions thereafter, even if unconsciously. An autobiography is also not an isolated write-up of one person's life. Since an individual is an essential ingredient of society, one's life cannot be narrated leaving out the happenings around. This is true of all people, even those who may not think about life that way. Even if the author wishes to keep the autobiography purely personal, a person's life is so context-dependent that this will not be possible.

Once I began writing the first lines, places, people and events flowed into my mind from all sides. Mine has been a long life. From a rather happy childhood in Kollam, a small town in the princely state of Travancore, it traversed through many places and countries. I remember with affection all those who have gone before me and who are still here with me. I thank all those who have welcomed me in their midst and allowed me to be what I am.

I have often, especially in recent times, thought about life in general. I have felt that it is a journey. Poets like Rabindranath Tagore and Harindranath Chattopadhyay have sung about vagabonds seeking or searching for something or somebody. Are we all, not vagabonds? We do not know where we come from. We do not know where we go to. We don't bring anything. Neither do we take anything.

My journey continues. Read on…

❖

CHAPTER ONE

Early Childhood

I had to take a trip down memory lane to dig out some interesting events in my childhood.

After a rather eventful life spent in various locations, it was not easy to make this journey which made me go back several decades. I was born in Kollam, an old port town in southern Kerala, and my childhood was mostly spent there. Today, when I try to write this book which is the story of my life, childhood seems ancient. My schooling was entirely in Kollam and higher education, Intermediate and BA (Honours), in Trivandrum. I went to Madras for an MPhil degree and France for my PhD A large chunk of my adult life was spent in Delhi. Hence, this trip back to that period called childhood was like peering into a kaleidoscope of events, people, languages, cultures, flora and fauna. In a sense, the attempt was audacious.

I was not unlucky. The very first memory I could recall was of a time when children found joy in the beauty of nature. It would be sometime in the beginning of June, as rains in those days came meticulously on the day of the reopening of schools. My friend Lily and I, roaming in the school compound, were spotted by the teacher. We were enjoying the rain, but the authorities did not think so. We were called and made to stand outside the headmistress's room. I am certain that the two of us could not have been the only girls wandering about in the compound. My immediate elder sister who was in the final year of school was called to look at us as if we had committed a 'crime'. We were let off with a warning. I do not remember that incident becoming an issue at home. The rain was fascinating. Most adults of my generation would have memories of rain.

Our school, St Joseph's Convent, right in the heart of Kollam, was one of the oldest girls' schools in town. The eldest of my two sisters, who was eight years older than me, had by that time finished schooling and was studying at the Women's College, Trivandrum. The headmistress found her the best of us three – she was gentle, quiet and never disobedient. My other sister, five years older than me, was the brightest. We also had a brother, nearly three years younger than me. He went to a primary school near our home.

On our school compound stood both the Malayalam and English schools, without any partition. When the episode with the rain happened, I was in the 'preparatory' class in the English school. In the Malayalam school, the classes were from one to nine, and all subjects were taught in Malayalam. In the English school, Malayalam was only taught as a language, and other subjects were taught in the medium of English. After the preparatory, the English school had six classes, which were called forms. At the end of the sixth form, we had the final examinations. Those who completed the eighth class in the Malayalam school could become needlework, art or music teachers. They could also choose to join the third form of the English school. Those who stayed with the Malayalam school and completed the ninth class could get government jobs or become teachers after teachers' training.

Education has undergone immense changes over the decades. There was a time children gathered around the village elder who taught them to repeat the alphabet, poems and songs under a tree or in a shed near his house. It was a different mode of learning, where reading and writing did not have the primacy they have today. It cannot be compared to the present-day nursery schools. Slates and notebooks became part of the learning process only later. Today's computer-savvy children may not even be able to imagine those days. Now, English-medium schools seem to be increasingly preferred by parents.

A few friendships from early childhood remain etched in my memory even today. Besides Lily Stephen, I had a few other close friends. I found myself among friends whom a bustling town like Kollam brought together. One was Jameela, whose full name was Jameelunissa Begum. She and her sister, Mehrunnisa, belonged to a family that spoke Hindustani at home. Our families had known each other for two generations as our grandmothers were neighbours and childhood friends. Another close friend at that time was Anna Jyoti. Her father was an employee of Harrison's & Crosfield, a British company at Kollam. They were from Nagercoil, a place in the southern part of the then Travancore State and presently a part of Tamil Nadu.

Among these friends, Lily and I lived close to each other, and we used to visit each other during the holidays. By then more and more houses in our town were changing to tiled roofs. Lily's family had founded a flourishing business in tiles, and the Thomas Stephen Tiles were in great demand.

After school, life took the four of us along different paths. After having lost touch for years, it was a pleasant surprise when I came to re-establish contact with Lily and Jameela. But I never again heard from or about Anna Jyoti. Nevertheless, she and her antics remain cherished memories. Once, when the teacher asked how mosquitoes could be eliminated, Anna said that they should be caught one by one and killed by hand. For a long time, it was a joke among us.

Our school, St Joseph's Convent, still stands in the heart of Kollam. Times have changed the school. Today, it is a multistoreyed building that offers up to the twelfth class. To a young learner like me decades back, it was an abode of friendships, wonder and a few mysteries. There was a tile-roofed shed in the Malayalam school where we used to assemble before classes began. The sand in front of the shed contained tiny beads of all colours, and collecting those was one of our joyful activities. How so many beads came to be there was a matter of wonder to me. Later, I have heard talks and read books which refer to the presence of beads at excavation sites. However, whether those beads which coloured my childhood were the vestiges of a bygone era when Kollam was a thriving port-city remains an elusive mystery.

A moment of joy from childhood was the day I got a prize, in class two or three. It was for an exercise that used to be quite common those days. The teacher would read out words or sentences, and we were to write what was read out. Young learners like us would try to listen carefully to capture the word correctly. It was an activity that helped us to learn the nuances of a language like Malayalam with a large number of letters, including simple, compound and complex ones. There were several eliminations, and at last, I won the first prize. It was a beautiful bead necklace in a pretty wooden box, too good to make a child happy. Most probably, the nuns would have made both the necklace and the box.

I am not sure whether tests like the above are there now. Those exercises sharpened our listening and writing skills. When I find that more and more of today's children cannot pronounce Malayalam words clearly, it makes me wonder whether 'change', something we hear in various contexts, has actually improved our education system.

A year before I left primary school, my father was transferred to a place called Varkala. Currently an important tourist centre, the place at that time was known as Dakshina Kasi (Southern Kasi), and was famous for the local Janardhana Swamy temple. The topography of the place was fascinating. The temple stood on the top of a cliff very near the sea. During the rainy season, waves would swallow the beach and lash at the rock. That part of the sea is considered sacred by the Hindus. A big crowd assembles there to perform the customary offerings to one's ancestors on auspicious days.

My brother and I were taken along by our parents, leaving our elder sister with my mother's family. The shift from a lively town like Kollam to a place like Varkala brought with it a whole new array of experiences. The two were as unlike as they could be. Varkala was more rural, and the people there simple and poor. At that time, however, such thoughts never came to my mind. I joined the government school at Varkala. When I try to recollect the faces of friends, only one girl comes to my mind, whose name I have forgotten. She was tiny and always wore only a *thorthu* except when coming to class. Many girls were like that. Some of them wore a simple frock which may also be called a petticoat. Unlike today, shops displaying dress material or readymade garments had not come into being.

Ours was a big house in a large compound where there were many trees, especially coconut trees. The old-fashioned gate was like a sit-out where there was space for us to sit and play or watch the people going along the road. It was from there that I spotted many saffron-clad men going to the temple with bowls to collect alms. We called them *gosayi*s. Oil lamps were built into the gate, and they were lit daily in the evening to help people who walk along the road at night. Those were days when electricity had not arrived. Most of the time, my friend would come over to our house. Once, the two of us kept awake to observe Sivaratri.

A vague childhood memory today reminds me of the pomp of caste hierarchy that permeated society. The memory is of watching from a distance the Azhvanchery Thamprakkal, one of the topmost Nambutiri Brahmins, being carried in a palanquin from his *illam* in Malabar to Trivandrum, for his participation in the festival of

Murajapam at the Sree Padmanabhaswamy temple. Those were days when untouchability was severely observed. Those who carried the palanquin would shout 'hoi, hoi' for the onlookers to keep their distance.

Another memory about our stay in Varkala was a tea party arranged for my sister's boisterous and fun-loving friends and teachers from Trivandrum, when they came to spend a day with us. My mother was always very generous with food. They originally planned to come to our house, but as they overstayed at the temple and the beach, the food finally had to be taken to the railway station. Despite the hurry the party was a success, and after several years, I met friends of my sister who still talked about the size and taste of the *laddu*s.

My life's long journey thus began with an innocent childhood.

❖

CHAPTER TWO

Growing Up in Kollam

Though I have spent the bulk of my life in Delhi and Trivandrum, in my heart, I always think that I am from Kollam. It was my mother's hometown and the place where I was born. Though we did not go there often, this beautiful coastal town made me familiar with the beach right from a young age. Currently a city, Kollam was only a town in my childhood. My father came from Changanassery, a place further northeast and nearer to the Western Ghats. In those days, it was connected mainly by boat to the port-town of Alleppey, and was a trading centre for commodities collected from the surrounding areas. The place has changed with the times. Today, it has many schools and even colleges, unlike in my father's time. In my childhood, both Kollam and Changanassery belonged to the princely state of Travancore, ruled by a Maharaja.

My mother's name was Kunjulakshmi. Perhaps she was named Lakshmi and *kunju*, which means 'baby' or 'small', was added to give it a loving touch. Officially, she was K. Kunjulakshmi Amma. My father's name was P. Madhavan Pillai. I have never heard of a pet name by which he was called.

My mother's *taravad* or matrilineal joint family was in the heart of Kollam town. A sizeable section of communities and people following this system of inheritance lived in the state. The major feature of the practice was that the family name and property were passed down from generation to generation through women. Another aspect was that the property remained undivided, allowing large numbers to live together.

Though a small number of communities in certain other parts of the country too followed this system, the large majority in India followed the system of patrimony, by which the woman was 'given away' at marriage. With that, all her ties to the natal home were cut.

Amma's *taravad* had a name: Attupuram. She was very proud of her *taravad*. By the time I was growing up, it had disintegrated. Though I knew where it was and have gone there a few times, I never lived there. I had classmates who came from near our *taravad*. One family story goes that we were people from Malabar who escaped to the south when the Mysore rulers, Hyder Ali and his son Tipu Sultan, attempted to capture and control the southern regions including Travancore. This was during the late eighteenth century. The custodians of the temple which we consider as our *kuladaivam* or family deity confirm this idea. I talked to anthropologists to understand the concept of family deity and how disparate sets of families were linked to one temple, but I never got a satisfactory answer.

Amma's father, Ayyappan Pillai, was from a family a few kilometres to the east of Attupuram. They owned vast areas of land and also a temple. The families of Amma's father and mother must have been linked by marital relations over generations. The family story is that my grandmother Kochupillai was married at the age of eleven or twelve.

She gave birth to twelve children, all delivered at home. The first, a girl, was born when she was just thirteen. Two children died when they were babies. Amma was the fifth child. My grandmother's youngest child died a few years ago. I haven't heard much of my great-grandmother. However, the story goes that she had two daughters by two husbands and then declared that she did not want any more husbands or children. There was enough space in the matrilineal *taravad* of that era for a woman to be able to make such a decision, and many of them displayed courage and strength of character to do so.

My Amma was educated till the eighth class. She always talked about two uncles of hers with love and pride. She had stayed with one of them while studying in the government school for girls. Weekend returns to her home were often an unhappy affair for her as her uncle, an expert in Carnatic music, had arranged music lessons for her. I still have with me a book of music which belonged to that uncle, a souvenir of my mother's younger days. Surprisingly, I never knew their names or their occupation. The uncle about whom Amma often talked was referred to as Pandala Ammavan. Pandala must have been a short form of *pandakasala*, could mean a warehouse or godown. Perhaps he worked in one of these. The other uncle was called Kayamkulathammavan, which could mean that he was either

Grandmother Kochupillai, known as Mattemma.
(Photographer unknown)

living or working in a place called Kayamkulam, slightly to the north of Kollam. At our grandmother's house, there was a wooden board that was used to count coins in those days. It had small carved hollows into which coins could be spread at once so that their count could be noted without counting them individually. It could be that either one or both uncles had something to do with accounting or finance.

Amma's was not a *taravad* with a large number of members. There were *taravads* where several generations lived under one roof and ate from the same kitchen. Things had begun to change in our parts even before I was born. Maybe because of this, my grandmother was brought, even as a child bride, to live in her husband's place. Even before my sisters were born, my grandmother was living in a house with her husband and children near his *taravad*.

The house where we lived as children was not far from the one in which my grandmother and her family lived. Grandmother's house earlier had a thatched roof, but it was tiled by the time we grew up. Amma often told us that it was tiled after the thatched roof was brought down by a fire. The railway track to Madras ran very near to the edge of the house's compound, and the train was stopped upon seeing the fire. For a long time after I started travelling by train along that route, I used to wait to see the house and imagine the fire. I also used to wait for the paddy lands and shallow water bodies with thorny bushes growing in them. They were a landmark for me to locate the house.

My father's ancestral home is said to have been in Neyyattinkara. I have heard stories about Nair *taravad*s where a woman is said to have moved from her ancestral home and set up a family in a different place. Acchan's family, called Pothuvadathu, located in Vazhappally Panchayat in Changanassery, was far away from Neyyattinkara. My paternal grandmother died soon after giving birth to my father and his younger brother. Their aunts brought up the motherless children. Later in life, I met the aunts and their families who regarded my father with great love and respect. I must add that I got a share of that love, all because I was his daughter.

In those early *taravad*s, kinship had meanings and dimensions which are quite difficult to imagine today. It was a time when terms like uncle, aunt or cousin were not known or used. The notion of a slight difference between the children of two sisters and brothers, or a sister and a brother, could not be thought of. Even now, there is no Malayalam word that would readily correspond to the English words cousin, uncle or aunt. Instead, there are specific kinship terms denoting each relationship. For instance, my mother's elder sister was Peramma and younger sister was Kochamma to us. They were also called Valiamma and Cheriyamma or Chitta. Mother's brother was Ammavan to many. These kinship terms, with their numerous regional variations, suggested a way of life that was more nuanced and affectionate in its conception of family bonding. But things have changed. In tune with our changing concept of family life, terms like cousin, uncle, aunt or auntie have come to be widely used.

How did my father and mother come together? My father, a

brilliant student, had graduated in chemistry from Trivandrum College, which perhaps was a version of the present University College, then affiliated to Madras University. His teachers, many of them Englishmen, thought that he would go to England for higher studies. Unfortunately, he became a victim of a severe heart ailment at a young age, which prevented him from pursuing higher education. He tried to study law, but that also had to be given up. He joined government service. In those days, a BA degree was not common. While working in the district court in Kollam, he came to know of my mother, a colleague's daughter, from another friend. My mother was fifteen years of age and father was thirty. The marriage took place at night, as was the custom in those days. My mother wore a full-sleeved velvet blouse, a skirt and a cloth to cover the upper part of the body.

Family photo taken over a hundred years ago. (*Sitting, left to right*) Father with baby Devamma (Vally) on his lap, mother. (*Standing, left to right*) Mother's younger brother Kuttammavan, mother's sister Bai Kochamma. (Photographer unknown)

After marriage, my parents first lived in an outhouse at Attupuram and later shifted to a house near the Thirumullavaram beach. My paternal grandfather was with them while they were living in that house. I have heard from Amma that the names of my paternal grandparents were Rama Panickar and Ummini Amma respectively. A male help, Pachu Panikkar, was with Acchan for long. This meant that Amma did not have many chores to be burdened with. My parents had their first child after six years of marriage. In these six years, Amma learned to do housekeeping and to cook what Acchan was to be given, considering his health. Later in life, Amma would recount these days and narrate hilarious stories about her experiments in cooking.

All of us were born in Amma's home under her mother's care. Delivery in hospitals was not known in those days. Amma always said that I was born in the twelfth month of pregnancy and that too at mid-noon. For my birth, Acchan insisted and arranged for a trained midwife to come home and help. Acchan's extensive reading had helped him to develop his own views on many matters, including healthcare. Recently, while sorting out books and papers, I spotted and have saved like a treasure, a 1929 edition of *The Nursery Years* by Susan Isaacs, published by the well-known British publishing house George Routledge & Sons, sized 4 x 6.5 inches. This little volume, with Acchan's name written inside, stands out on my bookshelf as a window to the shifting notions of healthcare in Britain. The first chapter reads:

> Not so very long ago it was generally taken for granted that parents had by nature or tradition most of the knowledge needed to enable them to bring up their children well. The baby then wore swaddling clothes so that he should not kick, and a tight belt so that he could not breathe. He was kept carefully away from 'droughts' and fresh air, and heavily clothed so that he should not catch cold. He was fed when he cried, and given soothing syrup or a none-too-clean comforter when he could not be fed.
>
> Now we leave the infant free to kick and breathe; we not only put him to sleep with wide-open window or out in the garden, but we let him lie and roll naked in the very sun and air from which we used to shelter him so carefully. (p. 1)

I could not refrain from thinking of how, in those times, mothers and grandmothers in Kerala used to smear babies with oil and leave

Collection of father's books. (Photo by G. Asha)

them naked usually, in a spathe of the areca palm. They were left in the open and allowed to enjoy the sky, the sun and the breeze.

The book offers interesting insights to a curious reader. In the end, the author writes: 'It is a wise general rule to leave the children to use their playthings in their own way – even if this does not happen to be the way we might think the best. For play has the greatest value for the young child when it is really free, and his own' (p. 75).

The author's continuous reference to the baby as 'he' amused me. This book has a twin volume which deals with nursery days and health. Whether or not these books on parenting influenced the way we were brought up, we played a lot – with toys and without.

While writing this, I am reminded of what Alice Stewart – a medical doctor, researcher and lifelong campaigner against radiation, mainly from the use of X-rays on the baby in the womb and from nuclear installations – wrote about her parents. Both of them were medical doctors who preferred to work among the poor and deprived. They educated people along with 'treating' them. They particularly educated the mothers about childcare, personal hygiene, and the need for keeping the surroundings and the drinking water clean. In fact, they are said to have conducted 'bedside classes'.

Acchan was not just a great reader but also a traveller. In one of his many travels, he met Saradamoni Devi, the wife of Sri Ramakrishna, at her home in Bengal. I have been named after her. The little that I came to know about his travels and wanderings made me curious. An interesting story is how he brought a sadhu along when he returned from one of his travels to Agasthyakoodam in southern Sahyadri. This was after Acchan's marriage, and the sadhu lived with Amma's family for some time. My uncles took him out for morning ablutions and baths. He ate what was given. He never talked. It is said that my uncle one day asked himself how long the sadhu could be looked after and he disappeared!

Our eldest sister, whom we called Vally (short for *valia chechi* or elder sister) was named Devamma. My immediate elder sister, whom my brother and I called Chechi, was named Rajamma. I came to know that both were given the names of two of Acchan's aunts, but they were never used. My brother was named Ramachandran, and we affectionately called him Manikuttan. The story is that it was I who called him by that pet name when he was a baby. Officially, he was M.R.C. Nayar or just MRC among friends.

In the early twentieth century, there was no treatment for heart ailments. However, Acchan tried to know as much as he could from books. He read extensively on health, physical and mental well-being, various systems of treatment and spirituality, among other things. Some of the early books which he collected were *Health and Human Spirit: A Biological Study* published in 1923 and *Greek Biology and Greek Medicine* published in 1933. From a young age, we were familiar with nature cure, especially the German variety of Louis Kuhne. Acchan's instructions had even helped to cure a man from a nearby place, of mental ailment. I remember this man, Mayyanad John, coming to see Acchan after he was cured, to present his 'doctor' with a book he had written on Francis Assisi. Acchan was probably so interested in naturopathy that he wanted to practise it after retirement. He seems to have corresponded with the British Naturopathic College, hoping to undertake a diploma course there. The college had courses for students abroad who were not expected to go to England. I still have with me the positive reply from the college, a letter dated 10 November 1930 with the prospectus of the college enclosed.

Some elementary knowledge about health, in general, was imbibed by us quite early. As a young girl, I had a sweet tooth. A favourite snack in our home was a healthy Kerala preparation called *kinnanappam* – made by mixing and steaming rice powder, coconut, jaggery and banana. It did not contain oil or sugar and was not fried. However, one of my teeth had to be 'filled' by an Anglo-Indian dentist near our *taravad* as it developed a cavity, and I remember Acchan telling me that it was because I ate too many sweets.

Acchan used to buy books in Malayalam and English. In every one of them he wrote his name in full, and his writing never changed. He also bought books for Amma. A 1902 copy of a cookery book in Malayalam, titled *Pachaka Chintamoni*, written by an assistant school inspector and published by his wife, has survived the ravages of time and is with me even today. It includes, besides Kerala dishes, some recipes from states like Tamil Nadu, Maharashtra and so on. I occasionally use the book, though the paper is getting older. Each time, I am impressed by the care with which the author has arranged everything.

A book like that sheds light on the kind of book culture that must have flourished in our region. It was published by the Manomohanam Press, Thangassery – a press that I was not aware of. Thangassery was known to us as an Anglo-Indian enclave. Some of our teachers and friends were from there, and many men from the area worked for the railways. History says that the Portuguese and the Dutch had made this coastal area into a port for trading purposes. They also constructed churches before the place finally came into the hands of the British. I have not seen any other book published by that press.

I was more familiar with the publications of S.T. Reddiar Press in Kollam, one of the oldest in the state. Plenty of popular books came out from there. They included books by K. Narayana Kuruckal who used his pen to expose the deeds of the hangers-on around the palace. I read them early in life without understanding the context, but enjoyed them. At that time, translations from Bengali were available, especially of authors like Bankim Chandra. We also grew up reading children's literature written in Malayalam. One of my favourites among these was *Virutan Sanku*, a hilarious book, with the main character playing tricks on everyone. I have read it many times. Children's books from Japan – *Japan* and the *Land of the Rising Sun* – told me about Japanese children, their hobbies like kite flying, making dolls and playing with them, and the different Japanese festivals. They influenced me a lot in my childhood.

There were plenty of other English books as well in Acchan's collection. Some of them he won as prizes, many he bought, and some were gifted by friends. Broadly, his books included literature, both poetry and prose, philosophy, religious works on Sikhism and Buddhism, the Upanishads and many more. In those days, short versions of books by important authors in English used to be textbooks in high school. English schoolgirls' stories were also available in bookstalls and sometimes in the school library. Looking back, these books and the lives they narrated had nothing in common with the lives we led, but this did not prevent us from finding them interesting or enjoying them. One of the books in Acchan's collection which I found interesting and read several times was *Character* by Samuel Smiles. I did not take much to poetry, though we had Tennyson, Wordsworth, Byron, Keats and many others. However, I became familiar with some poetry from a series titled 'Rapid Reading', which contained summaries and extracts from the classics. Among them was Byron, whose fascinating first lines in the work were, 'Roll on, thou deep and dark blue Ocean, – roll', the verses I used to chant for a long time. 'Abou Ben Adhem' by Leigh Hunt was another poem which captured my mind. The essence of that poem was that god loves those who love and care for their fellow beings.

Acchan tried to teach Amma to read and write English, and bought books for that. Amma's strict resistance defeated him in his attempt. However, Amma knew how to pick from the shelf and bring to him any English book he wanted.

From the court, Acchan moved to the Registration Department. He became a sub-registrar, a high enough post in those days. This meant that my parents had to move out of Kollam. The names of a few of the places where they lived have been preserved in the family stories. Their travel to Munchirai, presently in Tamil Nadu, is a journey that Amma often recounted. She used to describe vividly the travel by private boat from Kollam to Trivandrum, the boatmen's songs, and their cooking their own dinner when they halted for the night at compounds on the banks of the lake or the canal. The rest of the journey was by bullock cart. I have tried to visualize this journey from sandy Kollam to a place whose soil and topography differed, a place where quietness and nature's beauty were in abundance. They also stayed for a while in Meenachil in northern Travancore, living near a river by the same name, where Amma struck up a companionship with Acchan's youngest aunt. Some other places Acchan worked were Haripad, Sasthamkotta and Kundara. Looking back, their journeys look like eventful ones to make in those times. They nearly lost their savings when a local bank in Haripad became bankrupt, but they moved on, refusing to accept the gold which was offered by the bank. The family never developed a great love for gold. A doctor at Haripad told Acchan that he had only six more months to live, a warning which he proved wrong by living for some more years. They must have had a serene life at Sasthamkotta, famous for its lake untouched by salt water. Recent news informs us that things have changed there.

During my school years we lived at Devi Vilasam, not very far from where Amma's family lived. That place was called Pattathanam. Today, one can reach most places in Kerala by bus, car or train. It was not so at that time. People used to walk long distances. Some people had bullock carts. We had a rickshaw, in which we two sisters used to go to school and Acchan to his office. I have a vague memory of us three sisters going to school in a bullock-drawn cart as well. We did not use it after Vally went to college.

Our house stood somewhat in the centre of a big compound. The roof and the floor of the house were tiled with terracotta. There was a wooden lattice for the front veranda which had two platforms at either end where one could sleep comfortably. I still remember that space. I used to spend long hours there sleeping, reading, looking out at the trees and enjoying the breeze. We never had a fan in the house. Though coconut trees were plenty, there were several varieties of mango, cashew, jack and other trees in the compound. On the eastern side of our house, where the distance to the compound wall was short, there were a few houses. They were our nearest neighbours.

As far as I can remember, ours was a peaceful family. As a child I was cheerful but also very shy – something that those who have known me later in life might find difficult to believe. Acchan's uncles and many younger brothers used to visit regularly, staying with us for short or slightly long durations. Amma welcomed them with great hospitality. In fact, 'Kollathe Chettathi' (elder sister-in-law from Kollam) was very popular throughout her life.

Amma used to wear only white clothes – a dhoti (*mundu*), a kind of upper garment called *raukka* and an upper cloth was her attire. The sari had not become common, and she never wore one. Acchan used to buy clothes in bulk. Though Amma never found it difficult, I was not happy with the many frocks I had, all made from the same material. I remember Amma making her own blouse while my frocks were stitched by a tailor. Acchan bought readymade khadi-silk blouses for my sisters. I was unhappy, and when he bought a dress with frills for me in Varkala, I did not want to wear it as most of my classmates did not wear even ordinary frocks.

It was while we were there that Acchan introduced us to the vegetable tomato, which was not common in those days. The brightly coloured beautiful thing attracted me, but I felt it to be tasteless. It was years later that I took to tomatoes. An interesting episode is how Acchan got the fear of lightning out of me. One night, when I was hiding out of fear from the thunder and lightning that was lashing outside, he took me to one of the verandas and asked me to look at the sky through the leaves. And that did the magic. The lightning appeared beautiful. We were also taught to chant the ten names of Arjuna – Arjunan, Phalgunan, Parthan, Vijayan, Kiridi, Swetavahan, Bibhatsan, Jishnu, Savyasachi and Dhananjayan – to make us fearless.

Footwear was not considered essential in those days. It nevertheless made its way into my life. There was a family of cobblers near our house. In fact, that area was named Chemman Mukku or cobblers' corner. A pair of *chappal*s was ordered for me by Amma. I would wear them to school but then leave them in the rickshaw. Amma gave them to a cousin of mine. It was nearly after two decades that I wore chappals again, this time also at Amma's insistence. She thought my daily walk to the University College from the Women's Hostel in Trivandrum on tarred roads in the sun would affect me. It was gradually that people took to footwear. I had a friend who started wearing *chappal*s only when she went to Calcutta after her post-graduation.

In our childhood, Acchan often used to bring new things to amuse us. I remember playing with a scooter-type toy which moved around once the screw was wound. Instantly the man sitting on it would beat with both hands the drum that was fixed in front of him. My brother was always curious to see the insides of the toys. He did not think that he was destroying them. I remember him throwing a toy into the well. Perhaps he wanted to see what would happen when it touched the water.

My mind still cherishes the games and amusements that kept us engaged as children. My brother and I played building houses and games like robber-and-police and hide-and-seek. Our compound, which was bound on two sides by a fence of plants and thorny bushes, was perfect for us as we could cut branches to build our playhouse. We also played games in the open sandy yard in front. For a game whose name I cannot remember, we drew either three overlapping circles or eight squares like a cross in the sand. Standing on one foot, we would strike a dry mango seed or a small stone, and we were not to touch the line. Finding this game mentioned in a beautiful children's book by Mulk Raj Anand was like reliving my childhood.

On our west, there was a similarly huge compound with a small house that was rented out. In one corner of that compound, there used to be a family which lived by pressing oil from coconut, gingelly and so on. Getting oil from the coconut was an interesting task. We would first break open the coconut into two halves after removing the husk, and spread them out on special mats so that the kernel got direct sunshine. In a couple of days, the dried *copra* would be cut into thin pieces and left once again in the sun, to remove what was left of the moisture. This would then be taken to the press, which worked either on the labour of bulls or on manpower. As we used only homemade coconut oil for cooking, this happened once or twice a year. As kids, we enjoyed the small tasks that we were assigned, such as driving away crows from stealing *copra* chips, collecting the dried chips in the evening, and watching the press at work. Gingelly oil had a simpler preparation. We had gingelly that was either grown in our compound or bought. Amma had aides who took it to the press and brought back the oil and cakes. Most probably, the man at the press was paid with a share of the oil and cakes, perhaps some money too.

Wooden presses like these, which were once a familiar sight in Kerala, are no more to be seen. With them have disappeared the essential jobs associated with them and the people who did those. Today's electricity-driven press does not have the ambience of the old wooden mill, the slow pace in which it went round and round. We were taught early in life to take a regular oil bath. Gingelly oil was necessary for the daily baths, lighting lamps and making *dosa*s. There was a time when snacks like chips made of banana or jackfruit, which we buy packaged in plastic bags today, were made at home – that too in huge quantities.

Amma was an expert in making various kinds of pickles. Her hot full-lime pickle was famous. A friend of my brother wanted no other dish if he got rice, ghee and one or two of these limes. We had huge jars where tender mangoes were pickled and used for more than a year. Amma used to make and store various types of *vattal*, from vegetables, sago and grains like rice. They could be preserved for months and were fried and eaten later along with other dishes or as a snack. Usually, they were made during summer and kept for the rainy season.

To prepare the *vattal*, grain and sago were turned into a pulp with a bit of salt and spices, poured on to a cotton cloth spread on the mat, and dried in the sun in different shapes and sizes, usually in the big yard in front of the house where there was good sunlight. My brother and I helped to spread the cloth or carefully roll it back without sand or dust. This way of life where snacks like these were either homemade or sold by sellers who went from home to home would be unimaginable for today's children.

Our childhood, thus, was mostly spent at home. Acchan was a man who had many friends and acquaintances from various walks of life and a broad range of interests, but we did not have a very active social life. Still, we occasionally went out. I can vaguely remember Acchan taking us to see Gandhiji when he came to Kollam. He also took us to see the Ashtamudi Lake being ornamentally lit up to commemorate the visit of some British official. Amma stayed at home during these outings.

Amma remained in charge of everything within the house. She had men and women to help and support her in various tasks. One such person was Kunji Chechi, a relative who attended to all demands. Following Amma, we also called her Kunji Chechi.

I cannot remember Amma and Acchan quarrelling or shouting at each other, though there were occasions when they differed. One such instance was over Amma's dealings with the domestic helps. Nevertheless, they did not exchange words over the matter.

Yet another instance was when Acchan started growing a beard. Amma accused him of being influenced by Tagore, pointing to a beautiful photograph of the great man we had at home. Acchan had met Tagore once at the Kollam guest house. I think Amma at that time did not know who Tagore was. Another serious dispute arose when Acchan one day asked the scavenger who came to our house to pull the rickshaw. To Amma, who grew up accepting caste distances, a scavenger was an 'unclean' man besides being untouchable. However, these did not in any way infringe on their relationship, and till her death, Amma thought of Acchan with a sort of adoration or reverence. All I can think is that Acchan always remembered Amma's age and background.

I cannot remember Acchan getting angry or laughing aloud. One day, however, I saw him furious at someone who came to see him. He shouted at him to get out of the house. Later, I came to know that he was running a petty journal, and making money by blackmailing people was his job. Acchan was not a man to be bullied.

This happy childhood suddenly turned upside down. One of those days, suddenly someone came to school to take me and Chechi home. My uncle went to Trivandrum and brought back Vally. My brother was already home as he was slightly unwell. Acchan's youngest uncle was also at our place with his son.

Acchan used to go to office after taking an early lunch. His official dress was dhoti, shirt, coat and a turban which was kept in a wooden box. Office keys, seal and essential papers were kept in another briefcase-like wooden box, which he carried daily to the office. That day, however, while getting the lunch ready, Amma looked through a window and saw Acchan's head falling forward. He was all set to go to the office in an hour, but that was not to happen. He died.

Our Amma, at the age of thirty-nine, lost her husband. She saw his passing away. She did not talk, did not cry.

Relatives and friends came. The customary cutting of mango trees took place. Acchan was cremated at a chosen place in the southern part of our compound. Today, as I write this, I have pain within me and feel the loss in a way I did not realize at that time.

Later, Amma told us that Acchan had asked her how she would manage if he were not there. At that time she did not respond. Perhaps she did not understand the seriousness of the question. Nevertheless, I think Acchan was aware of impending death, which he did not bluntly share with her.

Devi Vilasam without Acchan continued to be our home. Amma brought us up against all odds. Her younger brother Kuttammavan, who had earlier joined us after a spell of typhoid-wrecked tragedy in their home, later became her unquestioning support.

Amma became our guardian.

❖

CHAPTER THREE

A Home Without Father

I cannot remember when Amma got off her bed after Acchan died, but she did, and lived for more than fifty years without him. Neither do I remember her crying or feeling lost or even talking about the loss. For many years – more than four decades – she used to arrange the customary rituals for the dead on Acchan's death anniversary. On that day, she fed a large number of poor people from the neighbourhood. I don't think poor homes where that could be arranged were there at that time. The entire cooking was done at home, under Amma's careful supervision. Of course, Kunji Chechi was there all through.

When Acchan was alive, Amma was mainly a homemaker. In those years, she had become an excellent cook. She looked after Acchan's and our health like a trained nurse. True, she always had people to help, but the supervision was hers. The courtyards were always neat and clean. It was the same inside the house – everything including the bronze lamps that were lit every evening in the prayer room and the cooking utensils were washed spotlessly clean with ash from the hearth in the kitchen.

With Acchan gone, she became our sole guardian. Our school life continued as before. Vally went back to college. Chechi who was in the final year and I in the preparatory class, both performed well. At the end of the year, both of us won prizes – I got a children's book in English, and Chechi, two books by Dickens. One of them, *The Tale of Two Cities*, I still have. As our parents thought we were rather good students, there was neither over-eagerness nor anxiety on their part about our studies. There were times when I was somewhat upset over this. One instance was when I saw the parents of my classmate Leela coming out and seeing their daughters off to school in a rickshaw. Nevertheless, it never became an issue.

It was a time when the number of schools in the state was far less than a couple of decades later. But there were schools and most parents, except the ones in the lowest rungs of society caste-wise and money-wise, got their children admitted to them. Private tuition was not there either. There might have been rare cases where a master came home to help a child. For the children too, schooling was not just studies. It was closely linked to their other activities like playing, climbing trees, running around or talking.

After Chechi passed her school final, there was no discussion in the house about her higher education. At that time, there was no college in Kollam. In the case of Vally, what I have heard is that she cried and pleaded and made Acchan agree to take her to Trivandrum and admit her to the Government Women's College. It was not a time when all girls who finished school joined a college; colleges too were fewer in number than later. But Acchan yielded to his daughter's wish. Amma was not in favour of that, and she even asked an uncle

Rajamma, known as Chechi. (Photographer unknown)

of Acchan to bring Vally back. However he dared not attempt any such thing, and Vally's education continued. Acchan used to write to her regularly and visit her to make her comfortable. When Chechi's turn came, things were different. More than the possible financial difficulties in sending two children to study in Trivandrum, there was no one to take decisions on such matters. Amma did not have the necessary exposure to matters of the world like that.

Amma was not a person who disapproved of her daughters learning new things. Before Vally went to Trivandrum, a music teacher used to come home to teach both my sisters. Acchan was alive at that time. Though Chechi was not keen, Vally accepted the parental decision. I am sure Amma supported her. Amma had a good voice and had inherited a sense of Carnatic music from her family. She used to sing sometimes, and I also learned one or two *keertanas* from her. Though none of us became musicians, we did develop an ear for good music. Several years later, when Vally and I went to the Senate Hall in Trivandrum to listen to Yesudas, the lovely evening brought back those memories.

At that time, learning Hindi was taking root in Kerala as part of the freedom movement. The Dakshin Bharat Hindi Prachar Sabha had been set up with headquarters in Madras. Chechi began to study Hindi from a master who came home to train her for the examinations of the Sabha. She did very well in the examinations, completing the Visharad examination that was equivalent to BA. Each time, she received books as prizes, some of which are still with me. One of these was *Godaan* by Premchand. For the final examination, Chechi received a khadi shawl along with the certificate.

Around the same time, Vally completed her graduation. If Acchan was alive, perhaps she would have gone for further studies. That was not to be. She however got a job in the government, that too in the Registration Department where Acchan had worked. In this, Acchan's youngest uncle had a role. He also got a fee concession for me and my brother to continue our studies. Within a few years, Vally was married to a man in the same department. He had heard about her from friends.

Chechi too could have got a job easily. But that was not to be. She developed some ailment. It was the first challenge that Amma, who was not yet used to stepping outside the home, had to face. She and her brother took Chechi to the General Hospital in Trivandrum, the best facility in the state at that time. There was no medical college and the allopathy system of medicine was not as widespread as later. After some months of treatment in that hospital, Chechi was taken to a naturopathic centre near Kollam. It might have been at her suggestion. As I have already said, we were from a young age aware of that healing system. But there was no improvement in her health. Finally she was brought home and given ayurvedic treatment, but that too did not help.

By this time Vally had a son. The first grandchild in the family got all the attention. He was a cute, bonny baby and we happily looked after him. Chechi could not carry him but we made him sit on her lap, which she enjoyed. However, this joy did not last. One morning, she began to show signs of uneasiness. She said that Acchan was calling and that Yama, the god of death, was sending his messengers. She died peacefully. A highly talented and caring person, she was always there as our Chechi – playmate, companion and storyteller, when Vally was away. She was energetic and good at everything she did. How she yielded to such a deadly disease was a puzzle. Our house became silent. We did not talk.

Relatives were informed. As when Acchan died, there was no telephone or other means of communication, which have now become very common. Yet the news did reach many, and they came. In those days, there were barbers who would come regularly to cut the men's hair and shave their faces. Each barber was attached to a certain number of families. He also had the responsibility to inform the relatives of the family about deaths. Perhaps they did the same for births too. The present custom of offering wreaths was not known in those days. Again, a mango tree was cut, and Chechi was cremated in the same spot where Acchan was laid to rest.

Unlike the house where Amma's parents and siblings lived, we had a Christian neighbourhood. A group of women from these houses used to come and pray for Chechi. Faith was never a barrier for this practice that was born of care and concern. Amma did not have any problem with it. Among those who came to see Chechi, there was also a teacher who taught me at school. These memories remain with me; perhaps such concerns are almost non-existent now. Our neighbours on the southern side, across the lane, were Anglo-Indians. We did not visit each other, but exchanged gifts during Onam, Christmas, etc. After some years they left that house and a women's hostel came up there.

Amma, whose life and expertise were within the four walls of the home when Acchan lived, had an unbelievable transformation after his death. She was an efficient woman who rose to the needs of the circumstances when the time came. She started managing the affairs both within and outside the house. One such instance was when, at some point, she decided to keep a cow. A shed was made and a young cow came, perhaps from her family. She was there for a few years but did not have a calf. She was given away, free of cost, to another regular visitor, a Pentecost.

Vally gave birth to five more children, all boys. None of them was born in a hospital. She was given the best traditional pre- and post-delivery care by Amma. Everything needed for that, including separate oils for the head and the body and the various medicines used, were prepared at home. The women of the barber family also had certain roles. Before the appearance of the qualified midwife, these women helped in the delivery. The woman who was with us stayed on even afterwards to prepare special hot water – boiled with leaves or barks of certain trees which had medicinal qualities – and bathe the mother. These women were traditionally skilled in giving special hot-water baths and massages.

Even otherwise, Amma used to make ayurvedic preparations at home. We got used to medicated oils very early in life. She made not just simple medicines but also very complicated preparations including oils, *arishtam* and *lehyam*. On rare occasions, she would ask a neighbourhood *vaidyan* to come and do the last filtering of the oil. For this, a new *thorthu* and fresh sheathes from the coconut tree would be got. In all this, Kunji Chechi was Amma's right hand. There were select people who got a limited share of the oil. Growing up amidst these activities was exciting. Now, when I see people coming to buy herbs and other raw materials from the special *angadi* shops where these are sold, I go back to those days. We used to jokingly tell Amma that she could run a canteen or an ayurvedic medicine store. I have wondered how she learned all this.

Over the years, Amma learned to manage the affairs outside the home efficiently. We came to possess some land by chance when a person who had borrowed money from Acchan could not raise the amount and chose to transfer the mortgaged property instead. It was near the beach, on the banks of the canal. There was a small house, but it was mainly a coconut orchard. Amma learned to go there in a rickshaw and started supervising coconut harvesting, manuring the trees and the annual caring of the compound. With the money returned by another borrower, we bought paddy fields near our *ammayi*'s (uncle's wife) house. That meant that we started getting paddy regularly from the tenant. Amma did not go there, but the activities at home increased. The paddy was parboiled and dehusked at home. (Keralites, in general, prefer parboiled rice.) Decades later, two women who remembered Chechi told me how she never allowed the pestle to touch the mortar. Our belief in nature cure did not allow the bran to be removed.

The multiple tasks Amma had to tackle certainly injected positive energy into her. Acchan's presence as a companion, though short-lived, was another factor that helped her become who she was. Though Amma had a different educational background and refused to learn English, she continued to read Malayalam books. After our house was electrified, a brother of hers presented her with a radio. Though she preferred the newspaper for the news, she took to listening to music and drama which were special features on the radio. She narrated the stories to the women who came to work for or see her.

After Acchan's death, some of his relatives used to visit us regularly. The most frequent among them included Acchan's youngest uncle and his son. The latter stayed with us for long. He was a wonderful elder brother. Acchan's brother who was working in the court used to spend long spells with us during the summer vacation. He was a gentle, warm person and was very fond of us. We had never visited Acchan's *taravad*. After he died, his brother – our *chittappan* – decided to take us there during his vacation.

On that visit, Chittappan took us to many houses. Everyone remembered Acchan with fondness and respect. We, as his children, received a 'royal' welcome. We were taken to Acchan's father's family where there was a beautiful, loving grandmother who had arranged a special feast. Chittappan was keen that we meet people even outside the extended matrilineal family. We received a number of gifts, but the one that I remember clearly is a pot full of beaten rice mixed with jaggery and coconut which Chittappan gave us to eat on the return journey. I don't think that we finished it on the way. Chittappan's son, whom we fondly called Chandrettan, accompanied us. We started from Alleppey and travelled by boat through two of Travancore's biggest lakes, Vembanad and Ashtamudi *kayal*. Unlike the private boat

The family in later years. (*Sitting, left and right*) Saradamoni, Amma. (*Standing, left and right*) Devamma, Manikuttan (MRC). (Photographer unknown)

in which Amma and Acchan travelled in through lakes and canals, we travelled in a boat which was a means of public transport. It was a fascinating experience. At least, part of the travel was after the sun had set. We saw lots of places. We watched people getting out and getting in at the 'stops' on the way. I vaguely remember stopping at places like Prakkulam and Panmana. The changes in the colour of the water and its mood during different times of the day and night, especially on a moonlit night, was fascinating. Something that has always struck me during travels by boat or its cousin, the *vallam,* is the absolute quietness that prevails where they stop for the passengers to get out or get in. Those who get out simply walk away. I am talking of times when there were very few vehicles and hand-drawn rickshaws ruled the roads.

Another memorable episode was a bus journey, perhaps my first one. Amma's youngest sister had a daughter who was getting her first feed (*choroonu*) at a temple near Haripad. This is an important function and is not always performed in temples. This particular temple, Mannarasala, is famous for the snakes who are seen as divine. Another rarity is that the pujas here are offered by a priestess, a job done by men in most temples. The interesting part of our journey was that the bus came to grandmother's house to pick us up. I think I was the only one who went from my family. We left before dawn. I cannot remember if we were the only people in the bus or if other passengers were taken in later. That a public transport bus came home to pick up passengers is an interesting thing to recollect. Perhaps those were the days when the bus was being introduced. It was also a time when pedestrians could move around without fear of being knocked down.

Amma's mother, whom we called Mattemma, is another person who remains in my memory. She too had passed through trying times when her sons and husband died. She was a very beautiful, quiet person, and a great source of support to Amma. In our younger days, my brother and I went to her house many times with Amma's messages. We would run along a lane outside our gate, cross paddy fields, and walk through one or two short lanes to reach her home. Sometimes she would come along with us, but I cannot remember any secret discussions between Amma and her. Mattemma was always there when Vally's children were born in our house. We, the children, loved having Mattemma around as she allowed us to play with her long earlobes and hair. We also played a game known as *pallamkuzhi* with her. A matter of special bond between us was the fact that she and I were both born in the Malayalam month of *Medam* (15 April to 15 May), and we shared the same astral sign, *Tiruvatira.*

At one point in time, my brother and I took to gardening. We grew plants, creepers, bushes, crotons and different types of flowering plants. We had a well within an enclosed courtyard with less than ten steps and it provided us with excellent water throughout the year. Drawing water from the well and watering our plants was a task that we diligently attended to. As we spent quite some time daily among the plants, we came across many interesting moments. The birth of butterflies was one among them. They came gloriously out of a big oleander plant which had beautiful red flowers in bunches. It was a great discovery – the birth of butterflies. Slowly, we followed the sequence – the eggs on the leaves, the caterpillar which eats the leaves and the pupa to which it grows, and then out flies the butterfly, hovering around the flowers.

In a way, these wonders lessened the gravity of the losses and sorrows in our young lives.

I still remember the almost regular annual visits of Chinese and

Pathan traders. The former brought many things such as mats similar to our *pulpaaya* and silk. They had big dragons woven or embroidered on them. The Pathans who came from the North-Western Frontier regions which were part of India and Afghanistan brought things that Amma told us were rare in our parts. These were essential for many ayurvedic preparations. We believed Amma, as we had heard the story of Hanuman bringing the Kailas mountain itself with all the medicinal plants including those which brought the dead to life. We had also heard the story 'Kabuliwala' by Tagore.

Some moments of joy came from the festivals which we used to celebrate. All the festivals of Kerala, like Onam, Vishu, Mahanavami and Karthika, were celebrated by us. Occasionally we observed *ekadasi* (the eleventh day following the full moon), when we abstained from the normal food eaten every day. Instead, porridge made of broken wheat or a millet called *chama* with steamed banana fruit (the big variety grown in Kerala) would be eaten at noon. We would not use the usual plates either. A ring would be made of a strand of green coconut leaf. Banana leaf made supple by holding above fire, steam or under the sun would be given the shape of a bowl and kept inside that ring. There were also spoons made out of jackfruit tree leaves. We would scoop the porridge with that. Even on 'normal' days, about a dozen of such spoons would be made every morning to use for various purposes. Though we did not think about it then, everything that we used was biodegradable. Those were times when the world was ignorant of the present-day menace called plastic thrown around everywhere and resulting in serious health hazards.

Today, *ponkala* or cooked food offerings, mainly to goddesses, have become very common. The biggest *ponkala* at the Attukal temple in Trivandrum has attained the status of a great festival. I had never heard of the temple while growing up in Kollam or later while living in Trivandrum. We used to have *ponkala* occasionally cooked at home, but that was early in the morning, and the offering was to the sun. I remember that once it was done on a full-moon night in the month of *Vrischikam* (mid-November to mid-December) and the offering was to the moon. I still remember the moonlit sky, the cool breeze and the trees and plants which were slowly drifting to stillness. All these were festive occasions.

Amma was devout and god-fearing, but not a regular temple-goer. We used to light the lamp at home every evening and pray sitting near it. Although ours was not a joint family with several members, each of the above festivals was a joyous occasion. For Onam, we would have two *oonjal*s or swings hung up very early. These were done by the man who harvested the coconuts. One swing was made by tying two ropes made of coir on a branch of the jackfruit tree. A plank would be attached for us to sit on. The other was made by first tying a rope between two coconut trees and hanging a swing from that. The attraction of this was that it could take us much higher up in the air. Chechi was an expert at this. She could even swing with one of us – my brother or me – sitting on the plank, while she stood on it. I cannot remember us getting new clothes for Onam, but all our helpers – those who stayed with us to do domestic work, cleaned the yard around the house, worked in the compound, the man who harvested the coconuts – and some relatives got new clothes. Some of the elders like Mattemma got tobacco in addition. Those were the days when chewing betel-leaf and areca with lime and tobacco was very common. Tobacco from Jaffna was believed to be of high quality. Amma never acquired this habit. Some of those who received new clothes offered something back too. The coconut harvester brought a special kind of *aval* made from fried paddy which was different from the usual and very tasty. It must have been something that was not bought from the market.

There are a few faces which remain fresh in my memory. The coconut harvester Kunchen, probably Kunjan, was a person who made me aware of the distances in society early in life. We called him Kunchen Mooppar. Besides harvesting coconuts, he also played the drum in the local temple every evening during the main puja and when the deity was taken around (*sheeveli)*. Though he did these tasks for the local temple, he belonged to a lower caste that was considered untouchable. He did not enter our house or draw water from the well. I cannot say whether he kept a distance while performing his activities in the temple. I came to know that he drank toddy, but I never heard that he created problems anywhere. What I remember about him is his face where there was a twinkle coming from happiness and the kindly feelings he nurtured towards us, as well as a feeling of distance which always shaded his countenance.

Later in life, I have come across variations of this expression in others as well. They include people like cobblers who sit on the wayside and attend to our needs, like repairing a shoe or *chappal* which had minor damage. Perhaps a feeling of closeness and distance comes from the notions of both caste and economic hierarchy that prevail in society. Did they want to be friendlier or close towards us, and felt that they could not? I don't know.

Another face which refuses to fade from my mind is that of Baby. Many girls from around Mattemma's house used to come to our house, sometimes bringing milk or vegetables, or to meet Amma. She always welcomed them with something to eat. None of them studied much. As the years went by and they grew up, I stopped seeing them as frequently as before. But Baby continued to come, to spend some time with Amma. Even after leaving Kollam, I would often find her at home during my holidays. She got married and became leaner, anaemic and unhappy. The last thing I heard about her was that she had committed suicide. Today, the word has become common, but not in those days. I never understood the reason behind Baby's decision to take her own life. Baby and other girls whom I saw at Amma's place came from families where the mothers and even grandmothers went to work in nearby houses. Some of them made a little money from a cow or two that they owned, by selling milk and buttermilk. Those who were worse off went to milk cows in other houses and earned a small income. These women continued to live in their own houses after marriage. Neither did they leave the odd jobs that brought them some income. Their children were not educated to a level which would fetch them a small job. I never knew the details of Baby's life after I left Kollam.

Let me not end this chapter on a sad note. I shall present the man from the municipality who came every evening to light the street lamp outside our gate. He came on a cycle carrying a ladder, kerosene and of course a matchbox. The lamp-post was in a corner. The man climbed up the post, poured the kerosene and lit the lamp. The pedestrians got sufficient light to walk along the lanes, to the left and right. As the lamp-post was just outside our gate, we saw him daily – the man who brought light to us when the sun disappeared.

❖

CHAPTER FOUR

Me, Myself

The year Chechi completed the school final was crucial for me. I had just joined the first form and had another six years to go. The first major change I faced was that I did not have a rickshaw to take me to school anymore. I was only nine years of age and naturally needed some company and protection. A few senior girl students who lived a little farther away used to come home, and we would walk to school together. After walking for about half a mile or so, we had to cross the railway lines. We would walk through the railway compound and reach a road, across which was a boys' school run by the London Mission Society, a Protestant division of Christianity. More students coming along that road joined us there. It took another mile or more to reach school. I soon got used to this pattern.

Those days, children did not have uniforms or school bags. We had a satchel to carry books in. Most of us walked to school, though there were a few exceptions. The daughters of a rich cashew factory owner, Thangal Kunju Musaliar, and their friends from the neighbourhood came to school in a bullock cart. Daughters of another businessman, originally from the neighbouring state of Madras, came in a cart called a *jutka* drawn by a single horse. Our school also had daughters of Maharashtrian traders who had settled in Kollam for a long time. They, like the rest of us, walked to the school. On days that I did not have friends accompanying me, I used to run at least part of the way.

Though all this was enjoyable, I had some unpleasant experiences, at least one of which I have not completely forgotten. At a young age, I had started collecting stamps. At one time, I used to collect coins too. I cannot say how I chanced upon these hobbies. Perhaps I had read about all this somewhere. There were foreign stamps which gave us a lot of information. It was through them that I came to know that Helvetia was the name of Switzerland. They were difficult to get. The books Acchan used to order from places like Madras and Calcutta, and his national and international correspondence would have helped me. In the pre-Independence era, Travancore and Cochin had their own postal system called the *anchal* with their own stamps and other material. Some other princely states too used this option. A special stamp was issued to commemorate the Maharaja's Temple Entry Proclamation allowing the *avarna*s or 'untouchables' to enter government temples. Over the past decades, significant socio-political changes have come about in the world and to an extent, postage stamps reflect this. It is also true that the production of stamps has improved very much over time.

My stamp collection, precious to me, was not in an album but pasted in a thick notebook. One day, a very senior student who joined us on our walk to school expressed a wish to see that book. I gave it to her for a day, and she promptly returned it. But when I checked the book in the evening, some of the stamps were missing. Though I did not ask her about the matter or quarrel with her, the loss of my precious collection was deeply felt.

Another irksome experience of those years was a part of growing up. Some boys would follow us while returning from school. They were not wayside loafers but school students. We did not talk, but they might have made some remarks while walking behind. I was irritated when letters, sometimes with pictures and ribbons, reached home. Exchange of letters between boys and girls was not unknown in those days, but I was not interested and gave them to my sisters without reading them. I used to pray not to fall in love or get married. I cannot remember Amma telling us what we should or should not do. That was part of the unspoken and unwritten family code. Amma's philosophy that I can remember in Malayalam was '*poka vazhi pokarutu*' which in English can be, 'don't go along a path you should not'. We were never told what that path was. We were to develop our own sense of right and wrong. Today I can see the boys' behaviour as frivolous, but not at that time. I had enough things to make my small life happy and busy.

Moral science lessons, which are today part of many school curricula, were not there during our time. Our school hours were from 10 am to 4 pm with a break for lunch, but the Catholic students had catechism classes for an hour from 9 am. The rest of the students were left to play or do whatever they wanted. The big compounds in the schools of those times provided ample space where children could play in big and small groups, chat or walk around. We had a huge tree which gave shade and added beauty to the school buildings when its bright red flowers were in full bloom. We called it the Rain Tree.

Sports were part of the curriculum. Our school had facilities for badminton, volleyball, basketball and so on. However, the only game I was interested in was called rounders. There was a huge rectangle marked by lime, with circles at the four corners. The player hits with a bat the ball thrown by the opposing player, and if the latter catches the ball, the sides change. I was good both at hitting the ball and sending it far away and running along the rectangle, sometimes twice or thrice.

There were both nuns and others as teachers. In the English school, we had three male teachers who taught us science, mathematics and Malayalam. The last was a Tulu Potti from the present north Kerala. With his dhoti, black coat and an umbrella, he resembled the common man in R.K. Laxman's cartoons. The teachers who taught in middle school had studied only up to high school, with an additional certificate in the Teacher's Training Course. However, we did not find our teachers lacking. They taught us English, Malayalam, arithmetic, history, geography, hygiene, drawing and needlework. High school had more professionally qualified teachers who were graduates. Almost all of them had the training to teach, called an L.T. (License to Teach) degree. It was the forerunner of B.T. and what is now known as the B.Ed. degree.

We had teachers from Thangassery who were Anglo-Indians. They used to wear frocks unlike the women in the rest of the area who wore the traditional two-piece dress or sari. One of them, Merle Anderson, was my favourite. As her parents were dead, she lived with her guardians in Karunagappally, a few kilometres to the north of Kollam. She stayed in the convent and went home for the weekends. Even after she stopped teaching and got married, we used to correspond for a while. She had even sent me a copy of her wedding photo, but gradually we lost touch.

In those days, an inspector, an employee of the government, used to make an annual visit to the school. This was an event. When I was in middle school, I and some others would reach school early and help the nuns complete the work of those who had left their drawings and needlework unfinished. We did it not to get any favours but out of love for the work, and also because we wanted our school and teachers to get a good certificate from the inspector.

Another love of those years was our geography class. It took us to faraway lands and people: the Nile and the Amazon, the Tundras, the Steppes and the Poles. I loved these lessons so much that in my home, where I shared the drawer of a study table with my brother, I kept an igloo made out of half a coconut shell, polished and coloured using white chalk with a small opening and bits of cotton wool spread outside for snow. We studied geography at a time when an atlas or globe was not available. But our imagination knew no bounds.

An interesting incident when I was in the sixth form was when I found a mistake in the English textbook. I remember it was not a spelling mistake. Several batches of students including my sisters had studied the book but none of them, not even the teachers, had noticed it. It made me think, and one day, I stood up and pointed it out to our English teacher who was also the headmistress and Mother Superior of the convent. All that I can remember is that she accepted it.

The same year, I was hospitalised for an attack of dysentery. Though Amma stayed with me, I smiled only when I was told that I was going to be discharged. The illness cost me a share of my hair, which I had in plenty. Amma, in her wisdom, decided that the rest of the hair should be shaved off, and I had to go to school with a *mottathala*. But the hair did grow back to its old glory.

The convent was a continuum of the school, but we were not allowed there. Besides the nuns who were engaged in activities related to the school, there were others there whom we never saw. They managed the convent. Some did chores like cooking, accounting, poultry and gardening. In those days, the convent used to make and sell bread. They had regular customers. There was a window on the wall outside the school where bread was sold. We were not used to toast and sandwiches, but were given a special bread with crisp slices when we had a fever. The convent's bread was famous – a delicacy that they have now stopped making.

Two things from those schooldays that have not left good memories are the rooms where we used to have lunch, and the toilet facilities. In our time, unlike today, many of us had lunch sent from home. Amma had young boys or Kunji Chechi to help her in that job. The food would be packed in bronze tiffin carriers and served on a plantain leaf. The shed where we ate lunch had a gloomy look caused by a huge tamarind tree whose leaves and fruits covered the ground. We were supposed to eat sitting on the floor, which was always wet. Naturally, lunch break was not something we eagerly awaited.

The toilets were worse. Those were days when manual scavengers were employed to remove the night soil and clean the toilets. I cannot remember them coming when the school was functioning. I might have used the toilet a few times but developed the habit of controlling the urge to use it. The tiled shed where we used to have lunch is still there, but I do not know whether the practice of lunch being sent from homes continues.

It was quite difficult for my father to get me admitted to school. When I was five years old, he decided that I should join the school where my sisters were studying. He took me there, but I started crying loudly and would not stop. Finally, the music master in the Malayalam school came and took me off Acchan's hands. That is how I was finally admitted to school. I found myself remembering the good times I spent in my school when, a few years back, I met two students, a girl and a boy, who had just passed out of a prestigious school in Trivandrum in the early twenty-first century. They told me that their school days were nothing but intimidation. I hope that is not every student's experience. The lack of parental pressure and competition must have been a reason for our rather smooth school years.

The air those days was resonant with the mood created by the freedom struggle, of which khadi and Gandhian struggles like *satyagraha* were integral parts. Even before Chechi died, we had switched from mill-made clothes to wearing khadi. It must have come along with her study of Hindi. We bought a *charkha*, and all four of us began to spin. The local khadi shop was a centre of political discussions. Our brother, though young and still in school, brought cotton which we cleaned at home and made into yarn by hand through an elaborate process. This was then taken back to the khadi shop. It became a serious passion for us. I still have with me a folding charkha of those days.

I participated in a spinning competition held at the khadi shop and won a prize, a Malayalam version of Mahatmaji's autobiography. In the same area there were shops selling books and magazines in which we could read about our freedom struggle. Material from countries

Spinning khadi in the 1940s. (Photo by M.R.C. Nayar)

like the Soviet Union also started reaching us. Though enthusiastic groups visited these places, I cannot remember going there.

The same period coincided with the Second World War. All that I remember vaguely is a rumour about the possibility of a Japanese bombing. Kollam was a place where that could happen. Chittappan wanted us to move to Changanassery, but that was not to be.

I do not think we discussed any of the above at school. We were ruled by a Maharaja. We were told about the English king who was above the Maharaja, and who ruled us from a faraway place. He was the 'emperor'. We celebrated their birthdays by singing songs in praise of them. We observed Armistice Day to commemorate the end of the First World War (1914 to 1918). We used to pin a red poppy flower made of paper on our dress. But none of those occasions won a place in our hearts. They were nothing more than occasions for fun. I am certain that many of the girls in school would have heard about the struggles for freedom taking place in the country at home. That was not a matter of discussion amongst us at school.

Another unforgettable event of those years was Gandhiji's death. It remains a perpetual puzzle to me as to how we managed to get 'news' about Gandhiji's movements and the struggle for Independence that was taking place in various parts of the country. In 1948, we did not have an electricity connection. We did not have a radio either. Our neighbour, however, did have a radio. He was the founder of the

Quilon Radio Service, a major firm of electrical goods today. His wife, Rajalakshmi, was a gentle, pious, friendly person, and we knew her well. It was at their house that we listened to the details of Gandhiji's death. I was upset beyond words. I observed a complete fast on two days – the day of his cremation and the day his ashes were immersed in the sea. I drank only water those two days.

I do not remember having seen or read Gandhiji's *Harijan* at home. So I was surprised when I noticed some time back, inside an old book, a subscription renewal notice addressed to Vally from the *Harijan* office. It was a childhood dream of mine to go to Gandhiji's ashram in Wardha. Later, I came to know that some of the politically conscious young women, especially from Malabar, had gone to the ashram. But in my home the circumstances were such that I felt Amma may not be happy with such a decision. Moreover, I did not have any friend who thought like I did. So I wrote a letter to Mirabehn, the British-born disciple of Gandhiji. It meant so much to me when she promptly sent me a reply and a photograph of Gandhiji walking towards the daily prayer meeting. I still have them with me. It was in January 2011 that I finally realized my childhood dream, when I visited Wardha to attend the national conference of the Indian Association of Women's Studies.

After my schooling I took to serious reading and the habit of taking notes. I think it was a family preoccupation. Acchan also copied from various books. One of them was *A Book on Meditation* set in an interesting pattern where one page had to be read each day. There were notebooks where Chechi too copied extensively. I chanced upon a notebook in which I had copied from several books. I have also copied proverbs and Malayalam patriotic songs. Something else that attracted me were the sayings of great people. 'Believe in Yourself First, then Believe in God; Awake, Arise and Stop Not till the Goal is Reached' by Vivekananda was one of my favourite sayings. 'Aim at the sky and shoot at the stars' was another. 'Waste not, want not' and 'A stitch in time saves nine' remain with me even now, making me a stranger in a world where consumerism and a throwaway culture reign supreme. 'Procrastination is the thief of time' was another one because of which my children used to make fun of me for a long time.

Even in those days, there was the habit of collecting autographs. Many of the 'lofty' thoughts and sayings I had collected found a place in the autograph books of my friends. Besides all this, I had a book made with blotting paper where I used to press and preserve different kinds of leaves, creepers and flowers, which I still have with me. Today's children might not have seen blotting paper. Ours was a pre-ballpoint pen age. We used a pen with a nib which we dipped into the ink bottle and wrote. If a drop of ink was spilt on the writing paper, we used a special paper known as blotting paper to absorb the ink. The fountain pen was a luxury to some even in the high school classes.

After I finished school, there was no discussion about my future. Not everybody went to college. I was a good student, yet I was not particularly unhappy. I was enjoying a 'full' life, and one day, quite unexpectedly, my school authorities asked me to substitute for a teacher who was going on leave. I was a seventeen-year-old girl whose mind was still that of a learner. Still, I accepted the job and taught arithmetic and some other subjects. I earned my first salary, Rs 17, for a month.

I was again asked to take classes, for a longer period, for Rs 35 per month. I learned that teaching was not easy. One had to prepare not just mentally but write down in a notebook, step by step, how a lesson would be taught each day. I think I did my job well. Once, the inspectress came to my class when I was teaching arithmetic and appreciated my teaching. I continued to wear the same two-piece Kerala dhoti which I wore as a student in high school and remained happy among the teachers, some of whom had taught me.

When I was working as a teacher, Amma's youngest sister and her husband who was a station master in the railways were staying at a small station near Madurai in the old Madras state. I was invited to visit them. The station was near the once-famous Harvey Textile Mill. The workers were given 'quarters' and had a special train to take them from home to the mill and back. The labourers' quarters were not a new thing to me. We grew up seeing the official quarters of the railway staff. The siren from the cotton mill at Kollam, we knew, announced the shift of the workers on duty. But the special train transporting workers from their dwellings to the mill or workplace and bringing them back, that too for every shift, was new to me. During that stay, I remember visiting the hill temple of Thiruparankundram, which we managed to reach after a steep climb that tired me. Fresh water from a small spring quenched my thirst and kept me going. I bought two khadi saris in Madurai, which my colleagues taught me to wear.

Another experience of that time was going to see a film with some of the teachers. I think a cashew businessman called Swaminathan had built the hall where special films were occasionally shown. It later became the Municipal Hall. It was a Russian film called *Stone Flower*, about a sculptor who sculpts a flower from a big stone. The film ended with a picture of Stalin. I liked the film, especially the music with the accordion. The instrument and the attire of the people who played the music were new to me. Cinema was not popular in those days as it is today. There were no cinema halls or theatres. Temporary arrangements called *kottaka* were made, and mostly they showed Tamil films which sometimes ran for months.

Though we didn't see many films, I knew something about the then-famous film stars. The pictures of film stars and leaders of the national movement found their way into my notepad. Pictures of Gandhiji, Nehru, Sarojini Naidu and Rajkumari Amrit Kaur are in the collection. I don't think we used to buy English newspapers at that time. Still, I somehow managed to get them.

Looking back, Kollam in those days was a well-connected trading centre. There was a railway station, a bus stand and a boat jetty; the postal service of the colonial government and the *anchal*; hospital, schools, courts, police stations, jails, temples, churches for different denominations of Christians and mosques. There was no electricity, running water or drainage system. The British company, Harrisons & Crosfield, had their workplace near the sea. It gave employment to a large number of men in the area. I cannot remember any woman who was employed there. My uncle, one of Amma's younger brothers, worked there. A major source of employment for poor women were the cashew factories. The railways also employed a number of men from the neighbourhood. There were women sweepers as well to keep the area clean.

Kollam was a commercial hub even then. There were the Chinna Kada and Valia Kada, literally small and big bazaars. The latter mainly comprised wholesale merchants, while the former had smaller shops selling all kinds of things including medicines, soaps, biscuits, notebooks, paper, pencils, ink bottles and pens. Some shops had earned a name by stocking quality and 'fancy' goods. L.F. Fernandez was an example. By then the famous trading group, Spencer's, had a shop in Kollam, mainly catering to the British staff of Harrisons & Crosfield. But it was open to anyone with money. Just like the post, some 'native' states had their own currency. Travancore had its own rupee consisting of twenty-eight *chakrams* (today's paisa). The British rupee consisting of sixteen *annas* was also prevalent. It was worth twenty-eight and a half *chakrams*. I cannot remember whether the shops accepted both. However, conversion of the *sarkar* rupee to the British rupee and vice versa was a common question in arithmetic classes.

Kollam had another institution which induced fear and curiosity in us: the Free Masons. The rumour that spread among us was that it consisted of a group of men who secretly chopped off the heads of those who disagreed with them. We also heard that members who joined the group had to take an oath before a skull. I never came to know more about them, but I got rid of the fear long ago.

A most important event – the entry of a man into my life – happened during that period. I had a friend Padmavathi, whom we called Padma. Her family was from the suburban rural parts of Kollam. Her father's job as a Health Officer with the Kollam Municipality had brought them to the town. She was a good basketball player, and we used to frequent her house to drink water or to call her out to play. The hero of the present narrative was her cousin, the eldest son of her mother's sister.

His parents were away in the old Penang, where his father worked. They were five children, two older boys and three girls. The elder two were left with the grandparents to continue their education. The eldest was Gopinathan, called Gopi. To my friend, who was very close to him, he was Gopiannan, following the Tamil word *annan* for elder brother. His brother was Appukkuttan (Appu), but I did not hear Padma talking about him. Gopi spent a lot of time in their house, often helping his aunt with various chores including repairing the sewing machine. He had a way with children and so could relieve his aunt from taking care of the many small children in the house. Padma would have talked about me at home as a good student who was interested in reading and other odd things. He might have seen me in her house. His sister Ammu was my student.

The first bond which connected us was books. As mentioned earlier, books on the national movement and leaders were available in select shops – as also children's literature and illustrated books. The habit of gifting books was common during that time. Books from the Soviet Union on all kinds of subjects, for both children and adults, were there in plenty. Maxim Gorky's *Mother* was a great hit, a copy of which, though in a sorry state, I found recently in my collection. It may sound funny to give a copy of the *History of the Communist Party of the Soviet Union* to my brother as a birthday gift, but I did that. On another birthday, I gifted him a copy of *Gitanjali* by Tagore. During those days, Padma or Ammu occasionally brought me books to read. They were obviously Gopi's books.

Gopi was interested in politics and was politically active. After completing his schooling in Kollam and two years in college at Trivandrum, he joined the American College, Madurai for graduation. Though far away from the centre of national political developments, the temple town at that time was vibrant with messages of the freedom movement. Without any hesitation, he responded to the demands of the place and took on the responsibility of becoming the college union president. One of his friends and confidantes was a faculty member, Professor Subramaniam, who was a Brahmin from Thalassery and had married a Tiya student. In Madurai, Gopi met another Subramaniam from Thalassery too, who came to be popularly known as Sarmaji. He later moved to Trivandrum and remained a good friend of Gopi and our family. These like-minded friends gave support and encouragement to Gopi's activities while in Madurai, and stood by him when he took the crucial decision to become a journalist as part of his political life after graduation.

Spurred by the dream of being a journalist, Gopi took the train from Madurai to Madras and joined Goenka's *Indian Express* as an apprentice. After a few months, he and a young man who joined at the same time, C.N. Chittaranjan, were sent to *Eastern Express* in Calcutta. Both of them were idealists, and journalism for them was not a mere job. Both Gopi and CNC left Calcutta and the job after a few months, but their passion for journalism never left them.

Gopi's mind was fixed on journalism even after returning to Kollam. He worked with one or two papers published in the town for short spells. During this period he met five like-minded young men, and together they planned to start a journal. The investment to start a journal was much less then when compared to today, but the young group with dreams had no money.

Politically, things were changing in the country. Indian Independence became a reality. Developments like the formation of the State Congress, the merger of the princely states of Travancore and Cochin, and the election to the state assembly on the basis of adult franchise were welcomed by the people. But there was discontent and difference of opinion especially among the young entrants to politics. They came with conviction and expectations. Gopi, who was a Congressman in the beginning, had differences of opinion with the local Congress leaders who pushed him to the Congress Socialist camp.

Gopi's mother along with his three young sisters returned to Kerala from Penang when it became safe to travel during the war. There was a time when they had no news of his father, which affected his mother's health very badly. They returned to his family house Kuzhiathu, near the bank of Ashtamudi Lake. It was a joint family where once two sisters and their families had lived together. But later it was partitioned, and the younger sister and her family set up another house on the eastern side of the fence with a footpath leading to it. Before Gopi's mother came back, he, his brother and the grandparents were living in the house. Far away from the town, the place had few amenities.

When Gopi returned from Calcutta, his father was still away. In that circumstance, his primary responsibility was towards the family. His father was a practical man and 'modern' too. Otherwise, he would not have made use of the opportunities he got at that time and crossed the seas to give his family a better life. Like any parent of his class and generation, he too would have expected Gopi to look after the family, especially in his absence. Padma's father, who saw what Gopi was up to, was annoyed with his political activities. He made Gopi know of his disapproval when he shifted from wearing a shirt to a *jubba*. His mother, I don't think, understood what her son was doing. Moreover, she was not an authoritative person and would not have used any harsh words against her son.

Though the elders did not understand or approve of Gopi's decisions about life, the young people of his house, of his patrilineal and matrilineal kin, and even some neighbours saw a hero in him. They supported and joined his various ventures, like the handwritten journal, the enacting of dramas and spinning. Very many years later, some of them narrated the story of those days with joy in their eyes. Gopi had a collection of rare books, which disappeared over the years. He also loved music and cinema. They had a huge gramophone which they had brought from Penang and plenty of music records. Gopi was interested in collecting the choicest music of those times. He was also a keen sportsman. Though he did not find much time for sports, he keenly followed various sporting events.

One day, I got a letter from him by post. It was written on a thin, blue sheet of paper. Unlike the letters I have mentioned earlier, I did not show this to anyone. Chechi was no more. Vally too was away. My brother was studying in Trivandrum after completing his school. Amma and I were alone. I think I was growing up and realizing that our worlds were not the same. In a sense, I had no friend. Though he sent me letters, it was when I read the report of a speech he made at a trade union rally on the ground in front of Kollam railway station that he got a place in my mind. I saw in him an honest, upright man, and that greatly appealed to me.

I sent him a reply after some days. This exchange of letters continued for some years. A dozen of those, I still have with me. Those letters have made it possible for me to recollect many things that happened nearly seventy years ago. Almost all his letters were on the old-style light blue letter pad. The handwriting was steady and beautiful. I kept them in a special sachet of cotton khadi cloth made by me. It is destiny that they remained with me through the vagaries of my life. They have brought fresh memories, joy and pain.

The first letter was dated 4 *Kumbham* 1123 (16 February 1948). Gopi always used the Malayalam era. It could have been part of his nationalist fervour, or it could be that we had not switched to the English calendar. In the first letter, he addressed me as 'Dear Saradamoni' and used the word '*bhavati*', equivalent to '*aap*' in Hindi. It was not a love letter. He said that he happened to see a note I sent to his younger sister about a book. He not only did not have any objection to lending me books, but was also willing to order any book I wanted if it was available in any nearby bookstore.

We bonded over our interest in reading. He gave me a long list of journals he was getting and said that I could choose whichever I wanted from among them. On getting to know about my love and deep respect for Bapuji, he wrote that he did not think condolence meetings and fasting were fitting tributes to that 'Karma Chandran'; that would be achieved only by the successful culmination of his efforts to raise the life of unfortunate sisters in this country. He was interested in knowing my views and wrote that if sisters in our parts came forward for any service to the nation, he would be there to support them.

In my short reply after a few days, I asked him how he could be interested in a girl who was a total stranger. I might have felt that it was a bit harsh, so I sent another letter where I probably said that I was an ordinary girl and that he should not have any illusions or false ideas about me. Replies to these were quick. He said that he was upset when he did not receive a reply from me. But he did not find any reason to change his view that I was a politically minded person. He briefly told me about his vision of life and commitments. It was after a serious probing of heart that he took the courage to write to me, and he felt he was correct in his assessment of me. He went to the extent of writing the following in English: '. . . my soul has found its kindred spirit. An intuitive instinct, consciousness of having met one who will understand me, sympathize and feel with me, one whose joys will be my joys, whose pains mine own, one whom I could help, and one whom I could rely upon.' His letters would talk philosophically about human beings, their strengths and weaknesses. Once he added that there was no perfect human being, and categorically stated that he was not going to change his views about me. The letters were mostly in Malayalam, but when he wanted to quote from English books or wished to express an intense feeling, he switched to English.

Later, he told me that I caught his attention once while passing along the road in a car in front of our school. He saw me walking, clutching a heap of notebooks close to my chest, surrounded by students. It might have been during my teaching days. He was fascinated by a girl who showed a spirit of independence at such a young age. He did not know where I lived, and had cycled along the lanes and by-lanes in our area. When at last he spotted the house, I was watering the plants. When I started to write articles occasionally for the journal *Janayugom* that he and his friends started, they were published under the name K. Shakuntala. Without my knowledge, I got a pen-name. Much later, when I wrote in English, I used the pen-name Chetana, one that was chosen by me.

Gopi was keen that I know him fully. So he wrote long, loving letters where he told me about his life, views, commitments and interests. While at school, he was an arch believer in all the Hindu gods. He went to school with sandalwood paste or a *vibhuti* mark on his forehead. He had no sense of shame about that. The day started with a reading of the *Gita* and *Bhagavatam*. One day, while returning from Trivandrum, he bought a set of books by Pandit Nehru, whom he called Jawahar, and finished reading *Letters from a Father to His Daughter* before reaching Kollam. He wrote: 'In three hours, I became a rationalist, nay, an atheist, casteless, republican. The boy in me suddenly grew up. For the first time in my memory, I went to sleep without praying. That was its end.'

Some thought he was reserved, some considered him 'highbrow', and there were others who thought he was quick-tempered. He asked me to think dispassionately and decide whether it was advisable to link my life with someone who did not have a safe and secure life as society understood it. He did not hesitate to add how painful it would be if my decision was negative. He suddenly remembered some lines from Shelley:

> All things by a law divine
> In one spirit meet and mingle,
> Why not I with thine? . . .
>
> . . . The Sunlight clasps the earth
> And the moonbeams kiss the sea
>
> What is all this sweet work worth
> If thou kiss not me?

In response to a letter where I mentioned Vivekananda, he replied that he at one time was keen to join the ashram in Almora, especially after reading Swamiji's works and books like Romain Rolland's biography of Ramakrishna Paramahamsa.

> The fact that I am born in the land which gave him birth fills me with pride. At a time when we Indians were steeped in dependence and considered imitation as culture, he dared to raise the voice of India's prestige, standing on foreign soil. Thus he raised our self respect and self esteem. In this he was a forerunner to all the social reformers who came afterwards.

Gopi also wrote about his visit to Belur Math, away from the crowd and dirt of Kalighat. He vividly described the peace, serenity and inner happiness he experienced there. However, he could never agree with Swamiji's views on the role of Hinduism in resolving the problems of this country, and his ideas about *sanatana dharma*, *maya* and so on.

Often, he wrote about literature. He was very fond of poetry. This he had told me earlier. He loved Tagore and Shelley. When feeling low or emotionally tired, he would read Tagore as if he were reading the *Gita*. Among novelists, Thomas Hardy was his favourite. He had read *Tess* seventeen times and still, it remained fresh. Then there were Victor Hugo, Tolstoy and Upton Sinclair. So it went. In Malayalam, he loved G. Sankara Kurup the most – the poet who got the first Jnanpith Award. His mysticism was not easily understood by people. Humility was his virtue; in dealings too, he was equally charming. Gopi considered the poet to be Kerala's, even India's, prophet for the future. Thakazhi and Kesavadev, two well-known writers of that period, were personally known to Gopi. He had extensive discussions with them as he was also at some point involved with the progressive writers' movement. I have wondered why he himself did not become a writer.

From the two-page first letter, the page numbers began to increase. '*Bhavati*' gave way to very endearing terms. In the month of *Kumbham* itself, he sent me five or six letters, and we were convinced that we were born for each other. As I said earlier, he was keen that I know him well and fully. It was the national freedom movement that attracted him to politics. He admired its leaders like Nehru and Gandhi. Ideas like simple living and sacrifice, and socio-political goals like an egalitarian society along with national freedom, appealed to him. He was disappointed when he had to decide to return to Kollam. After returning, along with journalism, he got involved with State Congress politics and trade union activities. He was no longer the boy who went to Madurai, as he had seen and experienced more of real life.

Back in Kollam, he saw the realities around him with sharp eyes. They were the years after the Second World War. Unemployment, poverty and deprivations of all sorts pervaded everywhere. He could not think of a safe and secure life for himself. He wanted to use his pen and all his energy to eradicate social evils. But his experience with the State Congress turned out to be anguishing. Instead of working for the betterment of the lives of lakhs of working, unemployed and exploited poor, he found that the local Congress leaders, clad in khadi, were appeasing those who were anti-worker, pro-capitalist, casteist;

they were power crazy. After serious thought, he decided to leave the Congress. He knew that the alternative, the Communist Party, had lapses, but as things stood, they were committed to the deprived and have-nots. Gopi had much earlier accepted socialist ideas.

Gopi went through all the above conflicts and their resolution after we became acquainted. He genuinely thought that I helped him in the process. I think it showed the greatness of his heart. My knowledge about the real world of politics was extremely limited. Idealism and a world built around *Satyameva Jayate* was my politics.

His outlook on life was not that of a 'householder'. He had an impeccable character. He was amiable and could lend patient ears to those who wanted to talk. He was honest, highly disciplined, hard-working and, to a large extent, a Gandhian endowed with its positive attributes.

We had to wait for some years to have a life together.

Looking back, I have two regrets. One is that we never got to read these letters together. The other is that our daughters used to ask whether ours was a 'love marriage'. Gopi would have told them what it was, but he would not do it without my consent. And in those days, I still had my girlish shyness.

❖

CHAPTER FIVE

To Trivandrum, to College

My college years came after a five-year-long hiatus at home. In those days, instead of the several streams of school-leaving examinations that we have today, what one got was the English School Leaving Certificate (ESLC) after eleven years of schooling. Those who wanted to pursue higher studies did not have the large number of options one finds today. Higher studies were mostly in the pattern of a two-year Intermediate course followed by a two-year graduation course. I joined the Government Women's College, Trivandrum, for the Intermediate course.

By then, women from Kerala, especially from certain communities, had gone for higher education to colleges even outside the state. I remember hearing from friends and reading in magazines about such women whose achievements were many. Ambadi Ikkavamma, a government schoolteacher from the former Cochin state, translated Tolstoy's stories for children in 1926. The idea came to her from Gandhiji who had earlier championed the stories for their ethical value. She became an acknowledged author and translator, and had the privilege of meeting Gandhiji in person. She also translated President Radhakrishnan's book, *East and West in Religion*, into Malayalam. Janaki Ammal from Thalassery took a D.Sc. from the prestigious University of Michigan at Ann Arbor in 1931. True, they belonged to the upper strata of society; nevertheless, their achievements cannot be ignored.

To me, the college years brought the novelty of moving out of home and living in a hostel. For a brief while I stayed in a hostel run by the Ramakrishna Mission, which I soon left for the government hostel. The single-storeyed buildings with rooms of various sizes were not built to be a hostel; nevertheless, I settled in. There were beds in all the rooms, except those used as study rooms where we had a small table and a chair. Our tiny trunks were kept under the bed. Today, one of those hostel buildings has become the Office of the Commissioner of Police and another, a multi-storeyed edifice.

The Women's College in Trivandrum where I joined was set up in the early part of the twentieth century. I am sure that if I ever come across a directory of the women who passed out of this college, I will see many illustrious names in it. There were three groups to choose from: the first group with Mathematics, Physics and Chemistry; the second group with Chemistry, Botany and Zoology; and the third group with History, Psychology or Logic. I chose the last. This being a rather rare choice for someone who had scored more than 60 per cent marks in the school final, I was called to the college principal's office more than once to find out whether it was a conscious decision. But my aversion to cutting and handling animals like frogs and my love for reading made me stick to what I had decided. Apart from that, I had not thought much about what I would do with the college education I had come for.

The two years in Women's College, however, were a great experience. Our history lessons spanned from ancient Greco-Roman history to modern or Indian history. Our textbooks, even in 1948, were a leftover from the British period, and they were silent on the history of colonized India or the freedom struggle. Fascinating changes in the teaching of history, however, took place later. Malayalam and English were compulsory subjects.

I soon made new friends. Four of us formed a gang – Leela, Seetha, Vijayamma and I. Though we needed our local guardian's permission to leave the hostel, a group of us were allowed to go out for a short period without permission. None of us except Leela belonged to Trivandrum. Seetha was from a place called Kannadi in Kuttanad, one of the rice bowls of the state. Vijayamma was from Aranmula, the land of the famous temple and an annual boat race which attracts a huge crowd. Leela's home in Neyyattinkara, to the south of Trivandrum on the way to Kanyakumari, became one of our happy haunts.

Her house was next to the local temple, which was very famous. There was a hollow jackfruit tree in the area which is said to have offered asylum to a prince who was being followed by his enemies. He became King Marthanda Varma, the founder of the Travancore state. By the time we saw the tree, it was old and was known as *ammachi plavu*

The gang of four. (*Left to right*) Seetha, Vijayamma, Saradamoni, Leela. (Photographer unknown)

or grandma jackfruit tree. Leela's grandfather's brother was an intrepid journalist who was banished from the state for exposing the misdeeds of the Dewan. Remembered as Swadeshabhimani Ramakrishna Pillai, he has become a legend in the history of Travancore.

The many acquaintances I made at the college made me wonder that despite the geography taught at school, how little we knew about our own small state. Girls belonging to all religions and castes came from different corners. There were girls who came from schools in Trivandrum like Cotton Hill and Holy Angels Convent. A group of smart girls from Cotton Hill generally stuck together. Many of them were from known families in Trivandrum. But it was not difficult to get acquainted with them. For some of these girls, the one or two years in college were a waiting period before marriage.

When I joined Women's College, Ms Anna Nidhiri from Changanassery was the principal. Under her principled administration, there was never any talk about irregularities or nepotism. It was said that those who came with 'recommendation' for their wards' admission did not dare enter the college gates.

Our teachers were mostly young. Though there were a couple of foreigners in the faculty when Vally was studying there, by the time I joined the college, there were none. Our English professor was Ms Daisy Muthunayagam whose ancestors were from Tamil Nadu. She was pretty, gentle and friendly. Then there were Saradamma, Parukutty Amma and Janakikutty Amma who taught us History. Saradamma's sister Parvathi Amma taught Chemistry. On the whole, Nairs and Christians made up the teaching community. This was not surprising as women from these two groups entered the field of education even before women in England did so. Edgar Thurston, Professor of Economics at the Madras Presidency College, observed that Nair and Syrian Christian women from the west coast filled the women's colleges in Madras city. We also had Ezhava and Nadar Christian teachers. Ratnamma, who taught us Malayalam, was more of a friend. Of these young women who got jobs soon after completing their MA, many were unmarried. Some of them got married later.

Women's College widened my horizons in many ways. It was there that I saw Mrinalini Sarabhai and her dance troupe perform their production, *Manushya*. I also had the chance to hear Harindranath Chattopadhyaya recite his poems. Such experiences elevated my views on and appreciation of many things.

When I was in Women's College, a Frenchwoman, Madeleine Biardeau, came to Trivandrum to study Sanskrit texts with a Sastri. Our gang was sent by the warden to take her to our hostel where she had earlier obtained admission. We did our job, greeting her by shouting 'Madeleine Biardeau *zindabad*!'. She was allotted the room next to mine, and that was the beginning of a friendship that lasted more than sixty years. We used to spend a lot of time together talking about many things. She tried to teach me French. She later became a Professor of Indology at the prestigious Sorbonne University in Paris.

Debates and discussions held in the college were something that I loved participating in. In one debate, I argued vehemently against Changampuzha, the renowned Malayalam poet, maintaining that he

With Madeleine Biardeau, early 1950s. (Photographer unknown)

was a defeatist. Changampuzha was Vally's contemporary, and by that time, he had already published some of his early works. Later, after having read many of his poetic compositions and biographies of him and his friend Edappally Raghavan Pillai, I realized how stupid I was at that time. I started enjoying his poetry and bought his complete works in two volumes. There was a time I used to read one or two of his poems quite regularly.

Politically, important changes were taking place though they did not enter the Women's College the way they do at present. First of all, as per the recommendation of the States Reorganization Commission of the central government, the states of Travancore and Cochin were merged to form the state of Tiru-Kochi with Trivandrum as the capital and the King of Travancore as the *Raja-Pramukh*, which I think had the status of a Governor. With the Dewan gone and the region having become part of independent India, changes were naturally expected. However, the devotion to royalty and the old ways did not vanish immediately and totally.

Changes were not new to society. Much earlier, the voice of protest against practices like caste stratification and untouchability, which had denied access to education and employment to large sections of the 'low castes', was heard from their own leaders. Sree Narayana Guru and Ayyankali, two tall leaders of the movement, succeeded in instilling in their followers a sense of self-worth and pride, and the courage to demand the rights denied to them for ages. However, though this period is referred to as a renaissance, and certain changes did take place, it cannot be said that fundamental and all-pervasive transformation has come about in society at large or in the lives of the previous untouchable castes.

The young, mainly men from among the privileged communities, came forward with 'progressive' and 'modern' ideas about society, the individual and their interconnections. Legislation brought about changes in matters related to property and inheritance. I am not sure whether the changes that came about then can be viewed as social transformation.

In the newly formed state, power went to the State Congress, the state wing of the Indian National Congress. Socialist parties with shades of left ideology sprang up, attracting the youth. But they did not impact the daily life of the people like today.

It was during my Women's College days that I first met C.K. Susheela, who later married the communist leader A.K. Gopalan and became Susheela Gopalan. We met in college and bonded over several 'operations'. Among these were the tiffs we had with the new principal, B. Anandavalli Amma, who appeared to us as conservative and against the freedom of students. Unlike Ms Nidhiri, she was from Trivandrum. She was also the warden of the hostel where Susheela stayed. Perhaps she was the chief warden of a cluster of hostels where senior students stayed.

A disagreement over the toilet facilities was one instance. Trivandrum at that time did not have proper sewage facilities. There were scavengers who carried away the night soil. Water from the bathrooms and places where clothes were washed constantly flowed through open drains which crisscrossed the hostel grounds. This irritated many of us. The principal responded by asking us whether we had sewage facilities in our homes. Most probably not; but none of us had two hundred or more young women living together at home.

Trivandrum even today is a city with drainage facilities which may not be perfect. I used to think that the hostels for girls and young women are satisfactory. However, occasionally contrary news reaches us. It appears that they are not even safe in some areas. To repeat something said earlier, I had reason to believe that many girls learnt to withdraw urination right from their school days. In some cases, this continued through years of college and employment too. I have later written and spoken about this matter, pointing out the related health hazards. The fact that toilet facilities for girls and women remain a national problem after several decades in our sovereign nation is a matter of shame. It is also a reminder that we as women have failed to intervene on issues which demand top priority.

Though Susheela and I did not admire Anandavalli Amma while in college, in subsequent years I happened to read her writings in old Malayalam journals. One of them was titled 'The Freedom of the Eastern Women as Against the Western Women'. Her satirical dramatic piece, *Panikkarude Pinakkam*, had to be stopped halfway as it was seen as anti-men by male readers. We could have never guessed that she, whom we thought of as a conservative woman, had such a past! I never saw her after I left college. Several years later, Vally met her on the train while travelling. At that time I was studying in Paris. I was told that Anandavalli Amma, on hearing this news, remarked appreciatively that 'some *kuttikal* [children] are like that'. Susheela did not continue her studies in Trivandrum but remained active in politics, and we met again.

Let me note down two other experiences I had during the Women's College days. They had nothing to do with the college or the teachers. One was a visit to the home of a close friend of Chechi. Hers was a well-known family. Her father had been the head of the Kollam District Hospital. Theirs was a family of three daughters, like ours. The middle one, Chellamma, was a dear friend of Chechi. Both of them loved reading Sherlock Holmes. They went back to their family home in Trivandrum when their father retired. Chellamma Chechi came to know that I was in Trivandrum, and one day, she came and took me to her home. I had lunch and came back only in the evening. Whether I went there again, I have no memory. It was sweet of her to remember the younger sister of her old friend.

Another unexpected rendezvous which happened during my Women's College days remains a painful memory. From one of my classmates, I came to know that a nun who had been a teacher during my school days in Kollam was teaching in a convent in Neyyattinkara.

I could remember her. She was from Dharwar – she was friendly and a good teacher. The classmate, a former student of that convent, brought me a letter from the sister, and together, we went to see her. When we reached the convent, I was asked to wait in the visitors' room. After some time, the nun who was keen to see me came. But she had to sit at a distance, and it was not possible to have any conversation except one or two words and a smile. It was a very embarrassing situation, and we left soon. I never heard anything about her after that.

I later came to know some developments that had taken place in my school in Kollam after I left, which further opened my eyes to life within convents. Our headmistress, also the Mother Superior of the convent, was retained in the same convent even after her responsibility was over, whereas usually they are sent to some other convent. What was done to her was humiliating, and she chose to leave the convent. Those who supported her in Kollam were treated badly and transferred to other places.

Today, after having seen many new orders of nuns who try to make changes in their dress, activities and vision, and having heard and read stories like that of Sisters Abhaya and Jesme, these stories do not shock us. But in our student days we were young and ill-equipped to see what went on behind the closed doors of the convent. Simply because they accepted the robe, willingly or otherwise, they do not cease to be normal human beings. They live in a world of ego, rivalry hierarchy and exploitation.

By the time I passed the Intermediate from Women's College, the University College was starting a post-graduate course in Economics, a three-year (Honours) course. Unlike a regular postgraduate course, students like me who had passed the Intermediate could directly join this course. Those who completed their BA could join us when we entered the second year, which meant that we were gaining one year. Both the Honours course and the university that awarded the degree (Travancore University) do not exist today. The formation of the Kerala state and repeated reforms in the higher education system had an impact on them.

However, I must add that I did not join the new course knowing what it was going to teach me. My notion of professional life was vague, and there was no academic in my family. Though I cannot say from where I got the idea, I wanted to do something for the country and my insufficient knowledge about the subject prompted that Economics would help me to attend to the needs of the four-year-old free India.

Before joining University College, I had never studied in a co-educational institution. But I did not find it difficult to adjust either in the classroom or on the campus. Despite being a co-educational college, girls and boys did not mingle or walk around discussing, talking, quarrelling or romancing. Nevertheless, it was not a compartmentalized world.

The grandest event in the college right after the admissions was the elections, but compared to the present, it was a low-key affair. In the first year, I contested for the post of English editor of the college magazine. There were not many political parties in the state those days. There was the Students' Federation, an all-India body, and we were contesting under that banner. The opposing candidates were either supporters of the Congress or independents. I was defeated, but for the next two years, that post went to girls. At that time I heard that it was mainly the girls who did not vote for me. Anyway, I did not collapse. Our gang from Women's College joined different departments in University College.

The election experience, however, earned me a good number of male friends. One of them was K. Srinivasan who was elected the president of the college union. I remember he was made to treat our gang at the nearby Coffee House. This was not a common thing as it would be today, but it did not create any gossip or commotion. Srini, as he was known to us, became a Professor of English and continued to be a friend for a long time. There was also Mohanan who was the son of the renowned Malayalam writer Lalitambika Antarjanam, Kuttappan who became an advocate, and Anirudhan who remained active in politics and became an MLA and MP later in life. I came to know that some of them, while talking about their college days over the radio or writing for journals, remembered me. While the Women's College days gave me the opportunity to get to know many girl students from different parts of Travancore, University College opened out a different world to me with more male students and a friendly atmosphere. I shifted to a new building of the hostel and Vijayamma became my roommate.

Once the elections were over, it was time for the inauguration of the college union. As the inaugurator, a woman who had just come

Devaki Panikkar inaugurating the University College union, mid-1950s. (Photographer unknown)

from abroad was chosen. Her name was Devaki Panikkar, and she was the daughter of K.M. Panikkar, the well-known administrator, writer and diplomat. At that time Panikkar was the Indian Ambassador to China. They hailed from a well-known family, Chalayil, in Kavalam, Kuttanad.

Devaki was not the only woman to go abroad from this part of the world. Lakshmi Menon, after obtaining an MA degree, had gone to England and acquired a teacher's license. She taught in Madras, Bengal and Lucknow, and then she was spotted by Pandit Nehru. He absorbed her into his cabinet and she remained there till he died. Mary Poonen Lukose, whom I had the privilege of meeting at her house in Trivandrum a few years before she died, was a graduate of medicine from England much before Independence, and became the Head of Medical Services in the State Health Department, Travancore.

Devaki was studying in Oxford when the war broke out, and she had reached Kerala after living through wartime experiences in England. She had also spent some time in New China with her father on the way back. Many in Kerala had read Edgar Snow's book, *Red Star over China*, and people were excited about the happenings there. They were eager to hear from someone who had seen China. She seems to have also established contact with the Communist Party in Bombay before reaching Kerala. All this made her a celebrity. Naturally, she was the best choice to inaugurate the University College union. Devaki spoke in English, but those who could translate her were many. Though her parents were from Travancore, she did not grow up here and its ways were new to her. Despite this, she travelled from place to place and made speeches telling the people what they wanted to know.

Besides the Head of the Department, V.R. Pillai, we had a team of male teachers, most of them young. They were Lakshmana Panicker, Kesava Panikkar, E.T. Mathew and David. While I liked economic thought, economic history and Indian economy, I did not find economic theory and public finance interesting enough. Several years later, I came in contact with a group that ran the Centre for Popular Economics (CPE) in Amherst, USA. When I decided to organize a workshop on the subject and asked for funding from the Indian Council for Social Science Research, the chairman, an eminent economist, told me to demystify economics.

We also had Politics, which was taught by Easwara Pillai. Some of us had taken Statistics as an optional subject and used to visit the Statistics Department outside the University College campus, in the complex that presently has the Senate Hall. I vividly remember three illuminating and enjoyable lectures delivered by the Head of the Department, Professor U.S. Nair.

College life soon became interesting with many events. One was the socio-economic survey that our teachers organized at Ulloor. Looking back, I think it was like a child's game. But I enjoyed our regular visits to collect information from houses and small shops with wooden shutters that lined the road to Kollam. None of the women except a junior, Saktimayi, joined the team. For me, it sowed the seeds of my interest in fieldwork-oriented research. In a sense, it was the beginning of several extended field studies more systematically planned and conducted by me in later years. While travelling on that road after many decades, I have looked for those houses and shops. But I found that the road has widened and the shops had disappeared – modernization had brought many changes. I fear the people who lived there too may have moved elsewhere.

When I was at University College, independent India was just five years old. The nation was abuzz with debates on economic planning. As students, we had only vague ideas about the economic situation of the country and the vision and goals set by the leaders. Professor V.R. Pillai succeeded in attracting the National Conference of the Indian Economic Association to Trivandrum in December 1952, thus giving us the opportunity to meet many luminaries in the field. Among them were Professors Wadia and C.N. Vakil from Bombay, V.K.R.V. Rao from Delhi, and R. Balakrishna, Head of the Department of Economics at Madras University.

Students were recruited as volunteers and assigned in pairs to attend to the needs of the delegates. My team was entrusted with taking Hemalata Acharya and her colleague Deshpande from Dharwar sightseeing, including a visit to the Padmanabhaswamy temple. At the temple, men have to remove their shirts and vests and wear dhotis, and women who wear salwar kameezes, jeans or T-shirts have to wear dhotis over that. Our guest from Dharwar was so tall that none of the dhotis he tried on extended beyond his knees. This caused some amusement.

Another great figure we had the opportunity to meet during those days was P.C. Mahalanobis, the doyen of statistics. The Statistics Department organized a tea party in honour of him when he visited with his wife. It did not occur to me at that time, but many of the above moments were pointers to my later life.

In addition to our classes, we were expected to read in the library. The present University Library was not there. In our student days, the library occupied a smaller building across the road, along with the Malayalam and Sanskrit Departments. Later, when I saw bigger libraries, I might have thought how ill-equipped the University Library was, but not at that time. The librarian, Janaki Amma, was always friendly and helpful.

Before I completed the Honours course, Gopi and I got married. The wedding took place in my house on 4 May 1952. For a long time, we celebrated the day by calling it the 4 May Revolution. It was a typical Nair wedding. When I told Amma that I did not want a *tali*, she did not create any fuss. I did not think the *tali* was an essential part of a wedding. As Amma could not arrange proper weddings for her other two daughters, she did everything for my marriage. As usual, two *pantal*s were erected in our yard, one for the marriage and one for the

Wedding portrait in studio. (Photographer unknown)

feast. As per customary practice, Amma invited our relatives. Among my friends, Madeleine and Vijayamma were present. Mohanan and Kuttappan came with a beautiful gift. The bridegroom came with a huge crowd.

Marriage marked the end of my hostel life; we rented a house and Amma came to stay with me. Off and on, Gopi lived in the Kollam house as he was busy with the newspaper he and his friends had started, and my house was near their workplace.

When we were in the second year, the first-year MA students joined us. Some of the male students among them had worked for some time after the BA. But this did not create any distance either in the classroom or outside. My acquaintances soon grew beyond the ten women and ten men who made up our class. I befriended Rajamma and Subhadra from the Philosophy Department. After leaving University College in 1954, till the late 1980s I had no contact with most, but Rajamma and Subhadra were two friends I kept in touch with all through. Sugathakumari, presently a renowned poet and social activist, was also my contemporary at Women's College and University College. She was a student of Philosophy in the latter.

When I returned to live in Trivandrum after spending a sufficiently long spell outside Kerala, some of my classmates, whom I had lost touch with over the years, welcomed me with the same old warmth and friendship. It was Kunjukunjamma who took the initiative to arrange a get-together in her house.

Some years back, I came to know from the newspapers about the formation of a body called the University College Alumni Senior Citizens Association (UCASCA). I got in touch with them and enrolled as a member. I am one of the two of my batch to be in the association. True, we are the 'ancients'. Among the alumni of University College, there are very many distinguished and not-so-established women and men from all walks of life – professionals, civil servants, teachers, eminent artists and writers. My father was among the hundreds of science graduates who came out of the University College in its early years. Members of this association represent a small fraction of the

With old friends at a wedding, early 1990s. (*Sitting, left to right*) Lakshmikutty, Rajamma, Subhadra, Saradamoni. (Photographer unknown)

alumni living in and around Trivandrum. There are some members who live abroad. Those who are not members have their reasons, such as physical disability, not having anybody to accompany them and non-inclination to dwell in the past. I try to attend the three meetings that are annually arranged by the organizers.

We are proud that University College has had a glorious past and that this grandmother has crossed her 250th birthday. When we sit together and talk of new times, I cannot help remembering the debates we had and the college magazines which were a memento of those times, for which I regularly wrote when I was there. What did we think? Debate? It is for historians and researchers to find out.

❖

CHAPTER SIX

Madras University

First Steps in Research

In the early fifties, social science research had not become as common as it is today. For those who did a post-graduate degree, the first preference was a job. There were not many colleges and universities where one could pursue research, and there was no University Grants Commission to insist that a research degree was necessary to get a teaching job in a college. It was at such a time that I decided to continue my studies in Madras. The idea might have been planted in my mind by Dr Balakrishna of Madras University, who talked to me about research when we met during the conference at University College. Things became smoother when I got a fellowship for two years: Rs 100 per month in the first year and Rs 120 in the second year. Madras University was one of three universities set up by the British in their Presidencies, the other two being in Bombay and Calcutta. The university had an MLitt course which attracted students. It was a prestigious course. The renowned economist Professor D.R. Gadgil, of the Gokhale Institute in Pune, was an MLitt degree holder from Madras University. I decided to venture out of Kerala.

The day before I left for Madras, our Mattemma died. She was cremated following the custom, on the southern side of her compound. I attended the rituals performed that day. From the train, I could see the smoke rising from the funeral pyre.

The railway route from Kollam to Madras stretches through tunnels built across the terrain of the Western Ghats. I made the journey with Gopi; as he was an excellent companion, the travel was more enjoyable. The journey was a fascinating experience. Before entering the forest range, I watched with excitement the hanging bridge at Punalur. From the train, we could see the road far below and occasional buses. We spotted beautiful rivers, temples and rocks scattered everywhere. Making our way across these enchanting scenes, we reached the Shenkotta (Chenkotta) and Bhagavathipuram stations where the horizon changed. The vast expanse of land was dotted with fields and hamlets, small and slightly big, and the waterfalls at Kuttalam gazing at us from a distance. It was as contented travellers that we arrived at the Tourist Home, right across the Egmore Railway Station, to rest, bathe and change.

My abode during the two years in Madras was a hostel in Triplicane, not far from the university. It was conceived as a hostel for girls who were child widows. Since they were few, the hostel was opened to others who were students in colleges of the university or employed in Madras. It was managed by an Iyengar group related to T.T. Krishnamachari, a powerful minister in Nehru's cabinet. The hostel was named after Kamala Nehru. There was an open-air theatre in the vast compound which enabled us to watch many interesting programmes including drama, music and dance. It was also a venue for huge meetings where even world leaders including Chou En-lai of China and Bulganin of the former Soviet Union were given civic receptions. These receptions were grand affairs in which schoolchildren performed mass drills to music, creating formations that represented India.

The famous Triplicane temple was nearby. In our neighbourhood there were many Iyengar households, relatively poor. They worked as typists or ran small units where others came to learn typing. They were visibly conservative. The changes in the wider society appeared not to have entered their lives. The young men still retained their tufts of hair which marked their caste identity, and which their counterparts elsewhere had given up. Most of them were married, but we never saw any of them either going out with their wives or talking to them.

The life of these Iyengar women came as a surprise to me as women in Madras were by and large advanced in terms of education, employment and participation in public life. Every morning, we were woken up by the sonorous voices of women vegetable vendors who came from distant places carrying huge baskets overflowing with fresh vegetables. Even women from the upper strata seemed to have a rather engaging public life. The Dakshin Bharat Hindi Prachar Sabha, the Madras-based organization for popularizing Hindi in South India, was started very early as part of the freedom movement, and many Tamil women had developed an interest in the new language. One could find signboards in front of homes, sometimes more than one in the same street, advertising Hindi lessons. There were also notices about dance as well as music classes, both vocal and instrumental. The teachers were mostly women. Women could be seen stitching or reading Tamil magazines like *Ananda Vikatan* or *Kalki*. However, we did not see our next-door neighbours engaged in any such occupation.

I soon got accustomed to the new life. A short walk from the hostel took me to the road parallel to the beach, and a straight walk towards the north took me to the university. I had a seat in the University Library near a window through which I could see the beautiful Marina Beach and enjoy the sea and the waves. Most of the women researchers at that time were in the Departments of History or Political Science. I was the only woman student in the Economics Department. We had a room where we could meet each other or rest during free time. My guide was the Head of the Department, Dr Balakrishna. There were two more students from Kerala, both men, working with Dr Bright Singh, a former teacher at University College.

At the MLitt level, we had more flexibility in our work. Though the guide followed our research, we did not meet him/her daily. Regular classes, lectures and examinations were not held. All that we had was a written examination at the end of two years, and a *viva voce* in addition to the dissertation. All this left us with ample time to attend the seminars and talks organized by different departments, depending on our interests. Some students, who were civil service aspirants, registered for the MLitt course so that they could have access to the library. We were learning to be independent.

I made friends outside the research arena. Among them were two young women from Kerala who were doing a course in Library Science. They were my roommates in the hostel. At that time, Professor Ranganathan, well known for his contribution to classification and coding, was Head of the Department of Library Science. My conversations with mainly one of them, Chandrika, piqued my interest in the subject. She remained a friend for long; I briefly lost touch with her but later renewed contact when she was employed in Trivandrum. I became friends with young women from Kochi, Malabar and Mangalore. Inmates of the hostel who were from Ceylon brought embroidered fabrics and cotton voile which many of us bought from them.

My decision to continue education in a place far away from home did not create much of an issue at either of our homes. Gopi's mother would have liked him also to continue his studies at least up to a law degree. My hostel roommates were surprised and curious about a married woman returning to study.

Life alone in a new city exposed me to new situations, some of them challenging and some, funny. Before coming to Madras, I had never gone to eat alone in a restaurant or hotel. The first time I went to the university canteen, I did not know what to ask for. *Puri* was not something I was familiar with. Hearing the bearer mention it, I asked for four *puri*s and he brought four plates of *puri*s, smaller than we normally see, in sugar syrup. I did not know what to do but to sit there and eat them. I soon learnt the ways of the new life and avoided such blunders.

I explored the city, sometimes with friends and sometimes alone. When Gopi visited, we stayed in the same Tourist Home across Egmore station. We had a memorable evening at Marina Beach where we stayed for a long time watching the sea and wetting our feet in the waves. We explored the outlet of a famous hotel in the city, Buhari, and tasted a Persian drink called *faluda*, heavy but delicious. Slowly I became familiar with Parry's Corner, Mount Road, High Court and the eateries across the road. The Udipi restaurant facing the statue of Annadurai, the founder of the Dravida political party DMK, was one of my favourite haunts – their *badam kheer* was simply delicious. I also explored the wholesale vegetable market with more varieties of vegetables than in Kerala.

Life in Madras had another impact on me. I fell in love with train journeys. I became familiar with the stations where one got excellent coffee and *vada*. I began to look out for landmarks such as small village *kovil*s where one found terracotta statues of horses, and sometimes small churches. Before reaching Madurai, almost halfway, we came to Rajapalayam, known for a specific breed of dogs. Another station was Sivakasi, the famous centre for making matches and firecrackers, from where one could go to Kodaikanal, the mountain tourist centre. I never got out at Trichinappally, a station with a puzzlingly low platform, where the train usually reached late at night. But even in those late nights, I got to know an old man selling soaps, combs and bangles. I never saw this man, but from his voice, I presumed he must be old. The sing-song '*soappu cheeppu kuppivalai*' in his sturdy and clear voice still resounds in my memory.

One day, Gopi telephoned me and said that I should come home immediately as Amma was slightly unwell. I was at that time not very familiar or comfortable with telephones and did not know how to use them. I was attending to this call in the office room where the manager sat. I did not hear anything very clearly but decided to go home that very evening. I had by then become an expert in rail travel. My practice was to reach the station early, buy the ticket, spread a sheet on the upper berth as soon as the train pulled in, and buy a packet of *tair-sadam* which was splendid as dinner. After eating that, I would climb to the upper berth where I had spread the sheet to sleep. On this particular journey, I was anxious about Amma. Gopi, without informing me, had come to a station beyond Shenkottai, and asked me to join him as I was travelling in the 'ladies' compartment. He comforted me and said that he thought she would improve faster if I was near her. Otherwise she was being looked after well by my brother and his wife.

My first visit to Delhi, the city where I spent a long part of my life, happened during these years. Gopi was visiting Punjab via Delhi to attend a Communist Party Congress. It was the year Indian Railways had introduced the three-tier sleeper coach, and I can still see the short Sikh superintendent who travelled with us, looking after the passengers' needs, unlike the guards and ticket examiners. In Delhi, we stayed with Gopi's friend and comrade M.N. Govindan Nair, an MP at that time. The government accommodation where we stayed was in South Avenue, one of two locations for MPs' quarters. The other was North Avenue. On one end of the street was the President's Estate and on the other end was Teen Murti Bhavan, where the Prime Minister lived. The city was beautiful, with neatly laid-out roads, tree-lined avenues and historic monuments everywhere. Though I had lived for some time in Madras, which had bigger buildings, office blocks, shopping streets and wider roads than Kollam or Trivandrum, Connaught Place and its Inner and Outer Circles impressed me.

MN, as our host was popularly known, was living with his wife Devaki whom I had known from my University College days. I explored the city with her. We made the day memorable with a film at Regal Theatre and a huge helping of ice cream at the nearby Kwality Restaurant. Kwality ice cream was the king of ice creams at that time with many flavours and fancy names.

Gopi had a friend Crispy, who was at that time working in All

India Radio. His full name, Constantine Romanz, was known only to a few. He was Crispy to all others. Gopi's classmate from his American College days, this friendly man with a sense of humour was part of the group that dreamt of and planned *Janayugom*. The three of us took a taxi to Agra and saw the Taj Mahal during the daytime and by moonlight. Our dinner at the army mess afterwards gave me the first scare of the day. As we were entering the cantonment area, a guard asked, 'friend or foe'? Only after Crispy said 'friend' did he let us in. The whole setting was unsettling, and it increased when Crispy and the friend started drinking alcohol. Nobody in my immediate family drank alcohol or smoked – so I was shocked.

Gopi was a teetotaller and non-smoker, but he did not have any problem when others drank or smoked. He must have noticed the discomfort on my face. We remained silent on the way back. Sticking to his habit, Gopi did not talk to me about the matter. He wanted me to resolve the issue myself. Crispy either did not know anything or did not think it was an issue. He had a large heart. Today, when I think of that incident, I realize how stupid I was.

I made my return trip to Madras alone as Gopi was going to the Party Congress. The same short Sikh superintendent was there on the return journey too. I came back with the decision that I would never again go back to Delhi, the crowded city where I found the houses too close to each other and the lack of compounds a major flaw.

While I was in Kollam for the summer holidays in 1956, I received a postcard redirected from the hostel, which announced that I had won the first prize in the essay competition conducted by the Sahitya Parishad. The competition was on *Aikya Keralam* or united Kerala, which was the dream of a large section of people in the region. Gopi and I went to Ernakulam to collect the prize, a gold medal, on 18 May 1956, a few months before the state would finally come into being. My essay was published in *Jayakeralam*, a journal published from Madras at that time, the copy of which I seem to have lost sometime during the vagaries of life.

Soon after, we made another trip to Madras, this time to collect the prize for another essay written in connection with the All India Congress for Peace and Asian Solidarity. The prize was a book titled *People, Be on Your Guard* by Julius Fucik. I did not realize that the person who gave me the prize was the famous freedom fighter and campaigner for peace, Dr Saifuddin Kitchlew. It was at that meeting that I saw Perin and Romesh Chandra who remained lifelong campaigners for peace. I have no idea as to how the word peace got into my head.

We bought return tickets for a roundabout route. Even some of the co-passengers and the ticket examiner, who thought we had made a mistake, suggested that we get off at a nearby station and catch a train that would take us to our destination sooner. But we kept to our plans. On the way, we met a young, handsome visually challenged man. His beautiful rendering of the Tulsidas Ramayanam remains alive in my memory. We stopped at Madurai, went to the American College where Gopi had studied, watched a football match and visited the famous Meenakshi temple. We also went around Trichinapally. I saw the platform which had always puzzled me, but did not meet the old man selling soaps, combs and bangles.

The grandest event during my two-year-long academic life in Madras was the centenary celebration of Madras University. Madras was the first of the three universities that were the pillars of British education in India. We witnessed its centenary celebrations taking place ten years after India became independent. For five days between 28 January and 1 February, a special *pantal* in the South Indian style of those days was erected, and the inauguration was done by the Governor of Mysore, His Highness Jaya Chamaraja Wodeyar. The celebration gave us the opportunity to see many important leaders of free India. Dr S. Radhakrishnan, the Vice President of India, delivered the centenary address. On 31 January, the Prime Minister of India Jawaharlal Nehru was conferred the Honorary Degree of Doctor of Law. I was sitting very close to the aisle along which he briskly walked to the dais and back. Seeing him at such close quarters was exciting! He later laid the foundation stone of the centenary building. Another dignitary present on the occasion was Sir C.V. Raman, an old student of Presidency College who became an internationally renowned scientist and recipient of the Nobel Prize. I saw him taking a walk alone on the pathway of the Marina near the road in front of the university. Interestingly, from a commemoration souvenir that quite accidentally popped out of my shelf recently, I found out that I had represented the women research scholars in the Research Scholars' Association, something that had eluded my memory.

Within two years, I completed my dissertation on 'The Cooperative Movement with Special Reference to Madras State'. It explored how the state had witnessed successful functioning of the movement, especially during wartime. For this, I had extensively read at the library and visited many societies to find out more about their history and functioning.

My second trip to North India with Gopi happened after that, for the *viva voce* which was held at Lucknow University. My examiner Professor Baljit Singh, a known labour economist, was friendly and considerate. The journey through stations and places unknown to me presented me with interesting moments to remember. Once, I was looking out when the train briefly stopped to store water and a few railway workers brought me some fruits, pleasantly enquiring about our trip. At a station, we turned eastward with a sudden change in landscape, and I saw many men entering the train with long sticks, most probably peasants. Later, I have seen this in many parts of North India, especially in the hilly regions. The stick helps people to keep balance and walk long distances.

During these years, my love for travel also took me to Tirupati, the famous temple town that attracts endless streams of devotees. The temple is located on the top of a hill surrounded by seven other hills. The train took us to a station a little further away from the foot of the hills. One or two buses were available for a short distance, for the passengers who needed them. Others trekked up the hills. We went by bus up to a level and then walked the remaining distance. The bus drive through the minor forests was a memorable one. The temple's wealth in terms of offerings, coins, notes or jewellery is huge. The friend with whom we made the visit was a teacher at the university run by the temple trust. Because of that, we had the privilege of having *ekanta darshan*, which meant that no one else was present when we offered our salutations to the lord. This was otherwise a very expensive matter. An official visit to Tirupati years later gave me a shock when I saw that all the hills and forests had been cleared, and that *pucca* roads and even a helipad had come to the temple town. I preferred the Balaji of Tirumala.

My friend Madeleine had returned to Paris after completing the two years for which initially she had the fellowship. But she began to come frequently for shorter periods. Once, she worked with a Sanskrit pundit at the Deccan College, Pune. But her field of study was South India, and she came to Madras and Pondicherry regularly. As I was in Madras, this enabled our spending time together, sometimes visiting friends or places. Once or twice, she lived in the hostel as a guest.

Once the MLitt at Madras was over, though my professor and friends were happy, I was not particularly excited. So I decided against continuing in Madras for a PhD, though I knew and loved the place well and felt that the years I spent there were not wasted. I was unsure as to what I would do after coming back to Kerala. I seriously thought about our life. In our concept of marriage, the husband was not just a provider and protector. To me, Gopi was a friend, a loving companion and a supporter, which he was all through our married life. *Janayugom*, which Gopi and his friends struggled hard to start, had by then become a daily with a record circulation. But finances continued to be a problem. The editors had no salary. All they had was the encouragement, support and a little money which friends, well-wishers and the community around them provided. I thought that if we wanted to have things our way, we should not be a burden to our families. I needed a job. Though my ideas about economics still lacked clarity, I returned to Kerala telling myself that I would earn.

In early 2014, during a brief visit with my daughter Asha in connection with a family function, I found that the city of Chennai I encountered had changed dramatically from the Madras I knew. The Triplicane temple was there, but we could not locate the Kamala Nehru hostel. Certain parts of the area had changed, but not everything. The smell of *kadambam* and jasmine flowers, and the various sounds – from vegetable-vending women to the electric train – remained with me for a long time. I do not doubt that at least some of my friends had done well in life and perhaps migrated. I was genuinely upset to find that the Tourist Home where Gopi and I had found a comfortable rest house had disappeared. Moore Market, a landmark in Madras city was gone, and so was the Dasaprakash Hotel where the marriage reception of two of my nephews took place. I could take all this only with a sense of loss.

❖

CHAPTER SEVEN

Again to Trivandrum

And a Job

I had resolved that I would look for a job when I returned from Madras. The questions of where, how and what started bothering me. Normally, a woman in my position would have looked for a teaching job. But the number of colleges was limited. I also had reservations about the teaching of Economics. At the same time, I thought that the subject I had studied would be of use in fields other than teaching.

I found myself in the grip of sweeping social, political and economic changes. A decade had passed since the nation became independent. We in Kollam, far south in the Indian subcontinent, did not experience the pain and loss of Partition which the people in the north or Bengal went through. Soon after, Gandhiji was assassinated. The central government tried hard to bring back normalcy to the lives of the dislocated people. After prolonged deliberations, a Constitution which declared India as a sovereign democratic republic was adopted. All citizens, in theory, were promised equal opportunities irrespective of religion, caste, gender or place of living. To convert the above dreams into reality, the Indian government embarked on a development strategy based on the method of Five-Year Plans.

It was not easy. The subcontinent was spread over temperate and tropical regions between the Himalayas and the Indian Ocean, and broken into many kingdoms and principalities, big and small, rich and poor. Besides this, there were the wounds of the past to be addressed. They included the exploitation by the mighty British empire and the ravages caused by the two world wars. The majority of the poor were engaged in cultivation as small peasants, tenants or labourers. There were also a large number of artisans: carpenters, the blacksmiths, potters and goldsmiths, among others. Often, the poor were under the mercy of the chieftains and their orderlies. It was under such conditions that the central government put forth its promise of a new social order based on equality and justice.

The shift in the political and economic landscape of Kerala was no less drastic. The state itself was new, having been born on 1 November 1956, following the central government's decision to reorganize the states based on the language spoken by the majority of the people. In the case of Kerala, Malayalam was that language. The new state was also the realization of a collective dream, *Aikya Keralam*, of the people. To the Tiru-Kochi state formed by merging Cochin and Travancore, Malabar was added afresh by separating the region from the Madras Presidency.

Before the formation of the Kerala state, many women and men belonging to the upper strata used to go and study in schools and colleges in Madras. Some had settled there for generations. Many got into government and semi-government services. Others, from the lower economic strata, went to work in hotels, shops and occupations which did not require higher education or special skills.

In the very first election to the State Assembly, the people elected a communist-led ministry to power. For the first time in free India, the Congress hegemony was punctured. The birth and rise of the communist movement in the state is well documented. The presence and strength of the communists and other left political parties were welcomed by the people.

Before proceeding, we have to remind ourselves of certain realities that pervaded the region. Agriculture was the main occupation of the people. The ownership of land was held by a small section of upper-caste families. The people who worked in the fields were tenants or labourers who came from all religions – Muslims, Christians and Hindus. In the case of the latter, they included poor Nairs and castes below them who were treated as untouchables. These latter sections were not engaged in agriculture. Pulayas, a numerically strong group among them, were mainly engaged in tasks related to paddy cultivation. There were no rules regarding the working conditions of these people. The landlords would dismiss poor tenants and workers without warning. They did not receive any compensation either.

There was distancing even among the untouchable castes. Anthropologists have written extensively about this matter. Compared to the Pulayas, castes like the Paraya, Kuravar and Vedar were numerically smaller. Izhavas, another group who were victims of social distancing, were traditionally engaged in the tapping and sale of toddy. But they were not as 'low' as the castes mentioned earlier.

Changes in all this began with broad socio-political changes that came about in society. The invasion of Malabar by the Mysore rulers Hyder Ali and Tipu Sultan, followed by the British rulers coming up with new rules regarding land ownership and cultivation, shook the social order that had prevailed earlier.

The freedom struggle gave support to the socio-religious questions that were loud and clear in the region. Besides what has been said earlier in relation to the working conditions of the low-caste people, they were denied the right to walk along public roads, enter temples and draw water from public wells used by the upper castes. Their children were not allowed to join schools either.

Voices against these practices began to be heard from some of the untouchable social groups themselves. Among their tallest leaders were Sree Narayana Guru (1856–1928) and Ayyankali (1863–1941). They were from two of the numerically strong caste groups among the untouchables – the Izhavas and the Pulayas, respectively. The Guru declared the slogan of 'One caste, one religion, one God' for the entire universe.

Ayyankali, who was more of an agitator, demanded that *sarkar* lands be made available for his people to cultivate. He also demanded that his followers be given the right to walk along public roads and enter temples. Above all, he wanted their children to be admitted to schools. He was a relentless fighter. At a time when the word 'strike' was not known, he asked the women working in paddy fields to stop work till their children were admitted to public schools. Before that happened, he started a primary school for deprived children in his native place.

There were occasions when the struggles of people like Ayyankali had to face strong and violent resistance from upper-caste groups. Changing times did not allow the latter to be always the winners. By then, the social and political atmosphere in the region was absorbing fresh ideas from the freedom struggle. Some freedom fighters of Malabar came from as far south as Guruvayur in Kochi and Vaikam in Travancore to support the agitation of the low castes to enter temples and also walk along public roads.

Besides Sree Narayana Guru and Ayyankali, there were others like Chattampi Swami, Thycaud Ayyaswami, the poet Kumaran Asan and others who spread the message against caste-based inequalities. They raised their voice against the system that kept a sizeable section of the population away from decent and respectful living conditions. These certainly had an impact on society even before the formation of the state of Kerala.

In 1888, the then Maharaja of Travancore, Sree Moolam Tirunal, formed the Sree Moolam Praja Sabha or People's Assembly. To this were nominated Kumaran Asan, a prominent poet, and Ayyankali. In 1936, the Regent Sethu Lakshmi Bai's successor, Sree Chithira Thirunal, issued the Temple Entry Proclamation, which enabled the untouchable castes to enter *sarkar* temples. These were important steps though they cannot be said to have initiated fundamental changes in society.

The educated youth of Kerala began to watch world events. Socialism and communism became topics of discussion. They naturally were supportive of sections of the population who were victims of discriminatory practices in society.

These developments coincided with the freedom movement in the country. An increasing number of men and women were attracted to the struggle against colonial rule. They took up the cause of the poor and the untouchables. The Indian National Congress followed by the socialist and communist parties could not ignore the socio-religious questions that arose all around.

These, without doubt, shook the foundation of Kerala society. Over the years, many from the old untouchable castes have received higher education and entered professions in both government and non-government ventures. Some became members of the legislature and other elected bodies. At the same time, it remains a fact that the many questions raised by Sree Narayana Guru and Ayyankali remain only partially resolved.

Unemployment has always been a problem in the small stretch of land of Kerala. This has meant the absence of a stable income for a large section of the people, even for a very simple life. In that context, the early attempts to set up industries were welcomed by people. A coir factory was set up by an American, James Darragh, at Alleppey. This was followed by other coir factories set up by the British. Tile factories soon came up in different places. Some British entrepreneurs opened engineering workshops. Harrisons & Crosfield, mentioned earlier, was testimony to the new penchant for setting up factories. In and around Kollam, cashew factories were set up by different people and large numbers of women were employed in them. Plantations, mainly of tea, were also started by the British across the Western Ghats. All this created a stir in the economy as it brought some amount of work and money to a section, particularly the poor and lower-middle-class households.

This increase in non-agricultural labour proved to be a ripe opportunity for the socialist and communist groups to spread awareness regarding the inequality and exploitation in the system, and the importance of the collective strength of the workers. Clashes between organized labour and the management became routine in many places. Though power was in the hands of the management, they were not always victorious.

The aforesaid developments in the region certainly helped the non-Congress political formation led by the communists to come to power in the new state of Kerala. The new ministry was sworn in on 5 April 1957. Besides the Chief Minister, E.M.S. Namboodiripad, there were six other ministers – five men and one woman – in the new cabinet. Challenges lay ahead of them as well. They were not people with prior experience in the administration and ruling of a state. Politically, they were not on the side of the governments at the centre and other states. The Princely States did have a relatively organized administrative set-up, but that could not be copied as such by the new regime whose vision was different. They had come to power with popular support, and this meant that the people's expectations could not be ignored. Nevertheless, the ministry consisted of a team of highly accomplished and committed people. They had to envision a mode of development oriented to economic growth and fair redistribution. The prioritized goals before the new ministry included reforms in land relations, education, administrative reforms and the nationalization of plantations owned by foreigners.

As a part of envisaging and executing these, the new government decided to set up the Bureau of Economic Studies under the Planning Department. It was this Bureau – in an airy, old-fashioned house on rent, not far from the Secretariat – that I stepped into for my first job.

In the small Bureau where I began my professional life as a

Bureau of Economic Studies. (*Sitting in the second row, second and third from left*) Saradamoni, Ashok Rudra, (*far right*) Krishna Iyer; (*standing in the third row, third from right*) Sreedevi. (Photographer unknown)

research officer, the atmosphere was friendly. The staff were not too many in number, and we all knew each other. My post was officially that of a gazetted officer with a salary scale of Rs 200–400. Many of my colleagues held permanent jobs in the government and had come on deputation. One of them was Lilykutty, a technician. Another economist recruited to the Bureau was Sreedevi, a gentle, quiet person who managed her responsibility efficiently. She later retired as the Director of the Bureau of Economics and Statistics. The Bureau where we worked was amalgamated with the Bureau of Statistics which had offices in each district.

The administrative section too had a small but efficient staff. I remember the precision and neatness with which Parameswara Iyer, the typist-cum-stenographer to the Head of the Department took dictations, mostly letters in shorthand, made a draft and typed out the final version after approval. In the small, job-starved state of Kerala, classes in typing and shorthand were very common. Many of those who were trained in them got coveted government jobs. There was a time when men with these skills went to places like Bombay and

Delhi. Some of them became journalists. The arrival of the computer age finally tolled the death-knell of typewriting and stenography. Parameswara Iyer's work was always neat with impeccable spelling and grammar. His knowledgeable, sincere and dedicated manners, and his ability to correct the mistakes in dictation made me think that he should have been in a better position.

Most of the people in the office were sympathetic to left politics. The new government roused a lot of excitement. On the whole, there was a feeling that something very new had happened. The jubilation spilled over the boundaries of the state. People from other parts of the subcontinent as well as from different countries of the world came to see this 'wonderland'. Many of them visited our office. A young Bengali, Ashok Rudra, was brought from Paris to head this small unit. Dr Rudra was small-built, talked and walked fast, worked hard and did not care for formalities, especially the hierarchy within a government office. He was friendly but argumentative. With him came his French wife Colette – a gentle, quiet and warm woman. The excitement that pervaded the atmosphere in the wake of the new state and new government did not leave out the office.

Among several aspects of Kerala that underwent transformation during these years was the city of Trivandrum as well. Both Cochin and Travancore, even before their merger, had administrative set-ups to look after their affairs. After the merger Trivandrum became the capital and it remained so when the new state of Kerala was formed. In the Madras Presidency, there were Malayalis who had reached the highest levels of bureaucracy. Besides the government, they were employed in academic institutions, semi-government offices and private ventures. With the formation of the state of Kerala, this office-going population was given the option either to remain in Madras or shift to the new state. Quite a number opted in favour of Kerala. So, there was a sudden rush into a relatively small place like Trivandrum. Among them, there would have been many who were coming to these parts for the first time. I feel that the city even now has not resolved the problems which were set into motion at that time.

The office was abuzz with the hopes and concerns of the new era. When it came to questions regarding development, the government could not ignore the expectations of the people. On the other hand, being part of the Planning Department, we were supposed to follow the guidelines set for the country by the Central Planning Commission. The Bureau took to its work under the guidance of Rudra, a mathematician-cum-statistician whose experience in research on development and planning had been with the well-known French left-wing economist Charles Bettleheim in Paris. In India, he was associated with the Indian Statistical Institute founded by Professor P.C. Mahalanobis, the architect of Indian planning. Hence, he was familiar with Indian planning and the issues at stake. The Bureau was a research unit and the work there was research-oriented. I found myself engaged in work that was assigned to me, such as preparing a daily hand-out regarding the wholesale market price of essential goods, and writing a monograph on the coir cooperative societies in the state. I also started frequenting the library attached to the legislature, then located within the Secretariat compound near our office. I came to know some members of the Assembly who willingly got me books which I could take home to read. One such person was the late Surendranath, popularly known as Asan. That friendship continued till his death.

With the new job, my family life attained a settled pace. My brother soon moved to Trivandrum and along with Amma, all of us lived together in a rented house. *Janayugom*, which Gopi was editing, had grown into a daily. The daily and its original version, a political weekly under the same name, had played a crucial role in conveying ideas about socio-political change and communism among the masses and bringing the party to power. Gopi and his friends did not think that the job was over. In fact, the significance of the paper in sustaining and strengthening the Communist Party (undivided at that time) only increased once the party came to power.

Under such circumstances, there was no question of Gopi moving to Trivandrum. He often visited during his free days, which were rare. Rudra, who stayed not far from our house, found in Gopi a person with whom he could discuss Kerala, including politics. The discussions often turned heated. The Rudras came to our Kollam house for Onam with a young visitor, Josie, a cousin of Colette. They enjoyed the Onam feast and a boat ride on the Ashtamudi Lake and returned happy, admiring the cleanliness with which Amma kept the house.

It was after I settled into the job at the Bureau that our first daughter Asha was born. Within a few months, a son, Alok, was born to the Rudras. Asha was born in the District Hospital, Kollam and

Alok in the SAT Hospital, Trivandrum. Rudra died in his early sixties at Santiniketan in Bengal where he had built a house. I still keep in touch with Colette who lives in southern France, and her cousin Josie, who was part of that trip and is now settled in Australia. Some years ago, Alok had come along with his two schoolgoing sons to see the place where he was born.

Asha was the first person in my family to be born in a hospital. The hospital superintendent, a lady doctor who was seeing me regularly, might have suggested this. She had great regard for Gopi. She herself gave him a telephone call after the baby was born in the wee hours of the morning. He came to see the baby after daybreak. I gifted him a set of original Parker pens which my brother had got for me through a friend. I went back to Trivandrum to work when the maternity leave was over. Amma, who knew it would be difficult for me to look after a forty-five-day-old baby on my own, accompanied me.

My office was still pulsating with activity as the new ministry had to act fast to cater to the expectations of the people. They needed reliable information about many things to think about and find solutions. Most leaders of the Communist Party were well-read and aware of the changes in other countries, especially in the Soviet Union and China. Their life was spent among the people. They saw how the people lived and what their expectations were. One method effectively used by the communists to educate people about the party's agenda were the pamphlets written in lucid language and distributed among the people. People's theatre and popular science also helped to enhance people's awareness of and vision for a new world which envisaged much more than a mere increase in work and income. The people, in general, received all this with enthusiasm.

My memory of a meeting I attended in the early years of communist rule is an instance of how the ministry's agendas tried to touch a chord in the lives of the people. At this meeting, Gopi was speaking on green leaf manure. Those were days when most yards did not have walls. There used to be green fencing made of small bushes and plants, some with thorns or plaited coconut leaves. But the government was propagating a plant called *seemakonna* to be used as fencing. This plant, with plenty of leaves, could easily be multiplied and the leaves used as manure. The meeting was followed by distribution of cuttings to those who wanted to plant them. It is interesting to think that such an initiative on the part of the government was long before we started discussing Monsanto or organic farming.

The government began to unfold their programmes. Educational reforms were a matter of priority, but it was also a field which posed challenges. We have seen that there were private schools in the state even when I was a school student. But over the decades, private schools and colleges had started flourishing in Kerala. One reason for this could be that the number of aspirants in higher education kept increasing, and the government found it difficult to satisfy that demand. Christian missionaries, who are seen as the pioneers in bringing modern education to the region, were the first to come forward to start new colleges. They were followed by other communities including the Nairs and the Izhavas. Unlike government institutions, these unaided institutions took donations from aspiring students and faculty. There was a time when it was widely heard that teachers who got a paltry sum as salary had to sign receipts for a much higher amount in these institutions. Teachers' organizations protested against this. The new government wanted to change these malpractices that had ensnared the educational system.

The land question, an issue more complex and older than education, was also a vexed one. The nature of land widely differed across the three regions which made up the new state. Paddy was the major crop. Cultivation by the owners of the land was not very common. Tenancy was the most common practice. Tenancy laws were not always in favour of the tenants, some of whom were very poor. The government decided to change the then-prevailing tenancy rules. The objective was to bring justice to the poor, the exploited tenants and the landless labourers. In other countries, especially in Asia, land reforms had resulted in increasing production and raising productivity, particularly in the case of paddy, the main food crop in those countries. But this did not materialize in Kerala. The land under paddy steadily decreased. Roads, railways, government buildings, etc., came up on this land. Years have gone by, and the word '*bhoo* mafia' has become common in Malayalam.

The Catholic clergy was the first to protest when the government came forward with the Education Bill. The protestors were not willing to allow the bill to be made into law. The protests became louder when the new Land Bill came up. The Kerala sky became ablaze with antigovernment slogans. The rumbles grew louder and louder, and it came to be called a liberation struggle or *vimochana samaram* in Malayalam.

On 31 July 1959, the central government dismissed the first Kerala government which had come to power with a popular mandate. More than half a century has passed since those historic moments. An impartial and dispassionate enquiry into that period can teach us many things. Though the first non-Congress government in India that the people had voted to power could not complete its five-year term, its ascendance seems to have set a precedence. Non-Congress-led governments began to be voted to power in other states too. The immediate way in which history affected my life could be seen in the way the excitement within the Bureau gradually began to die down. Its future became uncertain. Those who came on deputation began to leave. Rudra's term was going to end. Personally, I too began to feel rather low, more and more alienated in the changed circumstances. I could not get used to the chaos around me. My mind was in disquiet.

Rudra, who sensed my mental unease, suggested that I apply to the Indian Statistical Institute, which had a small unit in Delhi. Delhi was a place I had never wanted to see again. But when Gopi too offered his support, I decided to give it a try. The Secretary of the Department of Planning offered to send me to Delhi on deputation without giving up my job in Trivandrum. Though the offer was appealing, by then, I had mentally got out of working for the government.

Making a decision at this juncture in my life was difficult and complex. It was not the same as when I left for Madras. We now had a baby daughter. Amma, who had locked her doors and come to be with me, would have to go back – something that I struggled to visualize. Though Gopi did not share it with me then, he had certain reservations about the party's concept of a newspaper. A newspaper, for him, could not be reduced to a party gazette. Though he did not say anything openly, in those ten years, he had helped to raise *Janayugom* to the status of the third largest newspaper in the state in terms of circulation.

Looking back, I find that on ever so many occasions, when I was confronted with anxiety and doubts, there was something that helped me take a plunge into an unknown destination.

❖

CHAPTER EIGHT

To Delhi

Early in the year 1961, I decided to move to Delhi alone. The plan was that Gopi and our daughter would join me soon. Gopi's friend Crispy, employed in the All India Radio, arranged for my stay with a colleague of his from Kerala. I had not known Rosscote Krishna Pillai and his wife Moni earlier, but they made me feel comfortable at their home. After Independence, the government had constructed quarters in the capital for government employees who came from different parts of the country. They were classified into four categories – I, II, III and IV – based on their status and salary or remuneration. The housing complexes too were classified into four corresponding categories. My host had a house befitting his category. The locale also had a convenient bus service to take me to and from my workplace.

My office was in the Planning Commission, known as Yojana Bhavan to the public. Parliament Street, where it was situated, went straight from the Parliament up to Connaught Place. The latter was one of the most important shopping areas in New Delhi at that time. Yojana Bhavan had lofty neighbours. On one side was the Delhi office of the Reserve Bank of India; on the other was the Parliament Street Post Office, a model post office with all facilities. Across the road was All India Radio. Later, Doordarshan too was established in the same compound. Next to that was the Punjab National Bank. At this point where vehicles could turn left and right, there was a round called Patel Chowk to enable the smooth flow of vehicles and pedestrians. In this nice, cosy area there was a small park in which a statue of Sardar Patel stood facing the Parliament.

The Planning Unit of the Indian Statistical Institute (ISI) to which I came was attached to the Perspective Planning Division of the Planning Commission. It was headed by Pitambar Pant, a serious and hardworking man. I came to know that Pant, who signed my appointment order, was a protégé of Mahalanobis and had functioned as a secretary to Prime Minister Nehru, who was the Chairman of the Planning Commission. Interestingly, his wife Bhanumati was Vally's classmate in college. Though of Tamil origin, Bhanumati had grown up in Trivandrum as her father was the Pro-Vice-Chancellor of Travancore University, perhaps brought to that position by the then Dewan of Travancore who himself was from Madras.

Yojana Bhavan was a massive five-storeyed building with around 500 rooms. We had 'identity cards', which I was not used to in Kerala. Those were years before terrorism and terrorist attacks had become a matter of concern, yet we were supposed to show our identity cards to the security men as we entered the building. Of course, the big bosses just walked in while the security men saluted them. The same 'respect' was shown to the foreigners who came in the garb of advisors, experts and researchers. They walked in with their briefcases whereas

In front of the Planning Commission, mid-1960s. (Photographer unknown)

the ordinary Indian staff who might have had their lunch boxes and one or two popular weeklies with them were supposed to show what they were carrying to the security men. These images came back to my mind when I recently heard a senior advocate of the Kerala High Court mentioning, in a different context, that the Indian judiciary has a soft corner towards 'fair skin' and 'the rich and powerful'. An independent, democratic nation!

The main thrust of ISI in Calcutta was Mathematics and Statistics. But there were also elaborate studies going on in Economics, Sociology, Anthropology and Linguistics, all of which were considered essential ingredients in planning and development. The National Sample Survey Organization (NSSO), which is currently under the Government of India, was earlier a part of the ISI. In Delhi, many of the staff in the Planning Unit held a Mathematics degree and also had undergone a three-year course in mathematical techniques necessary for planning.

The room in which I was seated was on the fifth floor of the building, which we could reach by a lift. The room had a wooden partition and on both sides there were two persons with separate tables. I soon became accustomed to my new colleagues. There were a number of women and men from Kerala in the Planning Commission. In the Planning Unit too, there were a couple of South Indians. One of them was Pushpam from Thrissur, Kerala. From Madras there was Chellammal, who was earlier teaching in the Presidency College, Madras, and a man named Ramsundar. All the others were men from North India. It was their names that baffled me – Saluja, Kansal, Vohra, Sabharwal, Goyal, Mathur, Mathuria, the list went on. Kumar was a common name, and I was told that they mostly came from the North-Western provinces during the Partition and that these were not proper names but surnames. By and large, they were friendly.

In the Planning Unit, two young Bengali men, both from Visvabharati University, Santiniketan, and I were to work together. The younger of the two, Pankaj Dutta, had a brilliant MA degree in Economics. By the time I met him, he had worked in all the possible economics research institutions in India including *Economic Review*, a prominent publication of the All India Congress Committee. The other, Mrinal Dutta-Chaudhuri, was a classmate of the Nobel laureate Amartya Sen. Both of them were trying to go to the US, which they did. Chaudhuri stayed there for some years, took a PhD and returned to India to join the Delhi University. Pankaj left the US, and after a short sojourn in Germany where he married Regina, went to Canada where he is settled. His wife, who is a dear friend, came with her son when I was in Delhi. Pankaj has never come back to India.

In the short period we were together, no shared work took place. I was new to everything in the office. All that I knew about ISI was that its founder, Professor Mahalanobis, was the architect of India's Five-Year Plans when we launched the massive development exercise. By the time I came to Delhi, Mahalanobis was not visiting Delhi as often; Pitambar Pant lived in the government house allotted to Mahalanobis.

The early 1960s, when I joined the Planning Unit, was a time when we were trying to bring about big changes in a very large country which was greatly diverse – not just in terms of language, food, dress and culture, but also in terms of economic development. To cater to the diverse needs of the country, the Planning Commission had, besides Perspective Planning, divisions which dealt with Agriculture, Industries, Labour, Education, Health, Scheduled Castes and Scheduled Tribes, Less Developed Areas and so on. There were, besides the clerical and administrative staff, research staff that included officers and assistants.

The majority of people in our country lived in rural areas and depended on agriculture for their livelihood. The vagaries of nature like flood and drought plagued them. Their life was also made difficult by the fluctuations in prices and the greed of moneylenders from whom they had to borrow money. The challenge before us was that we did not have correct information regarding these people. Detailed data on their age, gender, caste and occupation had to be collected.

As we were not keen to copy the 'capitalist model', we tried to see how the Soviet Union and other East European countries approached economic development. When I joined the Planning Unit, there were two men, Mr Rao and Mr Verma, whose responsibility was respectively to translate Russian and Polish technical material relating to planning and development into English.

When India became independent and we started on this massive development journey, the setting up of an array of new institutions created the need for trained personnel to do technical jobs like typing. From the farming community that existed within and around Delhi, select young men were given training in such jobs. They were also given paid holidays during sowing and harvesting seasons. Later, I met one such person in ISI – Mehr Lal from Shahpur Jat, a village nearby. Shahpur Jat was a prosperous agrarian area, which today is a very chic enclave in Delhi. This has happened as part of the gradual 'urbanization' of rural areas. It has turned into one of Delhi's posh areas packed with designer studios, boutiques and cafes meant for rich youngsters. The fields have all vanished and so have the farmers.

When I joined the office, I saw a lot of technical work going on around me. There were those who had worked for years with the manually operated calculator called a Facet machine and a few square sheets of paper. These juniors were called 'computers'. The sheets of compiled data they produced were used for further analysis by the seniors. To the 'computers', what they did was a job that provided them with a salary at the end of the month. I had no problem with that, but to me, planning meant improving the life of the people of this country. I failed to see how the work I saw around me was helping in that process.

Meanwhile my personal life, too, was at a major juncture. I had taken the train to Delhi only because of Gopi's assurance that he would be coming too. It was not something we decided upon with a proper plan of action, but that did not bother us. He was to join me with our daughter whom he and Amma were looking after. I had to look for a house before they came. My hunt for a house with a colleague took me first to Malaviya Nagar. Delhi, besides being the capital of independent India, was also a place which had to absorb large numbers of refugees from the other sides of the partitioned country, and Malaviya Nagar was one of those refugee colonies. I did not take that house because I thought that it was too far from the office; also, I was yet to get used to houses which stood too close to each other.

At that time, Rudra and his family were staying in a place on the western side of Delhi, called East Patel Nagar. It was with Rudra that I went out looking for a house the next time. In those days, Delhi did not have multistoreyed flats, but there were big bungalows with spacious lawns. On the side of the main road at South Patel Nagar, slightly further away from where the Rudras were staying, we found such a house. The ground floor was rented to a convent to run a school and the first floor of that building was occupied by the owners, an elderly Sardarji, his wife and son.

I rented the first floor above their garage for Rs 150 per month. The elderly owner liked me and readily gave me the keys. Above us lived another son of the owner and his family. Rudra and I went out and bought certain essential things for the family. It was winter and naturally, we needed blankets, bedsheets and *razai*s. It was to this house that Gopi came with our daughter. My mother sent huge boxes of eatables like banana chips and provisions to help me. There was powdered chilli, turmeric, rice, pulses and spices to last us at least three months. This was the first time I was setting up a house on my own. Parcels containing eatables and delicacies unique to Kerala continued to arrive regularly till I found it difficult to go and collect the big Britannia containers from the railway station. Amma also managed to find a young girl, Radha, to help me.

Today, I wonder how quickly one managed to adjust to things. The whole house was perhaps as big as one room in our house in Kollam. It had two small rooms and a rather tiny veranda. One end of that space became the kitchen. A curtain separated that part and the rest became the 'dining' area. Still, the house was not cramped. All the houses on the side of the road had some land around and a garden. We saw the children of our rich Punjabi neighbours playing on their grounds whenever they were free. During the daytime, we saw the school in action. Sights like these made the stay at the new house enjoyable. I soon became acquainted with the headmistress, an amiable nun.

While travelling from Moti Bagh, where I lived earlier, to Yojana Bhavan, I saw quite a lot of Delhi, including Chanakyapuri or the diplomatic enclave. Many of the countries who had diplomatic relations with India had their buildings there. These buildings in various architectural styles showcased the distinctive culture and traditions of each country. They also exhibited the affluence of the home countries and displayed the country's national flag. The layout of the area was beautiful with wide and clean roads.

Slowly, I came to know that Delhi had many parks, gardens and avenue trees. We had learned in school that one of the administrative achievements of the Maharajas was to plant shady trees along the pathways to protect weary pedestrians from the harsh rays of the sun. One tree which could be found in plenty was *jamun*. It had fruit that was both delicious and had medicinal qualities. When it was time for the fruit to be plucked, traders, who looked like villagers, came with their families and did a neat job. A youngster would climb the tree and shake it. The others would spread a cloth underneath and catch the falling fruit in it. There was even a song about it: '*Kaale, kaale jamun wale . . .*' .

There was a direct bus to Parliament Street from my new house as well. It was during these bus journeys that I saw other parts of Delhi. One such area was Karol Bagh. A friend who had been in Delhi for long told us that when he first came to Delhi, Karol Bagh was like a mini-forest where jackals and other animals thrived. But by the time I was there, it had changed. The place had a sizeable population of South Indians, mainly Tamilians, who had migrated to Delhi for jobs. There were shops catering mainly to their demands. We also passed through Pusa Road. It was more or less like the road in front of our house with big bungalows on both sides. The Arya Vaidya Pharmacy, Coimbatore, had a branch there. Many non-Malayalis or non-South Indians used to go there for treatment.

Gradually, we settled down in our new home. There was not much for Radha to do. Her main job was to play with Asha. I also taught her to knit and to arrange newspapers and journals. I had not expected Gopi to have a regular paid job as soon as he came to Delhi. At the same time, to me, my work was not just about earning some money. Though I could not explain or define it, working outside home was as important to me as my responsibilities within the house. So, I went to 'work' without any guilt. I used to cook the meals for the day in the morning before going to office. Fortunately, Colette used to come and take Asha and Radha along with her son Alok to a small neighbourhood park to play. Gopi would bathe and get Asha ready before she came.

I came to Delhi after getting a job, but not exactly knowing what I would be doing at ISI. It was difficult to understand what the Planning Unit as a whole did. One man from Kerala who was there for a long time told me that the job assigned to him when he joined was to take foreign guests and visitors around to offices and tourist spots. When I met him, he did not have any specific work, and he was not the only one to be in that state. I later met a North Indian like him, who however succeeded in migrating to the US. Some technical staff from ISI, Calcutta came to discuss their work with someone in the Planning Commission or other ministries. I did not get to know them and could not discuss the work done there. On the whole, I began to feel uneasy, not knowing what I was supposed to do.

Fortunately, the Planning Commission library came to my rescue. The library on the ground floor had not just books related to Economics and Planning, but books of all kinds. Books on the social sciences, especially Sociology and Anthropology, were in plenty. I came across interesting annual reports and special studies like the *Scheduled Castes and Scheduled Tribes Commissioners' Reports. The Annual Survey of Industries* (ASI) piqued my interest as I saw that the data it provided on the location of industries, labour, wages and so on made an all-India comparison possible. I indulged in research, publishing the results in the *Economic and Political Weekly*. Though I enjoyed it and found it useful, I did not want it to be my lifelong work.

I found out that there were others like me in the Planning Commission who were not very satisfied with the work they were doing. I met and exchanged views with some of them. I remember a chemical engineer in the Planning Commission who left soon. People like us met either in the Coffee House inside the Planning Commission or along the corridors. The Coffee House in Yojana Bhavan became a haunt for me and my colleagues. Although room service was available, Pushpam and I became regulars in the Coffee House. Initially, we were the only women who went there. Gradually, this began to change. On several occasions, Crispy from across the road also joined us. I became acquainted with some of the bearers, most of whom were from Kerala. They lived frugally in the outhouses of houses allotted to Members of Parliament from Kerala. This enabled them to educate their children who were back home. At least one or two of them had daughters who had completed their Master's degrees. On the other hand, there was an elderly North Indian bearer who was trying hard to get a job extension or get his son absorbed as a bearer. I still remember his pleadings.

Gopi had come without ensuring a job for himself in Delhi. He knew some major figures including the prominent journalist Nikhil Chakravartty, and Mohit Sen. Mohit would have liked him to join the publications division of the Communist Party (then undivided), but Gopi was not keen on it.

His old friend C.N. Chittaranjan (CNC) was at that time working with *Link*, an independent left journal started by Dr Baliga, Aruna

Asaf Ali and some others who had a progressive left vision. CNC told Gopi that they were planning a daily, and asked him if he could wait as it may take some time. In the meantime, Gopi occupied himself with editing and translation work that a young Malayali friend gave him. It brought some money. He also became a member of the British Council, which became an abode for him. He dug into the corners of the library, which was conveniently located near Crispy's home, and discovered books by unknown authors. Through the books he brought, I got to know writers in English who were not from England or its principal colonies. I remember reading a fascinating book which dealt with the struggles of the rural masses with the advent of industrialization.

It did not take too long for *Patriot*, the paper CNC mentioned, to materialize. In fact Gopi joined the venture even before it was launched as there were young recruits who had to be trained. Those were not the days when journalism or mass communication was taught in institutions. Though many of the young men did not complete the training, some joined the new venture. One person on the editorial committee thought that Gopi did not have experience in English-language journalism. But Edathatta Narayanan, the editor and a confidante of Aruna Asaf Ali, was not concerned. Gopi proved that he was not illiterate in the language or unfamiliar with the ways of English-language journalism.

At that time, we had no idea how long we would live in Delhi. We always dreamt of coming back and starting a weekly or a monthly in Kerala. But each visit to Kerala made us realize the increasing hold of money and the moneyed on newspapers. Newspapers could no longer survive merely on courage or commitment. Sponsorship was not a word common at that time, but investors were. Which investor would come forward to let us bring out a journal according to our politics and vision?

Our Delhi days were memorable because of the many acquaintances and friends we made there. Soon after Gopi came from Kerala, we met a young Bengali at Rudra's place. Viswapriya was the third son of Prabhat Mukherjee, the chief librarian at Santiniketan and the official biographer of Rabindranath Tagore.

Gopi had earlier travelled to West Bengal and met many people, including Prabhat Mukherjee, as it was his great dream to bring out a biography of Tagore as a *Janayugom* publication. He had

With friends in Delhi. (*Left to right*) Prabhat Mukherjee, Sudhamoyee, Saradamoni, Gopi with Anu on his lap, Asha. (Photo by Viswapriya Mukherjee)

taken extensive notes but, unfortunately, that book never came out. Viswapriya soon became a good friend. At that time, he was a bachelor. As I was busy during the week, I used to have a 'Sunday morning breakfast' session, which Crispy, Viswapriya and often Colette joined. These mornings became a tradition that we looked forward to. They extended beyond the breakfast with Gopi reading out from Malayalam poets like Vallathol and Kumaran Asan. Due to his knowledge of Sanskrit, Viswapriya could enjoy them.

It was in Delhi that I came to know M.P. Narayana Pillai (Nanappan) who worked in the Planning Commission, and K.N. Shyamasundaran Nair (Shyamu) who later became the Vice Chancellor of Kerala Agricultural University. Both these young Malayali men were related to P.K. Vasudevan Nair (PKV) and P. Govinda Pillai, who were our friends and communist leaders in Kerala. Shyamu was working on a PhD at the famous Pusa Institute which was very near our house. When we met, Nanappan was staying in a house allotted to PKV by the government as a Member of Parliament. We used to meet at Yojana Bhavan. He later left the Planning Commission, worked as a journalist for some time and became an acknowledged writer in Malayalam. We lost touch with him and the news of his early death was a shock to us.

Many experts visited the Planning Unit and Mr Pant arranged talks by them. I remember a Yugoslavian linguist observing that there were people who would not open their mouths if asked to respond in such a gathering, but would talk nonstop outside. That observation contained a great deal of truth. I also remember attending the Hindi classes organized for non-Hindi-speaking central government employees and passing a couple of examinations. Training in first aid was organized when the Sino–Indian war broke out in 1962, which I readily attended. Years later, when the computer was introduced, I also attended the computer language classes offered at that time. I enjoyed these activities.

Gradually, things were changing in the Planning Unit and people were leaving. Rudra left. Pushpam and Ramsundar went on deputation to the Railway Board where they were later absorbed. Many were trying to leave. Did I think of doing so? The 3,000-kilometre-long trek from Kerala itself was hard. I had left the government for good and felt that such frustrations would be there everywhere. So I decided to stay on.

This was followed by a phase where new people joined Planning Unit. They were mainly from the US. They were T.N. Srinivasan, B.S. Minhas, C. Rangarajan and Suresh Tendulkar. Jagdish Bhagwati was also there for some time. He was working on a project on India's trade with Japan along with Alaknanda, daughter of the eminent economist A.K. Dasgupta and wife of the late I.G. Patel. Patel had held several top positions including that of the Governor of the Reserve Bank of India and Director of the London School of Economics. Among them, it was Rangarajan who became the closest friend and went on to become a friend of the family. He had a blazing career after he left ISI. He went to the Institute of Management, Ahmedabad and later became Governor of the Reserve Bank of India. Others like V.K. Chetty and K.S. Parikh joined ISI later.

Before Independence, young Indians who aspired to higher studies used to go to Britain or Europe where they were influenced by liberal or radical thinking. But a phenomenon of the post-Independence years was that many looked towards the US. Several among the early staff at ISI, including mathematicians and statisticians, held left political views. I also heard that in the beginning, appointments were only for eleven months and the same persons were reappointed after a break.

Even by the time I joined, there was no sharp hierarchy there, as was known in the government or other academic institutions. The only two categories were scientific workers and non-scientific workers. The relatively egalitarian culture of ISI was a legacy from its beginnings in 1932 during the height of the freedom movement. The values of that movement had permeated society at large, but that could not be expected to last forever. Still, in terms of the scale of pay and other allowances, ISI did not follow the government rules.

Things began to change with the coming of the new batch of staff at senior levels. They were established academics who expected better status and salary than what ISI was used to. They were trained in the American style of mathematical economics rather than the European Marxian political economics. I have heard that many of the well-known 'progressive' economists and social scientists from India have spent some time during their careers in ISI.

These changes could be felt in the most immediate of matters. Initially, there was no housing for the staff. A big building in Hauz Khas had been rented as a guest house, but a part of it was kept for Sri K.P.S. Menon who was then the Chairman of ISI, though he was not always in Delhi. The rest of the building was occupied by guests who came for a short or slightly longer stay. The cooks and other managerial staff lived in an outhouse in the same compound. Later, many of the senior staff began to be allotted houses rented by the Institute.

Today, I can realize this shift as a result of larger forces at work. It was not just that students and job-seekers from India or other third world countries began to prefer the US for higher studies or jobs. Institutions like the World Bank and the International Monetary Fund were beginning to attract the young. Even employed people from the newly independent countries were invited for short or long-term training programmes and seminars. This was not just propelled by the collapse of the British empire. There were forces twisting the countries that had freed themselves from the exploitative clutches of the empire. Looking back, it seems strange to me that I, who came from communist Kerala, failed to understand what exactly was happening. Now we are familiar with terms such as neo-liberal, neo-capitalist and corporate; it was not so then.

In my home, too, things were changing. Our second daughter was born in our Kollam house. I had come home on maternity leave.

The birth was looked after by the same midwife who brought me into the world. Amma, as always, took charge of the post-delivery care. Asha, our elder daughter, who was four years at that time, was with me. She was a bit restless and curious about everything behind the doors which were closed to her. However, the sight of the baby eased her. The baby was named Arunima (the glow before dawn). But Vally named her Mini after the child protagonist in Tagore's 'Kabuliwala' and continued to call her so. My eldest sister-in-law and her daughters too took to calling her by that name. To the rest of the world, she is Anu or Arunima.

When I returned to Delhi after forty-five days, Amma decided to come with me. She could foresee my difficulties in managing the home and office. We were returning to a Delhi which was in the grip of winter. Amma had no idea of the severity of the cold. She thought that it would be a little more than what we in Kerala felt during heavy rains. She thought that she could manage with a *kodi neriyatu*. By the time we reached Nagpur, she asked for 'something' to cover her body. Fortunately, we had bought a warm cardigan for her. Without any problem on the way, we reached Delhi. Looking back, I am impressed by the way Amma adjusted to our tiny accommodation, that too on the first floor, where she stayed for more than six months.

Back in Delhi, I met an old friend and contemporary from University College, Parameswara Kurup, who had completed an MA and PhD from Baroda and was working as an economist in the Punjab National Bank, just across the Planning Commission. During those days, a young Malayali woman named Indira from the Central Statistical Organization (CSO) nearby used to come over to have lunch with us or coffee at the Coffee House. Perhaps she knew Pushpam. Kurup saw her and developed an 'interest' in her. He wanted me to be the mediator.

Indira was from north Parur and a brilliant student. After a Master's degree in Mathematics, she was doing her PhD with a central government scholarship, not very common in those days. She was invited to ISI, Calcutta with the offer of a fellowship, and she later accepted a job below what she could have got with her qualifications and ability at CSO. Her father was a retired teacher and Indira, being the eldest child, had responsibilities towards the family, especially the education of her younger brothers. Besides this, she may have

In the garden at Patel Nagar, Delhi. (*Left to right*) Indira, Saradamoni holding baby Anu, Pushpam. (Photographer unknown)

accepted the job because a central government job was a big attraction to people in Kerala then. In today's Kerala, one can find young women and men who have no difficulty moving from job to job or from place to place. Still, a 'secure' job is the dream of the vast majority even today. I have often thought that Indira's decision to accept the CSO job was a wrong choice.

She had no objection to the idea of getting married. They got married in Kerala. Amma was with us to receive the couple. Gentle, quiet and simple, Indira gave birth to three daughters who are married and live in different parts of the world, like many young Malayalis. She retired from the CSO and returned to Parur where they started building a house. Unfortunately, she did not live to see it completed. Leaving Kurup to live alone in that house, she left us. I still miss her. She was a younger sister to me.

An important event while Amma was with me in Delhi was the

death of Prime Minister Nehru. The news began to spread like wildfire and reached the Planning Commission around 10 or 10.30 am, much before the official announcement was released. Years later, when I read Nehru's sister Vijayalakshmi Pandit's autobiography, I could understand the commotion at the highest levels of the administration. In one sense, Nehru's death was not unexpected. In fact, 'After Nehru, who?' was a question debated in the media and political circles. But one must not forget that they were very different from the debates that we come across today. Nehru was the unquestioned leader of the country even there were a few whispers here and there about his giving way to someone else.

It was a time when there was only the All India Radio and a few newspapers to give us news. As soon as the official announcement of Nehru's death came, I left the office and went to the house where my friends P. Govinda Pillai and his wife Rajamma were staying. That was in South Avenue, near Teen Murti, the official residence of the Prime Minister. From there, I could see people, individuals and groups small and big, walking towards the Prime Minister's house, only to find the gates closed. It was late at night that news about the cremation, which was decided for the next day, got confirmed. But the people had to be given a chance to have a glimpse of the mortal remains of the man they had loved, trusted and followed. The crowd was swelling fast. And suddenly, heavy rain and wind came from nowhere as if nature was mourning the death of her great lover. Still, the people waited patiently. The gates were opened sometime after midnight. I, too, stood in line to bid adieu to the man my generation had loved and respected. I must have either stayed in South Avenue that whole night, or gone home and then returned. We had no telephone at home, and naturally, Gopi would be in office on such a day. The next day we went to the *Patriot* office and saw from the roof of the building, the procession carrying the dead body of a man who had travelled the length and breadth of this country many times.

A few days later, the urn carrying the ashes of Nehru was kept in Teen Murti Bhavan just outside the main building for people to pay their respects. I took Amma and the children to pay our respects when there was less of a crowd. Indira Gandhi came out and greeted the people with folded arms.

It was the end of an era.

Before Amma returned to Kerala we took her to Kasi (Banaras), which is a very auspicious place for Hindus. It is also the place where ceremonial rituals to remember one's ancestors and seek their blessings are performed. There are people, generally called Pandas, who help with the rituals. We reached there late in the evening and stayed in a room that was arranged by them. I got to see the great River Ganga and her banks only the next morning. I saw, across the river, people, especially women clad in white, moving like ghosts. Even from a distance, I could see that they were undernourished and did not display any human energy. I can faintly remember the shacks from which these humans crept out. The first thought that came to me was whether these people and the likes of them ever had a place in the minds of the experts who contemplated and decided the destiny of the people of this country. I wondered how many in the Planning Commission knew that such people too lived here.

Another interesting experience in Kasi was watching a special train which brought pilgrims from the Salem and Erode districts of Tamil Nadu. They had brought rice, vegetables, other necessary things and gas cylinders to cook and feed large numbers of the poor who sat in rows in the lanes and bylanes. While looking at them, I couldn't help thinking that there could be cheats and criminals among them. I don't think such thoughts ever crossed the minds of the Tamil pilgrims who had come from far away, their hearts filled with piety and charity.

At Kasi, we did all that Amma wanted to do, mainly for the ancestors of the family who had died. But the place, including the famous Vishwanath temple, did not impress me. It was filthy, unlike the temples in Kerala. People were continuously bringing water in big brass containers and pouring it over the idol. The whole area was muddy and slushy. The newly built Birla Mandir was certainly different, though lacking the imprint and grandeur of age. What I loved the most was a Buddhist shrine some kilometres away at Sarnath. It was clean and peaceful.

Kasi held many attractions to a curious visitor. Banaras Hindu University was a vibrant place during the nationalist struggle against the British. Kasi was also a seat of music, arts and scholarship. However, we did not manage to see everything. The place was renowned for Banarasi silk saris, one of which I had worn for my marriage. We also took Amma some days later to see the Taj Mahal and Fatehpur Sikri.

At Fatehpur Sikri, we were told that the special *paratha* served at lunch was the same as during Shah Jahan's time. It had to be ordered as soon as we reached. I think Amma enjoyed the trip, as these locales already had a place in her mind after having read about them in a book in Malayalam, *Yamunayude Theerathu* (On the Banks of the Yamuna), written by M.K. Kumaran who was an MP from Kerala.

It was not the first time that we had taken Amma on a trip. When Asha was about one year old, we planned to take Amma to Madurai and Rameswaram, not far from Trivandrum. She made a big fuss saying that the baby was too small, but we did go. We took a train to Madurai, stayed in the railway retiring room and saw the temple town and the surroundings. The Meenakshi temple was impressive. But I was not pleased that the place was a hub of business, with people competing to show us around or make us buy things to offer to the gods. At that time such things were unheard of in Kerala temples. At Rameswaram, where rituals to propitiate the deceased are undertaken, the aspect of business was even more glaring. After that we went to Dhanushkodi. As I remember it, there was a train to reach this tiny strip of land jutting out into the sea. We were fortunate to see the place, as it was taken over by the sea after a few years. The interesting thing was that while the sea was roaring on one side, the other side was very peaceful and all of us, including Amma, washed our faces and feet in clear, calm waters. The colour of the sea too was different on either side. Marvels of nature!

We took Amma to a concert by the well-known Carnatic singer M.S. Subbulakshmi while in Delhi. Amma enjoyed the concert. She had seen one film, *Avvaiyar*, a Tamil musical starring the legendary singer K.B. Sundarambal. It was in Kollam, and my brother had taken her to see the film.

I cannot remember Amma ever complaining in Delhi, though she had many things that she was not used to, including the lack of space. We changed to cooking gas while she was there. Gopi took Amma back to Madras where my brother met them and took her to Kerala. Though she went back, she was concerned about us. After some time she found through Chandrettan's family a young woman, Rajamma, to stay with us and look after the children. She was with us for several years both in Delhi and later in Trivandrum.

This chapter would not be complete without mentioning a

cherished friendship that started while I was in the Planning Commission. As part of an Education Commission set up between India and England, a team of Englishmen were in India. Two of them shared the room with me. We used to greet each other when we met on the corridor of the Planning Commission building. One day, I encountered one of them at the nearby bus stop. In the course of our conversation, I told him that my husband was a journalist. He said that he too was a journalist. I suggested that he could visit us at home. He asked me whether he could bring his wife. Not knowing that he had a wife with him in Delhi, I replied that he could. He came out with another surprise when he asked, 'Can I bring our children?' I gave the same reply. He did not stop. He wanted to know whether he could bring the young girl who looked after the children. I gave the same reply, that he could if he had an ayah for the children. He kept his word and came with the retinue. It was a very enjoyable afternoon and the beginning of a long-lasting friendship and an extended familial relationship. The person I am talking about, unfortunately, is not with us today. His name was Tyrrell Burgess.

Tyrrell's parents, Ivy and Jack Burgess, were middle-level functionaries in the UK who were strong supporters of the Labour Party. They had two sons who went to a state school. The younger one became a botanist. The elder brother went to Oxford and became the president of the University Students' Union. I think that it was the first time that a student from a non-elite school background had reached that position. Tyrrell had many interests – politics, journalism, music and art. This was his first visit to India, and he was trying to grasp as much as he could. He wrote to his parents almost daily. His lifelong interest was education. He was a champion of the state school system and a relentless critic of Margaret Thatcher. He chose to remain a professor at the Polytechnic, while others with lesser qualifications and ability would have managed a position in one of the 'prestigious' universities.

During the days we first met, he had started to write a story or novel based on his experiences in India, especially at ISI. He named one of his characters Brinjal. He used to tell me bits and pieces of the story, and we used to laugh a lot. Sadly, the book was not completed. He died of cancer in 2009.

After some time, we moved from Patel Nagar to a more spacious house in Hauz Khas towards the south of Delhi. Our landlord, the

With Tyrrell and Joan Burgess in Stonehenge, 1983. (Photographer unknown)

elderly Sardarji, was not happy. Fortunately, we could arrange for him a Keralite, a cartoonist who was an old associate of Gopi, to rent the house we vacated. We liked the new house. It was on the first floor with two big rooms, a kitchen, bathroom and toilet. But what we liked the most were the verandas in the front and back, the latter spacious and airy. From there, we could see a pond surrounded by big trees whose branches touched the water. Peacocks and peahens used to visit this place regularly. We arranged more than one Onam feast in this house. Those were delightful moments. It was from that veranda that we could see the farms of Shahpur Jat village. Cabbage and cauliflower, uncommon at that time in Kerala, were the main crops there. We watched them being grown and harvested around winter. Big trucks came and carried away the harvested vegetables, which sold at four *anna*s (sixteen paise) per kilo.

Our time in that house was enjoyable, but brief. The landlord asked us to vacate the house, giving us some reason which we thought was genuine. We shifted to a house on the ground floor, not far from the earlier one but with no scenic beauty. It was a twin house – one of two identical houses with a common wall. This was something I had not known in Kerala. Otherwise, the houses were separate and had different gates too. The landlord stayed on the first floor of the house.

The occupants of the adjacent house were from the north-western parts of undivided India, an elderly couple with their two sons and a daughter.

By the time we settled down in the new home, it was time to think about the schooling of our children. Our elder daughter had been admitted to a pre-primary school in Patel Nagar where we first lived. However, we had not thought of it as a permanent arrangement. We had our own notions about schooling. We did not want them to go to a convent school. My sisters and I had studied in a convent, but after having seen the schoolchildren in various types of schools in free India's capital – the snobbishness of some and the deprivation of another section visible even in their uniforms – we looked for a school that came in between. We ruled out the Kerala School as we did not want our children to remain exclusively Malayalis. Later, I came across students from Kerala School who spoke Hindi and not Malayalam among themselves, and sometimes even at home.

Our search took us to Lady Irwin School, one of the oldest girls' schools in Delhi. It was started in 1927 during the British period, mainly for the children of middle-level Indian officers. During the summer, when Delhi became too hot for the whites, it used to be shifted to Simla from where the administration functioned. At the time we came to know about that school, its primary wing was in a place called Defence Colony, and the main school was in the heart of the city, on Canning Lane, now renamed as Shrimant Madhav Rao Scindia Marg. The school was different and interesting in many ways. In primary school, rabbits and pigeons were raised. Children had to bring food for the pets. I have bought carrots and spinach for the rabbits many a time. One thing that attracted us was that the school did not have uniforms. The principal, strict in an old-world sense but with atypical ideas about schools and students, believed that inculcating the values of simplicity in clothing and lifestyle among students was more worthy than insisting on uniforms for a few hours every day. Her name was Ms Kamala Sengupta, and her centenary was celebrated in 2011. Though we did not know it then, students from that school have occupied many top positions as teachers, doctors, artists, scientists, lawyers and bureaucrats.

Our younger daughter Anu's first school was decided more by chance. In Hauz Khas itself, there was a play school run by a mother–

daughter team, which we used to pass regularly. They had a van which used to be parked on a road near the Hauz Khas market. Whenever we went to the market, Anu would touch the van and say that she wanted to go to that school. The demand persisted, and we admitted her there. Later, she too moved to Lady Irwin primary school. Both girls graduated from the same school. Even at that time, schooling and studies were far less taxing and more relaxed than what they have turned out to be today.

A big event that we witnessed in Hauz Khas after we moved in was the wedding of the only daughter of our neighbour from the north-west. Theirs was a friendly family. The father ran a business in Connaught Place. The year we moved in, the daughter was studying in college. While we were there, she got married to a young man she chose, outside their community.

Before we left for Delhi and during the several years we spent visiting Kerala, weddings in the state were relatively simple. I had not known or seen dowry being given. The weddings we saw in Delhi were contrary to these. Our neighbour in Delhi stored all the dowry items in our living room. One cot worth Rs 3,000, other furniture and all other items of household goods would have cost many thousands. It was a typical Punjabi or Delhi wedding. The *pantal* or the *shamiana*, as it was known in those parts, was erected blocking the road. As it was an accepted practice, nobody protested. The bridegroom came on the back of a mare by dusk, accompanied by family and friends with great gusto. North Indian weddings are usually accompanied by lots of merrymaking and are not matter-of-fact like those in Kerala. The first part of the wedding – the bride garlanding the bridegroom – is a delightful event. Then comes the feast, invariably, a buffet. Most of the guests leave after that. The real marriage takes place late in the night with a *pujari* performing the rituals including a *homam* in front of close relatives. This continues till the wee hours of the morning. After the *kanyadaan*, the girl leaves her parents' home, and the groom and his family take with them all the dowry.

Out of curiosity and because the house was so close, I decided to watch the ceremony. In the end, I saw what it meant to be a 'bride giver'. The girl ceased to be a member of her household in every sense. Even when I was in Delhi several decades after Independence, I have seen families where the bride's people did not drink even a cup of tea from the son-in-law's house. Some people paid an amount if they accepted any hospitality from the bridegroom's family. It was a world of men where the worth of boys was far superior to that of girls, even if she was equal to him in terms of education and salary. Just as the bride was leaving, I heard her elderly father pleading to be excused for any lapse. I could not control myself and asked him not to say such humiliating words. I have not forgotten that incident.

I did not realize at that time that calamities were awaiting my neighbour's house. It had nothing to do with the marriage of the daughter. In the years that followed, the younger son of the family who was with the Air Force as a trainee pilot died in an accident. The body was brought home before the cremation. He had just been married, and this was naturally a big blow to the elderly parents.

The other calamity was a more devastating one. We used to give a lift sometimes to the senior neighbour up to a point near his office. One day, he came with us as usual. Gopi dropped me off near my office and they went to the city centre. He did not return home that night. The search led to his office where his body was found hanging from the ceiling. We never knew that when he came with us in the morning, he was carrying the belt of his housecoat for that purpose. It was a sad day and its memory remained with me for long.

Another unforgettable memory from those years is a surgery which I underwent. I had developed a thyroid problem after the birth of Anu. Vally noticed that I had some difficulty in swallowing even liquid, but I started taking it seriously only when more people began to notice it. I went to the All India Institute of Medical Sciences (AIIMS), which was not such a VIP hospital at that time. There I became a patient of Dr Ahuja, the Head of the Department of Endocrinology. I was put on medication after some tests, and this continued for a couple of years at least. Actually I was not bothered, but was slightly disturbed when people remarked about it, and more so when the doctor told me that medical science could not promise that it would not develop further. It was then that I decided to have it taken out.

The surgery was under the joint care of Dr Ahuja, the physician and the late Dr Atma Prakash, the surgeon. AIIMS being a research institute, the patients were sometimes examined in front of students. The operation was under full anaesthesia. But something scary, yet interesting, happened. I did not feel any pain, yet I heard everything the doctors were saying. I was conscious that I was on an operation table and that I was not supposed to hear anything. During my stay at the hospital, which continued for some more days, my brother came from Kerala to be with me. He slept in the room adjacent to mine and took me for morning walks. I used to hold my neck out of an subconscious fear and he used to gently remove my hand. In the evenings, the children and Gopi came to see me. My food was provided by the hospital, from which I used to save the sweet dish for the girls. I had to pay for the food and stay; the rest of the treatment was included as part of the research and hence free. I am not sure if this practice continues. I believe that I got very good attention and care in the hospital. This spell in the hospital too was an indelible part of the years I spent in Delhi.

While we were in the second house in Hauz Khas, there was an unexpected addition to our family. The children conspired with Nikhil Chakravartty, a great lover of dogs, and brought home a puppy. I use the word conspired because I was not fond of pets. Besides, I knew that the children's enthusiasm would not last long and the responsibility would fall on me. Indeed that happened. Soon after he was brought, everybody at home except me came down with chicken pox. He was not to go near the sick, so he developed a closeness, and later love for me. When I returned from office he would hide himself under my sari and play with my feet or chappals. During my occasional migraine attacks, he would patiently sit near my bed and wait till I got up. In fact, I thought for a long time that he would one day call me 'Amma'. But alas, that was not to happen. He was named Zippy by Anu. In the course of time, it was upgraded into Zipparanean and then to Zipparanean Nair.

❖

CHAPTER NINE

To France

It was sometime in the middle of the 1960s that life suddenly threw a surprise at me. One day, I got a telephone call from a person who introduced himself as a friend of Madeleine. He asked me whether I could meet him in the place he was staying. He turned out to be Professor Louis Dumont, the renowned French social anthropologist who had worked in South India and produced a study on the Kallar community – a study that was widely acclaimed. After talking for some time, he abruptly asked whether I would like to go to France. The question was so unexpected that I was taken aback. He was at that time engaged in building up the Centre for Indian Studies (Centre d'etudes de l'Inde), and facilitating the exchange of scholars between India and France was one of his plans. Later, it became the Centre d'etudes de l'Inde et de l'Asie du Sud, or Centre for Indian and South Asian Studies. I told him that I had never thought of going abroad, and would do only if I could do some serious work. He was insistent and asked whether I would think about the matter if he took responsibility. I had no reply to that.

After returning from a brief visit to South India, he approached me once again. This time, he called Gopi at his office. Gopi invited Dumont for lunch the next day at our house. The same question about my going to France was raised. Before I realized what it was all about, he started moving on the procedures, and I began to get forms to be filled out. With that I went through extreme agony, the like of which I had never experienced before. Friends like Crispy encouraged me by pointing out that while there were many who were trying hard to go abroad, here the chance was coming my way. On the other hand, Amma wrote to remind me that the children and Gopi would find it difficult to manage without me. I myself found it difficult to face the reality before me. I had never travelled to such a distant place. True,

Gopi was good with the children, but the question, 'This is for a long stretch of time; how will they manage everything?' bothered me day and night. My mind was turbulent for nearly three months, till, one day, Gopi in his characteristic manner said, 'Sometimes in life, one has to take painful decisions.' That meant a lot to me. I decided to go.

I was called to the Cultural Counsellor's Office attached to the French Embassy. There, I met three Malayalis who helped with the procedures and made things easy for me. They were from Mahe, which used to be a French enclave. Raghavan was the seniormost; then there was Devarajan. The third was a much younger person, Raghavan's younger brother Mukundan, who later became renowned in the Malayalam literary world as M. Mukundan. We became close to Raghavan and his family. This friendship lasted till we left Delhi. I had off and on studied French since I came to know Madeleine. Once my trip to France was decided, I again went to the Alliance Française in New Delhi.

My momentous journey to France took place towards the end of September 1969. My ticket was arranged by the French government, on an Air France flight. I was shocked when a member of the crew asked me to remove the jasmine flowers that my daughters had given me from my hair. I quickly removed it – it upset me, but I was not dispirited. The plane had a stopover at Tel Aviv, where those of us who wished to go out were given a slip to do so. I took one and went out, took a quick round and also got a free cup of black coffee. Next we landed in Paris.

An annoying experience during my maiden travel to a country away from India opened my eyes to how the procedures of international travel are often blind to cultural differences. We had to fill out many forms, in each of which we were to write our name, country of origin and so on. In the space for names, we were supposed to give our first name and surname. Officially, you would be known by the surname, something which changed after marriage in the case of most women. This was not something that could have always worked for an Indian as many people in India have the name of the family or village as surname. I coolly wrote my first name as my surname and that served my purpose. I came to know from friends the funny ways in which they tackled the issue. I was irritated because it was a pointer to how the so-called developed or advanced countries from where these rules originate failed to recognize the fact that there are variations in naming practices between peoples and countries.

In France, I would have naturally sought out Madeleine before anybody else. We had never lost touch. She was in Paris but was resting after undergoing treatment for breast cancer. She had sent a friend and student of hers who was also looking after the library and documentation at the Centre where Dumont was the Director. This young woman, Marie Louise Reiniche, was holding out a book with a blue cover when I entered the lounge so that I could easily identify her. Madeleine had arranged my stay at the Maison de l'Inde (India House) at the Cité Universitaire (University City). The Cité was a big complex where different countries had built hostels or residential accommodation. However, there was no rule that they would accommodate students only from their own countries. One of the biggest hostels was that of the US. Some of the smaller Asian countries had smaller buildings which were architecturally unique. Sri Lanka had a small but pleasing hostel. Chandrika Bandaranaike, later Kumaratunga, who rose to become the Prime Minister of that country, was a student in Paris while I was there. The first three months were mainly spent on orientation. Besides Paris, there was one more place students could opt for during their orientation. But I had not known about that; besides, I was not ready for any adventure.

As one entered the Maison de l'Inde the concierge or the receptionist would welcome you and provide you with all the instructions. The same person remained the concierge through the two years I lived there. It was in his enclosure that we found our mail and other notices. The French workers were an organized force. I lost count of the number of postal strikes that were called for during the years I was there. It was not easy to get news from home, but we survived. The truck workers were another organized group. Their frequent strikes hit the economy, and made big news.

French law insisted that all foreigners report to the police within a stipulated time. Madeleine had arranged for another young woman, Teresa, who knew both English and French, to take me to the police and other relevant ministries that I was supposed to visit. Teresa was not French. We became friends and met often. She fell in love with a young worker from Yugoslavia named George and married him. They soon had a baby and after some time moved to Australia where Teresa's

Outside the Maison de l'Inde, 1969. (Photographer unknown)

parents lived. Though we lost contact, I still have fond memories of her.

I was keen to continue studying French and the government readily agreed to meet the expenses. I opted for an early morning class, which was at a place quite far away. There was a direct underground train – the metro – to take me there. The travel was easy for me as there was a metro station just in front of the Cité inside a huge park. I used to have a small cup of coffee (*petit café*) and a croissant from the Italian house in the Cité on the way to the station. Now various types of continental food are available in India, but the croissant was not that common in those days, and I liked it a lot. The metro was the real wonder. It was different from the rail travel I was familiar with. Commuting daily, I had to walk a lot, and go up and down the stairs many times. Besides the staircases, there were escalators as well, where one stood steady on one step and the rest was done by the machine. It took some time to get used to it, but one soon did as I encountered them at the airport, supermarkets and other public places. The metro I took in the mornings crossed half of its distance above the ground and the rest, underground. We crossed the River Seine and saw the sights of the city. What impressed me was that there were many women and men who went to work very early, and there was a sense of discipline everywhere. While ascending from the metro station one saw several legs, and while descending, all we saw were heads. Winter was waiting around the corner. Madeleine saw to it that I had proper footwear. As I wore a sari, she made a woman tailor-stitch a coat to suit that. It was stylish, and I had it for long.

I found my French lessons interesting. We were taught to speak, write, raise doubts and answer questions. I found them easy and enjoyed the classes. There were students from many countries. They were curious about me. It was difficult for many to believe that I had a husband and two children back at home. Usually, women came away when there was some trouble at home, particularly in their marriage. I remember meeting a young couple from the US, both Jews. The woman was from Israel and the man was from the US. She did not want to stay in the US, so they were spending that year in Europe. She told me that she was envious of me. She thought that we, Indian/Asian women, had more freedom.

After a while, I stopped going to the early morning classes but continued my lessons with an elderly woman, arranged by Madeleine, to strengthen my ability to handle the language. I can never forget that I found settling down in Paris relatively easy only because I had such a caring friend in Madeleine. In those days, the allowance in foreign currency provided by the Government of India for those who went abroad was meagre. Many students spent the whole amount on the first day itself, on taxis, coffee and snacks. Yet, I met a young woman who told me on the very first day that she did not wish to return to India.

There was a small but lively community of Indian students in France. Fewer students from India chose to come to France as compared to England. The language was a problem, which might have deterred them. Still, to me, Indians came across as quite good at learning new languages. Even those who came to France with no prior knowledge of French picked up the language very quickly. At the India House, I met many Indians who had come to France for a short period. Among them were students, as well as those who were employed as scientists, social scientists, French teachers and artists. Not all of them came with any specific goals; many of them somehow lingered on. In the India House, I also came across a number of Indian students from widely differing backgrounds. Perin Mistry and another Parsi woman, who later married a South Indian Christian, were scientists employed in Bombay. They were friendly, sociable and welcoming. There were also Diamond, a Bengali scientist, a Rajasthani girl named Rajkumari Shankar and a Bombay-based artist, Nalini Malani. Some of them later settled in Paris. Akkitham Narayanan, a Malayali artist from a well-known Nambuthiri family in Kerala, chose to settle there with his Japanese wife and son. So did Savitri Unni, a dancer who married a young man from Andhra Pradesh and had a daughter who is today an established dancer.

There were also students from Kerala who lived outside the Cité. I came to know one such student who lived with his family. They had rented a small apartment near the Cité. I visited them many times. Several years later, he came to a meeting in Thrissur where I was speaking. Sadly, I missed meeting him. There were others, both students and employed persons, from India with whom I got acquainted.

Those were the years when young women from poor Catholic homes, especially from the farming areas in the high ranges of Kerala, were sent to convents in Europe. This happened as there was a fall in the number of young European women who were willing to join the convent. I met a couple of these Malayali girls when they came to India House to meet some of the inmates they knew or because they wanted to meet us from Kerala.

The French government was keen that the foreign students benefit from their stay in France. They tried to expose us to the country's history, natural beauty, art and culture. Every month, we received a brochure with a list of events which included music, dance and theatre. My stay in France was relatively short, but I made use of these facilities whenever I could. France was not a highly expensive place at that time. For those under thirty-five years of age, everything including food was very cheap. Even for us who were senior students, there were many concessions. On most weekends, we were taken out of Paris. I have gone on many such trips. These *sorties* were either for a day or over the weekend. Surprisingly, I did not find many Indians, especially from the Maison de l'Inde, at these outings. However, I met many Bangladeshis, Pakistanis, and scholars from countries like Afghanistan, Turkey and Greece. We made an amiable crowd. From among them, a medical doctor from Greece, a professor from Yugoslavia and I made a trio who were together for most of the trips. We kept in touch even after we returned to our respective countries, though I have lost touch with them in recent years.

On a trip to Marseilles. (Photographer unknown)

A weekend *sortie* that I enjoyed the most was to the birthplace of Joan d'Arc. I also remember the last of these trips – to an extended meadow, a grassland surrounded by many small hills and dales. We were taken there to see the making of cheese, chocolate and wine. Some of the famous monasteries, chateaus and palaces found a place in our itinerary. There were many groups like ours that went on these weekend sojourns.

Many a time, my stay was arranged with families. Post-war France saw a decreased population and a very large number of widows. Naturally, the government initiated several policies to encourage families to have more children. France is primarily a Catholic country. Many of the families that welcomed me had widowed mothers of both husband and wife staying with them. The fact that I was a vegetarian and teetotaller did not appear as strange to them. As France had colonized Muslim countries and also had a not-too-small section of Muslims among its population, they knew that there were religious strictures against certain practices. But they were curious about me and the place where I came from.

These households were not the only places where I was faced with unexpected questions. There were many small shops, with mostly women as shopkeepers, which sold practically everything that one needed for daily use – sometimes postage stamps too. Those women were always curious to know more about me. They had not heard of India or Indians. When I said that I was Indian, they would ask, '*peau rouge*?' (or 'red skinned'?), by which they meant the Red Indians of America, who today are called Native Americans. I clarified their doubts, and they heard from me about India and Indians.

I gradually realized that many had vague notions about the nation that is India. Besides the scholars at the Centre and the people I met during the *sorties*, I also came across people who had visited India. To many, it was a country known for its poverty and spirituality. In Paris, one could buy tropical fruits like mangoes, bananas and pineapples which came from their old colonies. Yet there were people who found it difficult to believe that India had plenty of fruits and vegetables grown in temperate and tropical climatic conditions. Our poverty had made such a strong impact on their minds.

I used to go for music or sightseeing within Paris on my own as well. There were many parks and monuments in Paris which were quite easy to reach. I think it was on such an occasion that I went up the Eiffel Tower, a great attraction in Paris. I cannot remember whether I went to the Versailles Palace away from the city with a group or alone. The beautiful and huge monument, which is also called a *chateau* or fort, is situated far away. The structure and extensive gardens have been listed as a World Heritage site by UNESCO.

An observation that struck me were the subtle class divisions that could be seen around. When I saw foreign women travelling and staying alone in hotels in my younger days in Kerala, I had thought that they were free and fearless. Their similarities in appearance gave me the impression that they had lives that were more or less equal to men. Moreover, the land I had come to had proclaimed the three words '*liberté, égalité, fraternité*' (liberty, equality, fraternity), and that fascinated me.

Once in France, I had reasons to know that I was not fully right. Early in the morning, I saw plenty of women coming to the Cité to attend to various chores. A large number of them worked at the big cafeteria where students, staff and others came to have food at different times. Others worked as *femme de ménage* (cleaning maids) in the houses in the Cité. A woman who worked at India House became a friend. She was middle-aged and used to come in a car. She used to dust and clean every room including the furniture, and make the bed. She liked me and took me to her house one day. She fondly gifted me some of her costume jewellery.

Many women worked as domestic help in homes. Some of these women were from Spain and Portugal, and they came to cities like Paris to work and earn some money for their families. Madeleine had a Portuguese woman who would make her a pot of soup which lasted for four or five days. All of these women who worked in homes, at the restaurant in the Cité, shops or eateries were always greeted with a '*bon jour*' (good morning), and when they left after work, they were sent off with a polite '*merci, madame*' (thank you, madam). These gestures were certainly well-meaning, but the women belonged to a distinct class. True, they cannot be compared to the poor in India, but encountering these women opened my eyes to the fact that France was not a classless society.

The documentation centre of the Centre for Indian Studies directed by Dumont impressed me. Here I came across many journals and books in English that I was not familiar with. The librarian, a Frenchwoman, knew English, and we became good friends. She had married a Caribbean and had three children. One day, she took me to her house. Years later, she met me in Trivandrum when she came to India as part of an official visit to the libraries here. I came to know many other members of the staff, students and visitors at the Centre. I also went to the École Pratique des Hautes Études, where Dumont used to give talks. There I met Daniel Thorner, who also used to give lectures on India. He had visited Kerala when I was at the Bureau, but I had not met him then. His wife Alice Thorner used to attend her husband's lectures and took copious notes. Several years after his death, she brought out a book based on them. My acquaintance with Alice, a warm and generous woman, lasted till her death in 2005. The Thorners were Americans who had been driven out of the country during the McCarthy era. Mahalanobis had given them 'asylum', and they spent the bulk of their days in India in Bombay and Delhi. They moved to Paris at the invitation of Dumont to be with the Centre.

The talks of Dumont and Thorner attracted many others besides those specializing in studies on India. Among them were women and men who were lay public, as well as persons from disciplines other than Sociology, History or Anthropology. I even met a medical doctor and his wife at one of these talks. Many French people were curious, if not fascinated by India. In those days, they seemed to be more 'attracted' by spirituality or mysticism, perhaps also the art and culture of India, than India as a reality. Things have changed over the years, and today, one can find serious researchers and scholars from countries like France interested in various aspects of India.

My first Christmas in Europe was spent with Tyrrell and his family. At their suggestion, I flew to a small airport near Croydon where they lived. After returning to England, they had a second daughter who was named Radha. This family with four children became a home to me. The next day Tyrrell's parents, Ivy and Jack, came with plenty of gifts. They took me to a nearby market as they wished to buy more things. Joan, a good cook, had got ready a Christmas cake, pudding and turkey. They had a spacious kitchen from where one could walk into a garden. Near the wall were fruit-bearing trees. The children were happy with the presents. I was not forgotten either. Every evening, they had many visitors and enjoyable conversations. It surprised some of them that I spoke English so well, a compliment which I had heard at other places as well. I am sure it's not something that I alone have heard.

With Ivy and Jack Burgess in front of their house in Croydon, 1970.
(Photographer unknown)

During my stay in France, I got the chance to visit Geneva. Savitri, my friend from the Maison de l'Inde, had a brother in Geneva and arranged my stay with them. A great wish of mine came true when the welcoming hosts helped me buy a camera. I thus became the proud owner of an Olympus 42 with which I used to take photographs for a long time. Those days, I wanted my children to know about all that I saw on my travels. I cherished a secret dream to take them to Switzerland, the home of Heidi, a character we all liked. Time and money did not allow me to realize that dream, but both my daughters have travelled quite a lot on their own.

I also visited Colette at Thonon, almost on the banks of Lake Geneva on the French side, a mesmerizing place at the foot of the Alps. Through the window of her room, we could see the snow-clad mountain range. It was a nice day, which we celebrated by going sightseeing and skiing. She also sent me on a visit to her mother, who lived in Basle, Switzerland. I travelled by train from Geneva, crossed the River Rhine – and there was Colette's mother, wearing a hat, waiting for me at the station. I spent two or three happy days with her. She was a friendly woman who talked a lot. I did not feel a stranger in her house. I had always felt that Jews tried to keep family ties intact, guarded the sense of being a community and were generous in introducing us to friends. When I returned to Paris, I had the address of a cousin of Colette and his wife who lived not far from the Cité.

By that time, I had learned to locate houses with their addresses in the Paris directory of streets and lanes. I vividly remember walking along the street and looking at the door numbers to find the one I was looking for. At last, I entered the gate of the complex where Colette's cousin Jusieu (Joseph) Storper and Audrey were staying. They lived on one of the top floors. I rang the bell for the lift and waited. To my surprise, Jusieu came down in the lift. He took me upstairs, and his wife greeted me warmly. She was busy teaching the English language to some students, and suggested that her husband and I go for a walk and come back. We went to the garden in front of the Cité, and Jusieu told me the remarkable story of his life. He told me he was an engineer and how, several years back, he had met with an accident which caused serious memory loss. He narrated in detail how Audrey had looked after him and helped him recover his memory. It was a strenuous job to be looked after like a child and be taught everything from scratch.

With Audrey and Jusieu Storper in their flat in Paris, 1971. (Photographer unknown)

When we returned from our walk, Audrey had got ready a soup, salad and bread. We had a quiet dinner. During those few hours, a friendship blossomed which lasted till the passing of both of them. Audrey came to India several times as she was interested in ancient civilizations. She was a tourist who visited a place only after she had read about it in detail. One of her trips was to Rumania, from where her husband's family had spread to the rest of the world. She brought back some bricks from his ancestral home. The Storper household soon became a home for me. It took me just a short walk along the pathway of the park in front of the Cité and then another few minutes after passing through a side entrance to reach their place.

My stay in Paris was not just about sightseeing and making friends. Dumont not only gave me time to get used to the place and people, but also the freedom and responsibility to do meaningful work. The only suggestion he made was to work on a topic of socio-economic relevance to Kerala. Besides reading in the library, I attended lectures by Dumont and Thorner. Hearing people like Dumont was inspiring because the talks were on a higher intellectual plane. Even aspiring to that was not easy. I always thought that the French language was more musical than English.

I was sent to London to look for research material in the India Office Library (IOL). The library fascinated me as it opened up a treasure-trove. It was unlike the University Library in Trivandrum which I regularly used to visit, the library in Madras where I had a fixed seat, or even the Planning Commission Library. The staff were courteous and helpful. Among them were men earlier attached to the Viceroy's House in Delhi. Many had been attendants, and they had many interesting stories of the time they spent in India. All this added a human touch to the library. It was here that I hit upon the topic for my PhD thesis.

It all began with my finding a dilapidated file with the caption, 'Slavery in Kerala' – something I had never heard of. Neither did I have a deep knowledge of slavery or the slave trade. The file aroused my curiosity. I found more books, reports and documents on slavery in general and with particular reference to Kerala. Another library I used to visit was the one attached to the British Museum. One had to reach there early to make sure to get a seat, and requisition books. Readers had no access to the shelves, but the books came to the reader without delay. One of the seats (perhaps number 1) was said to be the seat which Karl Marx used during his prolonged research in that library. Naturally, all of us wanted to sit on that at least once. I managed that.

While doing this work, I lived with the Burgesses in their house in Croydon. From the house I took a bus, mostly a double-decker, to Croydon railway station, from where I got a train. I got off usually at Charing Cross station and walked for about fifteen minutes to reach the library. On the way, there was a 'round' where I saw some men every day. I think they were squatters. From their looks, it was obvious that they were human beings discarded by 'civilized' society.

Before going to England, I had heard that people there are very reserved, and that they would not enter into conversations with persons sitting next to them on a train. But I met many women and men who proved this wrong. I never felt that they carried bits of the imperialist past within them. In fact, there were occasions when I felt that among the ordinary people, there were many who did not know much about their past. Each of these train journeys came across as a genuine experience for me.

Gopi came to England once while I was there. He was in Europe in connection with an International Conference on Peace and came over for a few days. As he could not manage a visa to France, we spent our days sightseeing in London. Jack and Ivy drove us to Stratford upon Avon, the birthplace of William Shakespeare, where we spent some time. The place was dotted with many visitors like us. The thatched house where Shakespeare is said to have been born is preserved as such. We also went to Bernard Shaw's residence, a big house in a big compound. In one corner of that place was a small airy room where Shaw worked on his books. The visitors were orderly and respectful of their past. Another place that I explored on my own during my stay in England was the cemetery of Karl Marx in London. There were some other eager visitors like me, and we managed to get photographs taken by each other.

My return trip to France, interestingly, was by a hovercraft. I did not know what that mode of transport was. Most probably, I was driven by curiosity and a spirit of adventure to use it. From London, I went by bus to Dover on the sea coast. There I found the hovercraft, an air-cushion vehicle which was neither a boat nor a ship. We could feel the water around, and from inside, we felt that it was sliding on the water. Just before landing, the base of the hovercraft was deflated and the air was let off. We sensed the bottom of the craft flattening while landing at Calais in France.

From Calais to Paris was again a long bus drive. We drove through small towns which occasionally offered interesting sights on both sides. In the 1970s, the world was different. One could spot many petty traders and town centres with trees and benches for the elderly to meet and for kids to play around. The drive from Calais to Paris appeared never-ending to me as it was severe winter. At many points, there was nothing but bleakness. The snow made the entire world around look whiter than normal. As if to break the monotony, the black stumps of grape plants peeped out here and there. Even the rare bird that dared to come out could not break the stillness. It was an occasion when I learnt how the surroundings could affect the soul. Delhi winters did not come anywhere near that.

However, snow was not something I disliked. I remember seeing snow for the first time – it was a soul-elevating experience. I was in my room in the Cité and all of a sudden, the mood outside changed. I thought it was about to rain or drizzle. I looked out through my window and, lo and behold, it was snowing. It reminded me of our old Lux soap-flakes. It continued for a while as I stood still, taking in one of the glorious sights of nature. I have seen waterfalls, rivers that gently flow and mightier ones that conquer the land through which they flow. Nature enjoys throwing surprises at us.

After a year or so in France, I came to India, to Delhi and Kerala, to collect additional data for my research. I talked to some people, interviewed some others and went to libraries. This was different from the type of research I was used to. For this research, places, people and events got priority instead of numbers. True, I had stumbled upon the topic among old documents, reports and books at the India Office, which were not readily available in Kerala. But it was during this visit to Kerala that I began to seriously think of Kerala's history and development. In this, Gopi helped me in many ways. He read a lot and bought plenty of Malayalam books. He also knew most of the authors and people who could be of help. He would give suggestions, nothing more.

I returned to Paris with more material, and started writing drafts of chapters. I worked very hard. When I felt tired or wished for a break, I would lock the door and go out. Often it would be to the Louvre, which I visited a number of times. I found the place a treasure house which I still cannot claim to have explored fully. If it was noon, I would watch the men who would be enjoying their extended noon break playing *boules* in the Dauphine Park between Louvre and Notre Dame. I saw the *Mona Lisa* several times. I saw exhibitions in the nearby museums. These were opportunities that life in Paris offered. I also walked along the River Seine many a time. Before returning, I took a night cruise on the river. If I wished to have a longer break, I would go to one of the cafes on the Left Bank. One can take a book and read sitting there for any length of time, watch the crowd or dream. One trip, somewhat disturbing, was to the catacomb. When I wished to be away from tourist spots and have a quiet corner to myself, I would go to a park slightly away from the Maison de l'Inde. These trips gave me renewed energy when I returned to my room.

Almost all the information I had was in English and the thesis was to be written in French. I knew that my knowledge of French was insufficient for that. Yet, I decided to give it a try. I took the help of a friend, Sylvie Keller, who was immensely helpful in finalizing the thesis in French. She was a young Frenchwoman who had visited India, and used to frequent the library as she wanted to do a PhD. We sometimes met and talked about all kinds of things. Once she told me that she was in favour of arranged marriages. Her reason was that under such a system, the girl retains all the love within her and has all that to offer when she gets married. She felt that under the French system, where the girl and boy have to find their partners themselves, the girl often has to go through several relationships, and in the end, if one clicked, the girl by that time would most probably have lost all the finer sentiments within her. Very seldom did the first affair end in marriage and that too in a lasting relationship. I felt that things must have been different in the case of the previous generation. I had met Sylvie's parents, who were married for long. Madeleine's parents died after completing fifty years of loving married life. I had also met Tyrrell's parents and others of an earlier generation who had lifelong relationships. This does not mean that there was no marital discord in those countries, but they were not as common as today. My observation is that it is after the Second World War that these societies became what is called 'permissive'. This change seems to be more advantageous to the boys and the men.

Sylvie and I kept in touch for long after my days in France were over. The last time I heard from her, several years back, she was working with UNESCO. I also came to know that her parents, who were Protestants, had moved to the south of France, where Protestant Christians were more in number, from a region where Catholics dominated. Sylvie and I had good times together. It was a beautiful evening when I took her to see the Russian ballet *Swan Lake*.

Before submitting my thesis, I had reviewed a book as part of my assignment as a scholar. The book, suggested to me by Dumont, was *Social Revolution in a Kerala Village: A Study in Cultural Change* by A. Aiyappan, an eminent anthropologist from Kerala. In a moment of daring, I decided to do the review in French instead of English, and Dumont was immensely pleased. I gathered courage and did the defence of the thesis too in French. Besides Dumont and Thorner, another professor and some students were present. Jusieu Storper had come to support me. He took me to lunch later and stayed with me till the result was announced in the afternoon. I cannot say that I was elated, but Gopi, the children and my extended family were very happy. It was from Gopi that I got my first letter with Dr as a prefix to my name. The French government had allowed me to complete the work in such a short period because I had an MLitt degree, and also nearly ten years of research experience. My thesis in French was titled *Histoire sociale et économique du Kerala depuis 1800: étude des Pulayas*. After I returned to India, I rewrote the work in English and published it as *The Emergence of a Slave Caste: Pulayas of Kerala*.

The French government allowed me to travel across the country, to observe regional variations and cultural diversities. I collected brochures, made notes and took photos as memories of the places I visited. Sadly, they seem to have disappeared. But my mind still retains the images of the countryside that I saw, including the property of the famous artist Claude Monet: a countryside speckled with small peasants, plazas with plenty of trees and airy spaces where elderly people and children gathered to meet friends and enjoy the mornings and evenings. I also went to a Mediterranean beach where I went into a cave. I returned to Paris via Grenoble where Perin Mistry was living at that time.

I sent a trunk filled with books – some of which I had bought and some of which were gifted – records and some clothes by ship to reduce the luggage on the flight. One of the books was a French cookery book. My family already had a taste of France as I used to send home souvenirs from the country. Within months of my reaching France, I had sent chocolates to my children through an Indian I met in Paris, who was kind enough to carry them. I also sent Gopi a beautiful cardigan by post. But I felt that they must have a feel of the place where I lived. Before returning, I bought a tape recorder. I walked along the tree-lined avenues both within the Cité and the park across to capture the music of nature for my family to listen to.

I sent them more chocolates after going to Niort, Madeleine's hometown. The brief stay with her parents and the visits to her aunt and sisters-in-law were memorable. I had met her parents earlier in Paris for lunch. They were old, but her father, who had a transport business, was still active. To my surprise, I found in their house a photograph of Madeleine and me taken in Trivandrum. Her mother

With Madeleine Biardeau and her parents, 1970.
(Photographer unknown)

was struck by my eyes which she found very big. She was simple and warm. She did all the work at home and kept everything spick and span. After dinner, she would wash all the utensils and crockery, wipe them and keep them in their place. Madeleine used to carry back many metres of *kora* cloth, which her mother converted into large napkins used for wiping. I would stand by her side while she did the work. She never allowed me to help, but she talked to me. She liked me in a sari very much and told me not to give up wearing it. The reason she gave was interesting. She told me that she had lived through the years before the market made its all-pervasive entry into people's lives. Paris, considered the seat of fashion, had a hold on people's choices.

She found the social compulsions that made people accept changing fashions in their attire detestful. Her words, '*gardez la*', which meant 'keep' or 'don't give up' the sari, were sincere.

Our visit to Madeleine's house was during Easter. People there celebrated it with great gusto. I was surprised by the coloured Easter eggs and the variety of chocolates they made. I was given large quantities of green-coloured chocolates in the shape of animals and birds, which I sent home. They lasted there a long time, delighting many a guest.

One of the last trips I made before returning to India was to Belgium and the Netherlands. I came to know of a tour and booked my ticket. It was by bus. Belgium seems to have faded from my memory, but I remember the Netherlands or Holland as a place where I saw many world-renowned museums and the house of Anne Frank. We went on a cruise around the city of Amsterdam. The guide eagerly showed us around many things including a house with a tiny door that opens out into the water. The country is below sea level. I also went to the tulip gardens, where the flowers in a variety of colours and shapes were a breathtaking sight.

Before leaving Paris, I also went to listen to music in the Notre Dame and at the chapel inside the Palais de Justice (Supreme Court) compound. The church music was heavenly. Before I left, I treated my close friends to lunch in my room. I was also given a send-off by my friends at the Centre. Madeleine came to the airport to see me off. After my momentous sojourn in France, I landed in India where Gopi was waiting for me at Palam airport in Delhi. The children were away in Kerala for their annual summer holidays.

Once again, Dumont gave me a surprise. He happened to be in Delhi and we met at the India International Centre. I have forgotten the details except that we did some minor shopping. We also went to the Sociology Department of the Delhi University. What I remember vividly is that he was there in response to the call from Bharat Mata . . .

❖

CHAPTER TEN

Back in India

Before I left Paris, Gopi had given up the job at the *Patriot* newspaper. There was a workers' strike at *Patriot*, and the management refused to agree to their demands. In support of the strike, Gopi and his colleagues, Girish Mathur, O.P. Sangal and Shukla, all old-time communists, left the paper. Gopi had not informed me of any of this. I have never understood how he managed those months without a job. He did not tell the children either. They were taken out to watch films, visit bookstores and to Kwality's in Connaught Place for ice cream as usual. As an act of daring, he went and booked a car, a 1972 model Fiat. For the first time, we took a loan, from the Punjab National Bank. Both of us learned to drive. After my return from Paris, Gopi joined the United News of India (UNI).

Soon after I came back from France, we went to Kerala. From my family, I received a warm reception. At that time there were no direct trains from Delhi to Kollam. My brother came all the way to Madras to meet us, and shook my hands to show his love and appreciation. In Kollam, Amma and the children were happy to have me back. Gopi's family too greeted me warmly. However, it was my maternal uncle, a brother who was closest to Amma, who expressed the greatest happiness and pride. He said that a *veera sringhala* should be given to me. Vally presented me with a sari.

Before going to France, the Director of ISI, Professor C.R. Rao, whom I had met when he came to Delhi, had agreed to sanction me study leave with full salary. True, I had failed to get anything in writing as I was both busy and somewhat tense. When I returned, the ISI Delhi administration refused my request. I consulted a lawyer who advised me against going to court against the institution. However, my work was received well by colleagues like T.N. Srinivasan. He introduced me to Professor Dharma Kumar of the Delhi School of Economics, who was also the editor of the *Indian Economic and Social History Review*. She published two articles from the thesis in the *Review*. They were also published in the *Journal of Kerala Studies*. Dharma Kumar even wanted me to do a similar study for Tamil Nadu. T.N. Srinivasan supported the idea, but I was not prepared to take it up at that point.

The time I spent in France gave me, not just a degree and a thesis; I had developed fresh ways of looking at the society around me. I decided not to go back to analysing numbers published by the government. Not that I thought it useless, but I was keen to publish the thesis in English after reworking it. I was sanctioned a publication grant by the Indian Council of Social Science Research (ICSSR), but Comrade Mohit Sen saw the manuscript and said that the People's Publishing House would publish it. In their deft hands, under the care of the late Mr Rao, whom friends called Fatty Rao, my first book was born. I must thank them for the good job they did and Rao for the care he showed. The work was well received. Recently, a friend told me that she had quoted me, and added: 'It is not always that a thesis outlives twenty, twenty-five years.'* I have also been asked by several people to update the book and translate it into Malayalam. I could not do it because I was involved in various activities and hence did not get sufficient time to do the work the way I would have loved.**

There is also a memory associated with the book which bothered me for long. I wanted to have an introduction to my first book, and I felt the apt person to write one was V.R. Krishna Iyer – the Minister of Law in the first non-Congress ministry in Kerala who was by then a Justice in the Supreme Court of India. Gopi knew him. Without hesitation, he agreed to my request for an introduction. He even quoted from the book in the Ambedkar Memorial Lecture he delivered at the Jawaharlal Nehru University and was kind enough to send me a copy of the lecture. However, a reviewer in a Malayalam newspaper, who was also a historian, understood things differently. He did a good review; however, he attributed the introduction to my desire for a Brahmin's blessing. This bothered me a lot, and that was resolved only when I met and talked to the person years later in Trivandrum. Another reviewer called me a 'Seeker of Fortune', which I ignored.

My thesis was based on secondary data. I wished to know the real

* It has now outlived fifty years!

** The Malayalam translation is in the works, to be published by Sign Books.

lives of the people whom I had written about, and to study how the lives of the erstwhile agrestic slaves had changed. For this, I chose two panchayat areas near Trivandrum which had agricultural labourers from different castes. One of them was the birthplace of Ayyankali. This study became my second book, *Divided Poor,* published with the support of and a publication grant from the Indian Council of Social Science Research (ICSSR). The field study was an experience that opened my eyes to some of the harsh realities of Kerala. They left a painful impression in my mind. I met young boys who had basic education but were unemployed. They had desperation in their eyes. I struck up a friendship with them and chose some of them to help me to collect the field-level data. We met in the panchayat office. They told me in detail how the researchers who usually come to study their lives never got down from their cars or mingled with them. 'We have never laughed like this before,' said the youngest in the group at our last get-together. Those words still ring in my ears. In those times, the exodus of Keralites to the Middle Eastern countries was just beginning. However, that did not resolve the unemployment problem in the state.

Back in Delhi, I found myself busy with conferences and events which became a platform for me to meet a wide range of individuals working in similar areas. At the National Conference on Social Statistics, in one session, I asked a question. Before I realized it, I was led by someone to a woman. I came to know that she was Vina Mazumdar. We shall see more of Vina later. The person who introduced us was J.P. Naik, an educationist and Member-Secretary of the ICSSR. I also met A.R. Kamath from Gokhale Institute, Pune. He had read some of my writings and thought I was a Gandhian. We used to correspond for some years. I even visited him when I went to Pune. (By that time, I had become friends with Sulabha Brahme of Gokhale Institute. It was with her that I made that visit.) Sadly, he passed away suddenly. Two other people I met and interacted with during the conference on Social Statistics were Professor Sukhamoy Chakravarty, the renowned economist, and Kapila Vatsyayan, a leading art historian. We used to meet occasionally as members of a subcommittee on statistics related to arts and culture.

Another person who got me involved in new research engagements was Uma Roy Choudhury from the Central Statistical Office. Uma was a major figure in the study of national income, an essential input in planning. She was a woman with a slightly serious demeanour, which kept some people away. However, she became a good friend of mine, and introduced me to authorities in her field like Professor Moni Mukherjee from ISI, Calcutta. When I returned to India from France, she enrolled me as a member of the Indian Association for the Study of National Income and Wealth.

The conferences of this Association gave me the opportunity to see different parts of India, such as Shillong, Lucknow, Srinagar, Ahmedabad and Pune. I cannot forget the visit to the North East, during which we saw Cherrapunji, famous at that time as the place receiving the highest amount of rainfall in the country. In that remote place, there was a school run by the Ramakrishna Mission. This trip also gave us an opportunity to visit the Kapalika temple near Guwahati. The never-ending range of snow-capped mountains glittering in the early morning sunlight was a divine sight while driving back from Pahalgam in Kashmir. My restlessness and state of disquiet on the job front was somewhat eased by these engagements.

Despite my busy professional life, I had no difficulty in managing my home. I found time to spend on activities like stitching my children's dresses, something I did for long. While in Kerala, I had not cooked much; in Delhi, I started cooking both simple and elaborate meals. I was a vegetarian. Gopi's background was different, but he never insisted on anything and did not find fault with whatever he was served. However, when the children were growing up, I decided not to deny them non-vegetarian food if they wanted it. So I began to cook fish occasionally, which I found quite easy. In Delhi, one could get sea-fish flown over from the coastal regions, especially Gujarat. The shopkeepers sold us fish that was already cleaned and cut. What I often bought was Pomfret, which I found easy to handle. However, in the market, one had to walk past shops selling other kinds of non-vegetarian fare like meat and chicken. I did not like the open drains and smell in the area. I told myself that I would stop cooking non-vegetarian food if I found the smell and dirt revolting.

I also found time to make delicacies and arrange the children's birthday parties. I had always made special food on holidays and Sundays. After my stay in France, it became more elaborate and stylish. There were occasional candlelight dinners. I attempted some French dishes by referring to the French cookbook I had brought with me. One dish that became a favourite among many was the vegetarian *ratatouille*. We began to have more salads. It was fun! The children enjoyed everything. Friends like Crispy joined us often.

Meanwhile significant changes were taking place at the ISI. The Director, Professor C.R. Rao, who had been with ISI, Calcutta perhaps from his student days, left for the US. Gopinath Kallianpur was brought from the US as the new Director. I heard that he was a widely read man who could have become a great historian. As he had not brought his family, he lived alone in the quarters assigned to him. One room was retained for the Director in the Delhi guest house as well. The ISI Workers' Organization (ISIWO), which had problems with C.R. Rao on some issues, gave the new Director their full support.

By then ISI Delhi had got its own land in South Delhi, in the institutional area adjacent to the main road across the Katwaria Sarai village. Land acquisition by the government, displacing people and encroaching on villages and farms, had already begun. The institutional area in South Delhi, where ISI Delhi came to be located, was one such piece of land. Jawaharlal Nehru University (JNU) and the Indian Institute of Technology (IIT), Delhi, had already come up on one side of this area. The Delhi Centre of ISI was inaugurated by Prime Minister Indira Gandhi in a gala event. An American participant pointed out that there was no state in the US which did not have at least one statistician trained in ISI. What this move meant was that we left the Planning Unit and Yojana Bhavan behind. The Delhi Centre was thus formed with the Quality Control and Regional Development units related to ISI coming under one roof. New mathematicians and statisticians also joined. The Director hosted a banquet at the Qutub Hotel next door, which Gopi and I attended.

My association with the ISIWO was an important chapter in my working life. I was a member from the very beginning, but was not very involved with its functioning. However, once when I was away in Kerala on vacation, some friends from the organization telephoned and said that I had been made the 'president' of the Delhi ISIWO. It came to me as both a surprise and a joke! I found myself wondering on what grounds I could have been chosen for the position. I had heard a story that the previous 'leaders' were not popular as they would meet the authorities on the sly and get favours granted. I had seen the workers shouting '*hai, hai!*' (down, down!), gathered around the building.

My friends probably trusted me as the president of the organization because they understood that I had sympathies for the 'underdogs', or because I was not part of the 'elite' and those who wielded power. I therefore came back to Delhi with an additional responsibility.

In ISI Calcutta, there was an air of amity between the academic staff and the non-academic workers. Many of the former were members of the workers' organization, and they stood by the latter when they agitated for improved working conditions. In Delhi, the situation was different. The distance between the two categories was visible. Once the different streams came together under the roof of the Delhi Centre, the number of non-academic staff was higher than in the Planning Unit. The 'workers' began to feel that their grievances were never getting redressed. This was what made them think seriously about the organization.

I had a rapport with the workers even while in the Planning Unit. A friendly driver I knew at ISI was Tiwari. He was from Bihar, where his family owned and cultivated some land. When the new state of Jharkhand was formed in 2000, his home came within that area. Like in many other parts of the country, in Bihar too, small peasant

With the workers of ISIWO at ISI, Delhi. (*In front, left to right*) Tiwari the driver, K. Saradamoni, Dhora Ram the head gardener, Neeba, Darshana. (Photographer unknown)

households were cash-starved, which compelled one or two of the younger generation to seek work in towns and industrial areas to earn money. This was how most young men like Tiwari had come to Delhi. He often used to chat with me. At a later point in time, he was even keen that I undertake a study in Bihar. I too was interested, but sadly, it was never to happen.

Tiwari sometimes drove senior-level academics to the airport for their international trips. One day, he jokingly told me that for every five professors who went out, one driver should be sent. In his remark, I sensed something more than jest. I thought that the workers had a right to know what the so-called 'scientific' staff of the Planning Unit was doing. I discussed the matter with others, following which Rudra gave a talk on the work that was done at the Unit, explaining its relevance for Indian planning and its goals vis-à-vis the masses. Arranged under the auspices of the ISI workers' cultural wing, the talk was well attended and well received, though the higher-level scientists did not attend. Sadly, it was not repeated.

These early experiences probably came to my aid while working for the ISIWO. One of the first things I did was to make the members realize that what we are demanding are our rights, and not crumbs or favours from the authorities. The new Director was given a letter listing the workers' demands. He was good enough to invite a 'delegation' chosen by the Delhi workers to Calcutta. Along with me, Raj Narain, A.N. Sharma, S.D. Verma and A. Damodaran were selected. We met the Director and he agreed to look into the problems we raised. Our travelling expenses were met by the Institute and our stay was arranged at the Institute's guest house. It was also my first visit to that city. At the Director's suggestion, the administration arranged transport for us to go around Calcutta. We saw the major places including Howrah Bridge, Kalighat, Belur Math and the Botanical Garden. I rushed back to Delhi in time for the twenty-fifth anniversary of our wedding.

On this trip to Calcutta, I was impressed by the sprawling campus of the ISI headquarters. Far away from the centre of the city, it had many buildings for offices and a section of the workers to live in. The architecture was not particularly stylish. The buildings were designed by Mahalanobis himself. Surrounded by plants and trees, the campus exuded an old-world charm. There were trees planted by famous scientists and others who visited ISI. J.B.S Haldane was a scientist who had stayed on at ISI till he founded his own Institute. Ho Chi Minh of Vietnam was another international figure who had visited the Institute.

The guest house was without frills, but the rooms were spacious and provided natural air and light. The entrance to the building was welcoming. The elderly Bengali women who served us in the dining area were a warm, friendly presence. The serving utensils were old-fashioned but pleasing. Mahalanobis and his wife Rani were close to the poet Rabindranath Tagore. They had certainly imbibed his love of nature. Though they did not attempt to conduct classes under the trees, they had adopted certain ideas from Santiniketan: to conduct the convocation of the Institute in the open, in the *amrapali* or mango grove, was one such. The notions of simplicity, love of trees and nature went well with the time when the Institute was started.

One major achievement of the Delhi ISIWO was to get residential accommodation for the staff. The Institute had already started providing rented houses to some of the academic staff. Some of the administrative staff who came from far lived in one or two rooms sub-let by government employees at the same level. Sometimes they had to share the bathroom or toilet. The most low-paid workers found places to live in small villages around. So the question of staff quarters brought hope to many minds.

Many of the top-level academics living in houses rented by the Institute were not interested in moving to the campus. Those who agreed to move there did not have big families. I, as president of the ISIWO, suggested that all houses be alike with the academic staff having an extra room as the study area. Dr S.K. Mitra, the Head of the Delhi Centre, was not unwilling to experiment with the idea. He was soft-spoken and mild-mannered, and I had no problem discussing any issue with him. My dealings with mathematicians and statisticians who served as heads of the Centre were always cordial. However, persuading some of the senior academics who were not members of the ISIWO was not easy. I heard one of them remark, 'We cannot have such revolutionary reforms: there is no such practice in IIT or JNU.' Both these were eminent institutions. I could not pursue the matter as the staff whom I stood for were in a dire state and wanted accommodation at the earliest. After these debates, the staff quarters became a reality.

It was a happy occasion when the accountants, librarians, drivers, cooks, office assistants, receptionists, messengers, sweepers, cleaners and *malis* came together as an amiable, happy community. They came from various parts of the country, belonged to different religions or castes, and talked different languages. None of this was a barrier for them. They got more than what they had imagined. I visited many of them in their homes. Many kept small gardens, and one of them even arranged the marriage of a daughter there. However, there were some, like Meena, secretary to the Head of the Centre, who did not move to the campus.

Even after I retired I used to visit ISI, and my old friends welcomed me warmly. One day a *mali*, before I realized it, touched my feet and told the people around that it was I who got the poor workers everything – uniforms, hike in wages, houses. . . . It was a very embarrassing moment for me. What he said was not true either. They were poor, innocent people. I can still see the faces of Jedda Ram, Ram Dev Maurya, Ganga Ram and many others before my eyes.

Over the years, they began to leave. Many moved out after retirement, some passed away. But the saddest moment for me was when, years later, I found almost all the houses lying vacant. Our concept of development had changed. The lower-grade workers in the government and semi-government sectors lost permanency in work. With that, they lost the minimum security they enjoyed in life. The neo-liberal policies we accepted as part of the agenda of globalization have resulted in workers being recruited through 'contractors'.

In the 1970s and 80s, women's status became a topic of widespread debate in India. A similar atmosphere was prevalent all over the world, as the UN declared 1975 as International Women's Year and 1975–1985 as the International Women's Decade. The word *woman* acquired a new meaning. We were about to witness the birth of Women's Studies, and I found myself drawn to the momentum of the times.

This was not the first time that questions about women's life had become a matter of debate. Before the International Women's Decade, women did not remain totally ignored or invisible. The UN Charter in 1945 had adopted the first international instrument to establish a principle of equality between women and men. Women were at the forefront of many historic struggles, including the right to vote, abolition of the slave trade, the rights of oppressed and deprived peoples, as well as the freedom struggles of nations. Japan had a women's university established in 1901. Its noted alumnae include writers, philosophers and political workers. This is a fact that many of the younger Japanese may not be aware of. Concern about discrimination against women and the exclusion they experienced led to the formation of the International Congress for Women's Freedom at least two decades before the UN Charter, in 1945. An eight-member delegation from India had attended their Paris meet in 1926.

In India too, women's issues were debated before the advent of women's studies. The exploitation and neglect of women within and outside the family were major concerns of the national freedom movement. It drew women from distant corners of the subcontinent to participate in Gandhian constructive programmes as well as militant struggles for freedom and social justice. In our country with a history of untouchability, *sati*, child marriage and preference for a male child, there was a qualitative difference in the discrimination experienced by women across various sections and regions. Some of these questions were debated in women's journals as early as the beginning of the twentieth century, at least in some parts of the country. I have read Malayalam journals of that time which carried strongly worded articles on issues relating to women and society, such as education, work, employment, health, marriage, family and child-rearing, women and public space, property, inheritance and many related topics. Though they later became a significant source of reference for researchers, they were not formally labelled as 'Women's Studies'.

The world was different after the Second World War. India, Britain's biggest colony, became independent, followed by many other nations, big and small. Ideas of socialism, perhaps vague, were in the air. Demands for change in the unequal status between women and men were being heard from different parts of the world.

Vina Mazumdar, with whom I had become acquainted by then, played a major role in this new branch of study. She was the Secretary of the Committee on the Status of Women in India (CSWI), which finalized its report in 1974 before the UN declared 1975 as International Women's Year. Later she became the Founder-Director of the Centre for Women's Development Studies (CWDS). Once the CSWI submitted its report, Vina was absorbed into ICSSR by J.P. Naik. Along with a junior colleague, Kumud Sharma, Vina formed the Women's Studies Programme at ICSSR. The noted sociologist and anthropologist Leela Dube, who was also with the CSWI, was already in ICSSR. The ICSSR

With Vina Mazumdar. (Photographer unknown)

At a meeting to celebrate the twentieth anniversary of the Centre for Women's Development Studies, Delhi, 2000. (*Sitting, left to right*) Leela Dube, Neera Desai, K. Saradamoni, Lotika Sarkar; (*standing*) Rameshwari Varma. (Photo by Kalpana Kannabiran)

at that time was housed in the hostel of the Indian Institute of Public Administration (IIPA). The one or two small rooms of the new unit were always full of people, mostly women. Suddenly, the word *woman* acquired a new meaning, one that was different from what fashion magazines propagated. The Women's Study Programme initiated what was called sponsored studies. The ICSSR wrote to institutions and individuals asking them to submit proposals to do research or study problems concerning women's situation.

Strangely, this period of renewed emphasis on women's rights coincided with a black spot in free India's history. Emergency was declared across the country between 25 June 1975 and 21 March 1977. What is given below are jottings from my diary of that time. On 26 June I wrote:

> Early in the morning, Mohit Sen called to find out whether JP [Jayaprakash Narain] was arrested. Gopi called UNI. True JP, Morarji Desai, Piloo Modi, Raj Narain and others were arrested. Gopi went immediately to office and called to say that the PM would be speaking over the radio at 8 am. She spoke in a subdued tone and was faltering while reading. The main content of her speech was that democracy was threatened; there was violent opposition to the progressive measures she took for the common people. The institution of the PM was threatened. She did not mind whether she remained in power or not. The country has known her since her childhood.

We did not get the *Times of India* and *Patriot*. It was said that the power supply to the newspapers was shut down. I went by bus to the office. Nobody had heard anything. The next day, many colleagues thought that I would have news. During lunch a close friend came over, and we went to the coffee house near Gopi's office. He joined us and told us how the freedom of the press was being suppressed.

The fear that pervaded overnight cannot be captured or conveyed today. There were some who supported the Emergency by pointing out that it brought people to offices and other workplaces on time, and that there was more discipline everywhere. While I welcomed punctuality and commitment to work, I could never agree that the manner in which these were imposed was correct. Fear and suspicion among colleagues and those who meet and interact daily kill the ethos of a healthy democracy. I wonder whether the openness that existed among the people – colleagues, neighbours, fellow travellers on the bus and so on – ever came back after those dark days.

On a personal level, however, the day brought happy news as well. It was the day Emergency was declared that Asha got information about being selected for the Science Talent Scholarship.

The initiatives for women's rights continued unhampered. Within a couple of years after the setting up of the Women's Studies Programme, women's studies in India had a sort of launch in Bombay in 1981. A large number of women interested in knowing each other, hearing about issues concerning women and sharing experiences came together. It took place on the campus of the Shreemati Nathibai Damodar Thackersey (SNDT) Women's University. The gathering, at the request of Vina Mazumdar, was hosted by Madhuri Shah, the then Vice-Chancellor, and Neera Desai, Professor of Sociology. It was a gathering of nearly 300–400 women, young and not so young. The atmosphere was such that all of us felt comfortable though many were meeting for the first time.

That gathering gave me the chance to make many acquaintances. Some of them became friends. It was during the return journey that I met Vidya on the train. This young woman with a delicate body and pretty face seemed like a dancer to me. But she turned out to be a singer. We became very close and she used to visit me quite often with her young daughter. Music came spontaneously to her, and I have heard her melodious renderings many a time. She later became the Delhi chief of a prominent publishing house. Susie Tharu, a Keralite and a well-known academic and activist based in Hyderabad, was at the gathering. Susie and her friends including Lalita had already founded the women's organization Anveshi. It was at the Bombay meet that I met Devaki Jain. She got together women who had an Economics background or were interested in economic affairs. That group continued to be active for some time. Others I met at the gathering included Meera Velayudhan, Rukmini, Indu Agnihotri and Sahba.

In those years, many women initiated ventures that spoke up for women's rights. One among them was Madhu Kishwar, the founder of the women's bimonthly *Manushi*. I got to know her around this time. In fact, a women's journal was the collective idea of a large number of young women including some names mentioned above. Many left sooner or later. Madhu and her friend Ruth Vanita brought out the journal. Its launch coincided with the 10th International Congress of Anthropological and Ethnological Sciences in December 1978 in Delhi. Naturally, the journal received international attention. Eminent figures like the anthropologist Kathleen Gough were present. Our common interests including politics made Kathleen and me good friends.

There were many challenging questions before those who seriously took up women's studies. The Indian government had included questions of poverty and inequality along with economic growth in its goals set for the country. Though it was not easy, bulky reports were brought out on the life and contribution of the rural and agricultural population. Interestingly, women and children were confined to small paragraphs in a short chapter in these documents. These reports stated that women were engaged in relatively less strenuous work and that their contribution was supplementary. An important task before those who entered the Indian women's studies arena was to challenge these observations and to prove them wrong. They did it with evidence collected through painstaking effort and research. This led to the coining of the term 'female-headed household' at an international level, for households where women were the main earners even while there were able-bodied men at home.

Research in women's studies began to flourish. Women and men from colleges, universities and research institutions began to write research proposals. One reason for this was the financial support that came from bodies like the ICSSR, UGC, the Departments of Law, Agriculture, Rural Development and Social Welfare, the Department of Women and Children and the Department of Science and Technology. Newspapers began to run Sunday specials carrying articles on women and related topics. As someone who occasionally evaluated proposals for funding, I was amused to find that many aspiring entrants to women's studies submitted proposals with these newspaper articles as their sole reference. They did not try, I felt, to find out on their own how women are treated in their own or neighbouring homes.

There were some issues that were probing my mind for a while, and I sent a proposal to the ICSSR with the knowledge of ISI. Over the years, I had felt that despite the officially acclaimed high rate in literacy, education, employment and a sex ratio favourable to women, the status of women in Kerala was not remarkable. I had also developed some ideas about family, property, marriage and so on. These questions in my mind took the shape of a study proposal titled, 'Changing Land Relations and Women: A Case Study of Palghat District in Kerala'. I knew that some of the issues I was considering took place later in that region than in Cochin and Travancore. This was followed by my first visit to the area, during which I travelled extensively in Palghat and nearby Kannur. I met many women and men who, without hesitation, talked to me at length. They included people from all walks of life, ranging from politics and the bureaucracy to farmers, shopkeepers and housewives.

This study, along with another one, was published as *Women and Rural Transformation*, volume IV of the ICSSR's Programme of Women's Studies. It was only recently that I found out from Vina's 'Editor's Note' that the volume was meant to be presented at the Conference of Non-Aligned Countries held in Baghdad in May 1979. She mentioned my study in her note. She wrote that the evaluator who had been personally involved in framing land legislations had made the following remark about it: 'She has raised issues which had never been taken into consideration by us while framing these policies. They need wide dissemination to avoid similar blunders in future.' As I believed that the people have a right to know what the 'researcher' – from among them or from outside – does with the findings, a summary of the study, in three parts, was published in the Malayalam daily, *Mathrubhumi*. I did this so that all those who helped me or responded to my questions would be able to read about my findings.

Meanwhile the Indian Statistical Institute was changing under the chairmanship of P.N. Haksar, who was a champion of the Nehruvian ideas of 'scientific temper' and democracy. The different subjects – Mathematics, Statistics, Economics, Sociology, Anthropology, Linguistics, etc. – were brought under different divisions. The new Governing Council comprised of the Director, representatives of the Central Statistics Office (CSO) and the Finance Ministry. Two ISI workers' representatives, one each from the scientific and non-scientific categories, were elected by all the workers in each category at the ISI headquarters, centres and units all over India. I happened to be the first elected representative of the scientific category.

I took my responsibility seriously and attended the meetings that happened regularly every three or four months. I travelled by air to attend these meetings. The first time I reached Dum Dum airport and travelled to the Institute's guest house, I felt that I saw a peaceful coexistence between people and beasts. It was a rainy day. The roads were partly flooded. In addition to the uneven surface and potholes, the rain had added chaos to the mud and slush. I saw poor women sitting on the roadside selling rice, vegetables, flowers and much more. Cows loitered leisurely in the area or rested in the middle of the road. Dogs did not lag behind. This was several decades back; Calcutta airport may have now become 'world-class' like Bombay and Delhi airports.

When I reached the guest house, I received a message from Mrs Mahalanobis inviting me for breakfast the next morning. As someone used to respecting elders, I went to her house as she wished. I cannot forget the way she greeted me: 'I have heard that you are a fighter,' she said and added, 'I am a fighter too.' I could see that she meant it well. Once, while Dumont was introducing me to someone, he used the word *intrepid*. He too had meant it positively. There are people who use it to mean 'quarrelsome'.

She gave me a simple breakfast including the Bengali sweet *rosogulla*. She told me stories about how her husband had built the Institute. I remember her recounting the visit of the famous statistician Fisher to the Institute. They did not have the resources to arrange befitting accommodation for him in a hotel. After thinking about this for several days, Mahalanobis decided to invite him to stay in his house. An experienced Muslim chef who had retired from a top-level hotel was hired for the period. The guest enjoyed his stay, though there was no writing table in the house. The well-known host did all his writing sitting on an easy chair with a plank placed on the arms of the chair, an old-time practice for many.

Rani Mahalanobis had an impressive personality. I knew people who thought of her as a 'Tsarina' and feared her, and have heard stories maligning her. One reason I can think of is that when the Institute was being built, she might have been involved to the extent of being a stern watchdog. However, though my acquaintance with her was brief and peripheral, I found her warm and welcoming. I considered her to be a wonderful representative of her generation and class. On most occasions, when I went to attend the Council meeting, she would either come down to see me or ask me to see her at her residence.

Another amusing memory of the Council experience that lingers in my mind is the silence some members maintained when an important issue had to be resolved. They were 'renowned' statisticians and mathematicians who were coopted to be members. At the time, ISI was facing a very important issue. Kallianpur, who was the Director, had returned to the US without resigning, leaving the Institute without a functioning head. The Chairman, P.N. Haksar, asked for the views of members on this issue. If I remember correctly, the Director of CSO and I proposed that there should be a Director attending to the functioning of the Institute in Calcutta and the centres. The Chairman was authorized to contact Kallianpur and know his decision. Many of us liked him and we wanted him in India.

My visits to ISI Calcutta were also occasions when I met friends. One was Renu Chakravarty, who was a Member of Parliament when we first went to Delhi. During the visits to Calcutta, I loved taking long walks around the Institute and shopping. Sweet curd (*mishti doi*) in earthen pots, well-packed to carry home, was a favourite delicacy. I also loved shopping for handloom saris. There were specific localities suggested by friends for these. I was always amused if we went there around noon. The shopkeepers showed a preference for their siesta rather than selling saris. Those of us who cared enough for handloom saris from Bengal and nearby regions would go back to buy them.

The markets would suddenly become lively in the evening as women and men came out to buy whatever they needed – rice, pulses, vegetables, fruits, flowers and the like. Those were days when West Bengal was facing an acute shortage of electricity. Practically every shopkeeper, including the pavement sellers, had a private gas cylinder connected to a lamp or at least a bulb. I enjoyed loitering in the area, watching the transactions and occasionally making small purchases. All cities – whether Madras, Paris or Calcutta – have similar markets where they have things they shared as well as things that were unique to each. And the people who crowded such places shared a similar eagerness and enthusiasm, which sadly does not exist in the modern shopping malls. In a mall, what looms large in our minds is a sense of wonder, the fear of getting lost and often the decision to be a spectator rather than a part of the fair. Even after my days of association with the ISI Council were over, I frequently visited West Bengal, mostly in connection with a new project I took on.

That was a collaborative work with Joan Mencher, an American anthropologist at the City University, New York. I heard about her from friends at the Centre for Development Studies at Trivandrum. For her earlier work based in South India, she had been affiliated with CDS. At a later period, she conceived of a project titled 'Women and Paddy Cultivation' with a much bigger canvas, covering areas beyond South India. The new project included ten villages each in West

Bengal, Tamil Nadu and Kerala. For this, she needed a new institution to affiliate and a new collaborator. That is how I came on the scene. I had not undertaken any collaborative work until then, but as friends like Alice Thorner suggested that I participate, I decided to give it a try. I had come to know, while in Kerala, a young woman Janaki Panikkar who had earlier worked with Joan.

The project was approved by the ICSSR and ISI Delhi was to be the affiliating institution. The ICSSR sanctioned Rs 50,000 to me. For Indian institutions, it was not a small amount at that time. Later, an equal amount was sanctioned as a supplementary grant by the Council. When I met J.P. Naik for the last time in a nursing home in Pune, he asked me whether I had received the amount.

A project of this scale demanded a large space. Once the data started flowing in, five, six or more people were employed to tabulate the data. The Institute provided the space for them to sit and work. Storage space was needed to keep the filled-in schedules that came from different study areas, as well as the material that had to be sent to the fieldworkers as and when the requests came. Different schedules were used to collect data from the varying categories of respondents. The Institute was gracious in sanctioning the necessary support. The original idea was to have ten villages, two each in five districts of Kerala, Tamil Nadu and West Bengal, as study areas. However, we were compelled to leave out two villages in Bengal for reasons of time.

Before beginning the study, Janaki, Joan and I went to one or two of the Tamil Nadu villages to test how the women respondents would react to our questionnaire. Our idea was to discuss the major issues we were trying to study. Many women who came were neither landowners of paddy fields nor actual cultivators of any sort. Some were from carpenter households; some others made eatables at home and sold them. But they wanted to be included in the study. It was not the first time that I had seen such eagerness, especially on the part of poor women, when we went to collect data. They thought that it would bring them some benefits. Perhaps they got that idea from the 'welfare' programmes the government introduced from time to time. We explained to the women that such studies would not bring any immediate benefit to the respondents. We succeeded in making them understand that our study was on women involved with paddy cultivation alone who were a distinct category.

The first field visit we undertook was to 24 Parganas in West Bengal. What I remember about this particular place was the arrival of a small group of men from the panchayat office who were not aware of the fact that women were engaged in paddy cultivation.

Rural Bengal fascinated me greatly. The field-level investigator or supervisor who accompanied me and I often chose to stay in village homes. The village residents not only provided hospitality but enthralled us with their music, devotional and other. The young girls would change into nice dresses, plait their hair in two and tie them with beautiful ribbons. I have visited the villages of that state many times.

Tamil Nadu gifted us with equally fascinating moments. Once, we were returning from a village in the suburb of Madurai. It was late evening, and we were in a bullock cart. From a distance, I heard a woman speaking. The clear, beautiful Tamil attracted me so much that I got off there. It was a meeting to celebrate the centenary of the legendary Tamil poet Bharathiar. We waited till the meeting was over and I rushed to catch the woman speaker, whom we will encounter again in this book. Her name was Vasanthi Devi. Another unfading memory is a night bus ride from Thiruvaiyaru on the banks of the River Kaveri, famous for the temple where the Thyagaraja music festival is held every year. This area was part of our study in Thanjavur district. I am refraining from writing about the experiences on the Kerala front as I have recorded them well in many of my papers and books which the reader can refer to.

Though several papers came out of the work, the final report was delayed. Joan's period for the study was over, and she went back to the US. My files on the seminars and conferences tell me that my research was not restricted to questions about women. However, the women's issue was definitely a major concern as it deals with half the population.

Since the early 1950s, I have been writing about Kerala. Many of the pieces were on issues relating to women. It was Chittaranjan who encouraged me to write in English. I have written in the *Economic and Political Weekly*, *Mainstream*, *Indian Left Review*, the Sunday magazine of the *Patriot* and other publications. Besides research findings, I also wrote about the places I visited, the people I met and the events I witnessed. Finding two of my articles in journals published in Calcutta in the 60s took me by surprise, as I cannot remember having known anyone there at that point in time. One was the 'Industrial Structure of Kerala' in the annual issue of the Malayali Samajam Calcutta, in 1964. The other was a piece on working women which appeared in the 18 June 1965 issue of *NOW*, again a journal from Calcutta. The Independence Day issue of *Yojana*, a publication of the Government of India, in 1975, carried my article, 'Women in Employment: Low in Profile, High in Discrimination'. 'Harijans, Poverty and Inequality' and 'Need for New Economic Thinking' were two articles I wrote in 1974 and 1982 respectively. Research and writing were a kind of urge and passion for me.

Among my articles, there are two which were never published. Perhaps they never reached the right hands. One is a long interview with Mary Poonen Lukose, the first woman to be Director of Public Health in Travancore. She was quite old and living alone, having lost both her husband and children when we met, but it was a pleasant, warm meeting in which we talked at length. The other is a piece I wrote following Charles de Gaulle's death. It was autumn, and I can still remember the heaps of dried leaves over which I walked to reach the condolence book kept for us to sign outside the wall of the Presidential Palace. I never got back the manuscripts of these which I sent to the publishers. Sadly, I don't have copies either.

The 1980s were a rather hectic decade for my professional life. I was busy attending and often presenting papers at conferences. A major one was the two-day Conference on Women Studies and Development in August 1982, organized at the Kakatiya University, Warangal, in Andhra Pradesh. I was familiar with the place as it was on our train route to Delhi, but had never gone there. Many participants came from Delhi. I got to know many young women from Andhra. That get-together away from big cities like Bombay and Delhi was an enjoyable experience.

Another memorable meeting was the Indian Economic Association's Annual Conference at the Gokhale Institute in Pune. I also participated in the bi-national Seminar on Sex Discrimination in Gainful Employment organized by the United States Education Foundation in India (USEFI) and the Indian Institute of Education, Pune. The Indian Agricultural Economics Association and the Indian Association for Research on National Income and Wealth also had their annual meetings there, following the Conference of the Indian

Economic Association (IEA). At many of them, I presented findings from my studies. The IEA organizers had arranged a Hindustani classical music recital by the late Bhimsen Joshi. I remember this mainly because it was there that I learned to appreciate and enjoy Hindustani classical music.

One last episode has to be narrated before ending this section. It is a memory which still retains an element of joy, satisfaction and pride. In 1982, ISI celebrated its Golden Jubilee. Apart from the official ceremony held at Calcutta, a decision was taken to continue the celebrations for a whole year. Each division was given the freedom to organize a function in whatever way it wished. At the suggestion of B.P. Adhikari, the then Director, I decided to organize an international symposium based on my field of work. A mathematician with a left political leaning, Adhikari asked me to invite people from abroad including the socialist countries. He particularly suggested Cambodia. The Cambodian ambassador to India, a pleasant young man, received me warmly, but regretted his inability to help me. What deterred him was his inability to handle the English language.

Just before the symposium, I and a few others from Delhi went to Calcutta to attend the inauguration of the Golden Jubilee celebrations by Prime Minister Indira Gandhi. My younger daughter and I reached a couple of days earlier and visited Santiniketan. It was the time of their *Baisakhi* festival. There was a huge fair where tribal artefacts were being sold. It was a festive atmosphere. We also met a *Baul* singer under a tree. I visited Santiniketan again, more than once.

Back in Delhi, I made a programme for a two-day-long ISI Golden Jubilee international symposium and sent it to the Director. He approved it and sent it back with a cover letter. Once copies were forwarded to the invitees, the real problem started. I had planned the programme, inviting papers and presentations on topics such as the 'New International Economic Order and Women in the Third World' and 'Work and Status of Women in Capitalist, Socialist Countries'. The other two topics were 'Review of Indian Studies on Women and Work' and 'Database for Indian Studies'. In a way, these topics had not yet begun to be explored by women's studies scholars in India.

By that time, I knew that what the socialist bloc called 'women's liberation' was different from women's studies as it came to mean elsewhere. What impressed us in our younger days when Soviet books and journals reached our market were the pictures of women operating harvesting machines and engaged in similar tasks. Women's studies raised questions related to women and society. It certainly included questions not raised earlier including sophisticated critiques of patriarchy, but it has fallen short of solutions to liberate women.

Women's studies in India, which was quite nascent at that time, had not attempted a broad enough framework to discuss issues related to women as we aspired to in our call for papers. But these were questions which needed to be debated, as the Non-Aligned Movement was at its height and had raised the demand for a New International Economic Order (NIEO) where the world wealth between the rich North and poor South was to be redistributed. It was a period of great expectations for all those who dreamt of revolutionary changes for the newly independent nations. In such a circumstance, the demand was not unusually bold. In this, my major source of support was Sulabha Brahme, who was not a women's studies person. Vina Mazumdar's initial reaction to the topic of NIEO was sceptical: 'Who knows what it is? It is like *neti, neti*', she remarked. She nevertheless gave me the address of the chief of the United Nations International Research and Training Institute for the Advancement of Women (INSTRAW), and chaired the second session. A woman economist from a prestigious university whom I invited to chair the first session was hesitant. She was working on the problem of NIEO but did not know where to fit in women. However, I managed to convince her, and she came.

Getting responses from international participants was not that easy. Quite by chance, I came across a Yugoslavian journal which Gopi used to get. In the issue dated 5 November 1981 of the *Journal Review of International Affairs*, I found an article titled 'Position and Role of Women in Development' by Vida Tomsic. Yugoslavia was at the forefront of the Non-Aligned Movement and President Marshal Tito was a staunch supporter from the beginning. Tomsic was a member of the Presidency of the Socialist Republic of Slovenia. As it was a time before computers and email, I wrote to her, inviting her to present a paper. She not only agreed to write a paper but expressed willingness to come with a young student. In the end she could not make it due to her official responsibilities, but the student came with the paper. Another Yugoslavian who responded with a positive gesture was the INSTRAW chief, Dunja Pastizzi-Ferencic. She arranged for the participation of two women from Cuba, one a paper presenter and the other, a companion who knew English. At her suggestion, a participant from Chile too came. The second session also became successful with the participation of international paper presenters like Loes Schenk-Sandbergen from Holland and a young Englishwoman, Susan Balloch, recommended by Tyrrell Burgess. Loes and her husband were anthropologists.

Asia was not behind as Vietnam sent Tran Thi Hoan, the Vice President of the All Vietnam Women's Federation. There was no participation from the Soviet Union, China or the US. I wrote to Valentina Tereshkova, the famous cosmonaut who was at that time the head of the Women's Federation in the USSR. She acknowledged my request by telegram, but I did not hear any further from her. A Soviet woman at the International Labour Organization (ILO) with whom I had corresponded was interested in coming, but that also did not happen. I never heard from her again either; neither do I know what happened to the conference bag and papers I sent her through an Indian student studying in the Soviet Union. The lack of a representative from the USSR hurt me deeply at another level. Large numbers of Indian women of my generation grew up admiring the freedom and achievements of Soviet women. I still believe that despite the many failures which led to the dismemberment of the Soviet Union, they had many successes. One major weakness of the Soviet system, to me, was that instead of instilling in their people a sense of pride and self-confidence, they never outgrew the fear and suspicion spread by the 'Great Conspiracy'.

The third and fourth sessions had only Indian paper presenters. Four Indian women – three economists and one sociologist – who had established themselves by their contribution to women's studies were rapporteurs. There was no participant from China too, but they started inviting me to some of the functions in the embassy and were friendly.

The symposium was inaugurated by Jyoti Trivedi, then Vice-Chancellor of SNDT University, Bombay, and a doctor by profession. She was introduced to me by Alice Thorner. She and her husband were living in Delhi while we were there. We developed mutual regard, warmth and concern for each other. She came to Delhi by the morning flight and reached the ISI campus on time. The Director was also present at the symposium. Many of the participants stayed in the ISI guest house. Though most of them did not know each other and shared no mutually legible language, they got time to meet each other individually or in groups in the evening and morning. It turned out to be a good gathering of women who had common concerns. Many of the young Indian participants shared their happiness with me. Though the campus was small, it was beautiful. Delhi then was far less crowded and much less noisy and polluted than it is today. Special care was taken to prepare food with less spice and oil. It was done in the guest house, and the cooks got much appreciation.

At the end of the symposium, a statement, 'Women and the Quest for NIEO', was adopted and released to the press. We did not realize that scheming by stronger forces was cutting at the roots of the Non-Aligned Movement, and that our country, which had been at the forefront of the movement, would soon be receiving those forces with open arms. A country which was trying hard to reduce poverty and inequality began celebrating the increasing number of 'crorepatis' amongst us. Looking back, I have no regrets about having chosen those topics for the symposium.

With delegates to the ISI Golden Jubilee symposium in Delhi, 1982. (*Left to right*) Vina Mazumdar, two delegates from Cuba, Tran Thi Hoan from Vietnam, K. Saradamoni, Irma Arriagada from Chile, x.
(Photo by Loes Schenk Sandbergen)

The symposium concluded successfully. The Director was pleased with the deliberations. He found that it was one of the least expensive of the functions organized as part of the Golden Jubilee celebrations of the ISI. The small grant sanctioned by the ICSSR was used to meet the travel cost of the Vietnamese delegate, while the Institute paid for the air ticket of the young woman from England.

I decided to get the delegates' bag made by the Delhi branch of the Self-Employed Women's Association (SEWA). I don't remember how I found the woman in charge; her name and the many tales of woe she narrated to me seem to have eluded my mind. We went to the Khadi shop, bought the cloth and together designed the bag. The rest she did.

The young Englishwoman put me in a spot. She brought a bottle of high-class whiskey as a gift for me and gave it to me before leaving. Her friends had told her that was what Indians loved the most. I did not know what to do with it. I offered it to our young and new administrative officer, but he did not drink. Finally, I gifted it to my neighbour. Some years later, the same thing happened when a young South Korean woman who joined me on a short-term fellowship at ISI came with the same 'gift'. Sitting in front of the computer and writing this, the story of my life, I am amazed at the number of people who traversed one's path.

As a fall-out of the symposium, I struck up some sincere friendships, especially with the Ambassadors of Cuba and Vietnam. They came home for dinner, and their embassies became welcoming places for me. Those were times when people were friendlier and the topics we discussed centred on positive politics, peace and friendship between people and countries.

More than one publisher approached me to bring out a volume of the papers presented at the symposium. But the ISI decided to publish it. The ISI Delhi Centre was also listed as a Centre of Women's Studies, and the Institute had a publishing wing which published the ISI journal *Sankhya*. The editorial secretary of that publishing wing, K.B. Goswami, showed genuine interest and arranged for my visit to Calcutta for the final proofreading. The volume came out in 1985 with a foreword by the Director. I am happy that my work found a place in the history of ISI.

❖

CHAPTER ELEVEN

US, Africa, Europe, Asia

In 1983, I went to the US. A few years earlier, I had met Florence Howe and Connie Sutton, two academics from the US, at a binational American Experience seminar on Women and Development, held at Anand, Gujarat. Florence was the Founder-Director of the Feminist Press in New York. She had participated in the Civil Rights Movement and later became a major figure in women's studies. It was they who first invited me to visit the US, but I never seriously thought of it.

The seminar at Anand was an unforgettable experience. By then, Anand had become famous as the land of the White Revolution, a cooperative dairy development programme that involved the participation of a large number of women. Dr Verghese Kurien, the architect of the White Revolution, was present at the meet. We were shown the film *Manthan*, based on the story of the dairy cooperatives in Gujarat. Some of us went to see the Sabarmati Ashram on the banks of the River Sabarmati, where Gandhiji lived before he moved to Wardha. The place was peaceful.

My trip to the US in 1983 was funded by the United States Education Foundation in India (USEFI). The Head of USEFI, whom also I had met at the Anand conference, began inviting me to talk to Fulbright scholars from the US in orientation programmes organized for them. He sanctioned a generous grant for my five-month-long American trip, including the air tickets. My participation in the International Anthropological and Ethnological Conference held that year in both Quebec and Vancouver, Canada, was also part of the trip.

Joan was at the City University of New York (CUNY) and staying in Manhattan. They had a spacious flat. At the International House (IH) in Manhattan, a single room was arranged for my stay. Nearby there were two churches, one next to the International House and one slightly far away. One of the sights that caught my attention was the number of young women walking into the church with rosary in hand. Almost parallel to the road in front of International House was Riverside Park, where people walked or jogged throughout the day.

I had a shocking experience either on the day after I arrived in the US or the next. I was standing by the side of the International House, dressed to go somewhere. Suddenly, a car stopped next to me and out came two short, well-built African-American women. One was dressed like a policewoman. The other might have been the driver. The woman in the police uniform tried to put a bundle of currency notes into my hands and asked me to get into the car. I did not understand what was going on. I was in a sari, and naturally, they must have understood that I was new to the city and was from India. I don't think I shouted or ran, but it was a miraculous escape.

Joan took me to CUNY and introduced me to her colleagues and staff. In the beginning I used to go to her house often, but the joint work was not happening. Soon after my arrival, I gave a talk at Columbia University. I do not remember giving one at CUNY, but meeting Joan's young students was an amusing experience. A few of them were curious about India and wished to know whether all marriages here were 'arranged' by the parents. The students were non-whites. I responded by asking how many of them would marry white men. Not many, for their parents would not approve of that.

Before I left for the US, Alice (Thorner) gave me the addresses and contact numbers of some of her friends, and told me that I should get in touch with them. As mentioned earlier, Alice and her husband were from the US though they lived in Paris. She had friends and family there and used to visit them almost every year. Alice had lived in the US during the period of the Great Depression. She was from a wealthy family, but had many friends with left political leanings. The late Professor Paul Sweezy, the founder-editor of *Monthly Review*, was a close friend. I sought out her friends. Most of them were teachers at colleges or universities, and some had retired. Some of them took upon themselves the responsibility of showing me around. One of them got me a pass for the convocation at Columbia University, which was not far from where I was staying. Another woman with radical political leanings took me to the office of the *Monthly Review*. She was working there and it was the day of her retirement. The occasion was also Sweezy's eightieth birthday.

I also made friends on my own. International House had both short-term and long-term residents. Many of the latter were college students. A large number, both women and men, came from South American countries. One of my neighbours was from either Colombia or Brazil. Though all of us had single rooms, we often met in the corridor or outside the bathroom. I also had an accidental encounter with someone who would become a good friend for long. One day, I heard the voices of women walking past my door which was ajar. I thought I glimpsed someone wearing a sari. Curiosity prompted me to take a look. I was correct. I spotted them entering the next room. I must have gone there and introduced myself, or waited and caught the Indian woman while she was returning. Her name was Sakuntala.

Sakuntala was from a Hindu family in Old Delhi. Many Hindu families had been there for long, and represented a tradition and culture that went back at least a few centuries. Incidentally, Jawaharlal Nehru's wife Kamala belonged to such a family. Once we became good friends, Sakuntala told me about her life. She was married to a young Indian settled in the US and had come to the country after marriage. He was from a well-known business family. As many families in Old Delhi were into business, her family must have thought that it was a good alliance. But things went wrong from the very beginning.

With Sakuntala (*right*) during a boat ride around Manhattan, 1983. (Photographer unknown)

Sakuntala's story was one of shock and survival. She had come to a place in the north of New York State. To her good fortune, she met an elderly couple who rescued her. They were originally from England and were rich. They were good human beings who empathized with her situation, and were determined to take her under their wing. I never met them, but all that I heard of them from Sakuntala were good words, of love and kindness.

By the time I came to know her, Sakuntala was living in New York – not in a posh area but in a place where the relatively more disadvantaged lived. She had blacks, Hispanics and other immigrants as neighbours and friends. She was, by then, a teacher at a special school meant for the talented among underprivileged children. She was passionately involved in her work and took it very seriously. Naturally, many of the mothers liked her and thought it was safe for their children to be in her hands. Sakuntala and I met often, talked about many things and went sightseeing. More of that later.

During my stay in the US, I came to know a young woman working at the Ford Foundation office in New York who thought that she should acquaint me with her country. She arranged for me to attend a seminar titled 'Women of Color' in Memphis. Named after the city with the same name in Egypt, it was located in the state of Tennessee in the south and had a long history as the world's largest market for cotton and lumber. The cotton economy of the region depended on the forced labour of the Africans who were brought as slaves. By the middle of the nineteenth century, Memphis became a major centre of slave trade. It later turned into an important centre in the struggles against slavery as well as in the Civil Rights Movement. On 4 April 1968, Martin Luther King Jr was assassinated at the Lorraine Motel. Memphis also had a claim to be a cultural centre as many renowned musicians of that period, including Elvis Presley, grew up in and around the city.

The seminar I went to attend was arranged perfectly. All the participants stayed together and this gave us plenty of time to meet informally and exchange views over breakfast or dinner. One thing that surprised me was that there were participants who were African-Americans, Asians and Latinos, but no representatives from the Native American community. I raised a query on their omission. The answer was that it was a Sociology conference and Native Americans came under Anthropology. From India, besides me, there was only a Bengali woman, who was a second-generation Indian emigrant in the US. Her parents had migrated to the US, and the young woman was born there. There were similar participants of Chinese and Japanese origins. Perhaps their grandparents or great-grandparents had been brought to build roads and railway lines in the US. The one thing that disappointed me was that they were not interested in knowing anything about the India from which I came, including the status of women's studies here.

But this did not prevent me from making friends. One person with whom I kept in touch even later, for a long time, was a professor at Hawaii University. She was from North Korea and had moved to Hawaii when the revolution broke out. Like many others, she had relatives in South Korea, but I don't think she had gone there to meet them. From Memphis, she and I went to Ohio where the National Conference of American Women's Studies was taking place.

The International House, which offered accommodation for people from different countries, informed us about various activities taking place in and around the city. We could pick up notices and brochures from the reception or the cafeteria in the building. Within just a day or two of my arrival, I read a notice seeking students or volunteers for a strawberry-picking event. I was required to make a telephone call. I did try, but could not understand any of the instructions given at the other end. Most probably, it was an answering machine. Though I had improved from my Madras days when I used to fear telephone calls, I was not comfortable with receiving instructions from the machine. I gave up my eagerness to take part in strawberry-picking.

The International House also used to arrange talks and interesting events for its residents. Once, a police officer spoke to us on how to protect ourselves while out in public places like streets and parks. He suggested that women should be very careful with their handbags and hold them close. He was frank in telling us that there were pickpockets, loafers and petty criminals around, and the best way to tackle them was to remain unfazed.

Harlem was very near the International House. Originally a Dutch village formally organized in 1658, it became a residential, cultural and commercial centre for African-Americans by the early decades of the twentieth century. But the Depression years saw the successful among its residents moving out and the place sliding into decline. The shifting of industries out of New York City and the unemployment that followed affected Harlem badly; crime and poverty increased. We were warned not to walk towards that side. One day, looking through the city guidebook, I found that there was a tourist bus which took people to visit Harlem. I joined a group of people who were interested in seeing the area. I don't think I saw any non-black residents there. But the place showed no sign of violence either. We even got off at one or two places. There were many churches, and service was going on in one of them. We were welcomed. It was interesting to witness the service. The whole atmosphere, even the music, was African.

I found out that many Indians in the US did not feel comfortable among African-Americans, especially the poorer sections. Of course, there were exceptions like Sakuntala, who later married an African-American. Although the US has had a non-white President, no significant change in the lives of the poor has taken place there. On the other hand, it is seen as a country of opportunities, and many women and men, including the poor, especially from the South Americas, flock there to make a living. Understandably, all of them do not succeed. Once, I saw a relatively old Russian woman and her family living out in the open in one of the backstreets of New York. Many rich and highly educated Russians had fled to Europe and later to the US when the Russian Revolution took place. They were received with open arms, but not the poor.

Another slightly adventurous trip I made was to a nearby place, New Jersey, on an underground train about which I had read somewhere. None of my friends had used it, but Sakuntala and I decided to give it a try. It was different from the metro. We got off at a station which was almost desolate. We walked around for a while. At last, from a poor, old woman we understood that it was an area mainly occupied by poor Italian migrants. Before leaving for India, again with Sakuntala, I went to the top of the famous Twin Towers, without realizing that we would see it collapse during our lifetime.

Two other places of interest I visited were an Amish settlement and the Crystal Cave. The first was a trip I made alone. The Amish people had migrated from Europe two to three centuries ago and are spread in Pennsylvania, Ohio and Indiana. They are a peace-loving, non-aggressive people who follow their personal, social and family values and code of conduct. On going there, I remembered seeing a settlement of fishing people somewhere on the Belgium–Holland border before I left France – people who were treated as a showpiece for the tourists. The women among them, who wore dresses resembling that of Victorian ladies, ran inside the house when they saw strangers. Unlike them, the Amish were confident in their ways and were not a tourist attraction.

I made the trip to the Crystal Cave with Sakuntala and a friend of hers, Phyllis, who drove us to Pennsylvania. It was their first visit to the place as well. On another occasion, I travelled by train to Washington DC. Poduval, who had been a colleague in the Planning Unit, and another friend of mine were working with the World Bank there. I saw many interesting places in and around Washington.

Apart from the places I visited in the US, some of the people I met also remain fresh in my memory. One person I remember is Eleanor Leacock, a renowned anthropologist and a colleague of Joan at CUNY. She was well-known, not only on account of her research and academic accomplishments, but equally for her status as a staunch activist and fighter against discrimination on the grounds of race, sex and class. She had got a PhD from Columbia University in 1952 but had to wait till 1963 to get a professorship. The reasons for the discrimination she faced were that she was a woman, was married, had two children and, above all, was a Marxist. I cannot remember how and where I first met her. She made arrangements for me to attend an all-black protest meeting. It was in a hall. The meeting raised questions about unemployment and trade union rights. Eleanor also invited me to her apartment in Greenwich Village in downtown New York. It was an evening when a large number of friends and students met over wine and cheese. For those who did not drink wine, there was fruit juice in plenty. Many brought along books for sale, donation or exchange. The funds thus raised were donated to some cause. It was a lively evening.

Another group of women I met was called the WREE (Women for Racial and Economic Equality). I recall attending some of their meetings. It was a collective of white and black women who mixed freely and created a lively and easy atmosphere. I enjoyed their company. They were part of the Communist Party of the US. Some of them had gone through the Great Depression and remembered how it was followed by increased unemployment and poverty. As my stay was short, I had no opportunity to participate in their political programmes.

In the US, I got the opportunity to listen to K.J. Yesudas on two occasions. The first was in Philadelphia where an old family friend's daughter was living at that time. The audience was mainly composed of Keralites, the majority of them being nurses. It was an evening of film songs. The maestro and the troupe had come prepared with select popular songs. But the audience requested other songs, and they were not disappointed. The second time I heard Yesudas was in New York. This time it was a classical music concert. The flight which brought the maestro and the accompanying artists was slightly late, but Yesudas went straight to the stage and took his seat. During the concert that lasted more than three hours, he did not even take a sip of water. A young Malayali man who worked in a bank dropped me back at my place. His house was beyond the International House.

Another unforgettable occasion was listening to Zubin Mehta conducting his orchestra at Central Park in New York. It was beautiful! I suddenly got an idea. I imagined a large group of women regularly gathering once in three or six months at India Gate, in Delhi. They could be a mix of those who could sing well and others who were not very competent but could sing with the rest. I thought of Vidya as the leader. That dream did not materialize, but I do believe such groups will emerge one day.*

I met an interesting couple from Kerala in Philadelphia. They had both retired from state government service in Kerala as gazetted officers. It meant good money and high social status. They came to the US for their children's education. The woman had influential relatives. But for the elderly couple, the US was not a haven. When I knew them, they were working at one of the Holiday Inn hotels. One of them was engaged in counting and giving linen for laundering. The other was doing a similar job. The payment was according to the minimum hourly wages fixed by the state. This was very humiliating for them. I was amused by the man, when angry, shouting that while many others had come by ship, they came by air. He was furious. Later on, I met and heard about parents who go to the US or other countries either

* The MBS Youth Choir started by Sarmaji in memory of M.B. Srinivasan in Trivandrum completed 35 years on 6 August 2023.

to visit their children or to be of help to them. The loneliness and discomfort experienced by them is not something even their children recognize.

It was also in the US that I met and befriended Koshy, a highly educated Keralite who had a doctoral degree from a prestigious university in India. He was politically conscious and had been fully involved in student politics while in India. But when I met him in the US, he was without a proper job. Meeting Indians who were there like me, with whom he could discuss matters of common concern, was a pastime he enjoyed. His brother and mother were also there. Both the brothers had married nurses as such marriages opened a way to get a US visa for the spouse. The brother was far less educated. He was running an Indian grocery store and was making a success of it. He had a big house with a relatively large compound where, to my happiness, I saw some huge trees. It was in this house that I met their mother for the first time. She had not wanted to leave Kerala, but her sons had insisted that she could not be left alone.

I had been to Koshy's house too. We met and talked about many things, particularly politics in its broad sense. He told me many stories about the nurses from Kerala whose life was pathetic in more than one way. Most of them came from relatively poor backgrounds, and their main aim was to earn as much as they could. The American system of hiring and fixing wages was different from that in India. One could not call the nurses either part-time or permanent workers. They were hired on hourly wages, which was higher than what many other categories of workers earned. They were in great demand. Property dealers, car dealers and others approached these women once they crossed the initial settling down period and became financially stable. They became eligible for fully furnished apartments and a car. The agents offered them attractive deals. They found it easy to pay for these in instalments. They owned everything in their own name, and they became self-confident. Then came the question of marriage. It was easier than if they were back home. Their ability to sponsor a visa was valuable. However, only a minority of the husbands had the necessary qualification or skills to look for jobs in that country. The others sat at home indulging in drinks, playing cards and abusive verbal exchanges, while the wives worked a second or third shift. Koshy was deeply aware of the nurses' domestic situation and entreated me to take up a study on that serious human problem. I was genuinely interested, but the logistics were against my starting on that venture.

During our chats, Koshy also told me about the first conference of Keralites in North America. It was a gala event for the Malayalis. I remember attending a session organized for the youth. One of the organizers was the renowned scientist George Sudarshan. The session was attended by many Indian teenagers who were brought up in the US. The organizers had distributed a questionnaire to the young participants. A number of girls complained about not having the 'freedom' that others in their class or neighbourhood, mostly non-Indians, enjoyed. One of the mothers, who was also a member of the organizing committee, reacted vehemently to this. The boys, on the other hand, thought that in Kerala as well as in the US, they got the chance to meet and mingle with uncles, aunts and their children in places including the church. Hence, they did not feel their freedom was constrained in any way. A young boy, not a church-goer, said that he was made to write in Malayalam to his grandparents regularly, and that he was sent home to spend holidays with them. He appeared to like it. He also said that the teaching of mathematics in Kerala was better and on a higher level than in America. At that conference, I saw a nurse who was also a writer. Unfortunately, I could not get acquainted with her. Koshy told me that she wrote mainly about the life of nurses.

Before I returned from the US, I went to Canada for the International Conference of Anthropological and Ethnological Studies. It was held in two venues, one in French-speaking Quebec and the other in Vancouver in British Columbia. On my way to Quebec, I had to wait for long at the Montreal airport. I remember sitting in the spacious, glass-covered lounge near a window, enjoying the sun shining on the surroundings. My thoughts went to my childhood, to the days when I made Eskimo igloos with coconut shells and played with my little dolls. Musing about the wonders life offers to us, I wrote a letter home.

On the way to Vancouver I stopped in Toronto to meet my old colleague Pankaj Dutta and his family. While flying from Quebec to Toronto, I saw a lot of the uninhabited parts of Canada. Gina, Pankaj's wife, met me at the airport. They had a nice house with a swimming pool. Their two small children were at school. Gina took me out sightseeing. Pankaj, by and large, was quiet. He presented me with a fountain pen.

The conference was a large affair which brought together many delegates. These are occasions for many to travel, meet people and establish contacts. Many of the delegates had come from India for the Vancouver part of the conference. Leela Dube and Joan Mencher were there. It was there that I met a Kerala anthropologist, Vineetha Menon. She and her husband lived in Vancouver, working on their PhD. They had a small baby. That acquaintance turned into a close bond which has lasted over decades. Vancouver was a beautiful place. We went around sightseeing. We saw a salmon hatchery and the baby fish being thrown into the sea when they reached a certain age.

My return journey from Canada was eventful. I had planned to see the Niagara Falls on the way back, but this did not happen. When I got off at Chicago airport, the young woman who was to meet me and arrange for my stay and sightseeing was not there. I was given accommodation for the night at the Holiday Inn and the next morning, I got into a local tourist bus to see the city. The bus passed by the hall where Vivekananda had made his famous speech at the World Parliament of Religions in 1893.

This was almost at the end of my stay in the US. My return trip to India was via Paris and Amsterdam. Sakuntala and her friend Phyllis drove me to the airport. In Amsterdam, I stayed with Loes Schenk-Sandbergen.

Looking back, I realize I did a lot of travel in those years. Soon after my return to India, I went out again, this time to the east, to the Philippines. This was in September 1983, to attend a conference on Women in Rice Farming Systems. It was organized by the International Rice Research Institute in Manila. Both Joan and I had a paper each from the data collected for our study. The topic that the Institute decided to debate was relevant. Rice was a major food crop in India and many countries of the world. It was also the major provider of employment, especially for women. Agriculture's pre-eminent position came from its contribution to society and the economy in terms of food and raw materials needed for industries. The overall decline that has visited this sector during the recent decades has impacted the families who were engaged in agriculture in ways that could not be imagined earlier. The papers presented in Manila have come out as a volume, titled *Women in Rice Farming*.

Back in Delhi, I once again got caught up in seminars and

At the International Rice Research Institute, Manila, 1983.
(Photographer unknown)

conferences. Before I went to Kerala for a holiday, Leela Dube had talked to me about a conference on 'Women and the Household in Asia' which she was planning to organize. At that time she was looking for a venue, and I hoped that it would be in Bhopal where her husband, the well-known anthropologist S.C. Dube, held a high-profile office. I also hoped that the delegates would get a chance to visit the famous Buddhist sanctuary in Sanchi. But when I returned, to my disappointment, I found that Leela was still looking for a venue. Since her husband and she were known and respected in academic circles, I had thought that she would find a place easily.

Finally, the conference took place on the ISI campus towards the end of January 1985. It was inaugurated by the Chairman of ISI, Haksar, and the venue was a big *pantal* put up for the purpose on the lawns of the campus. However, the delegates took over the auditorium, several classrooms and several rooms in the guesthouse.

An acquaintance I made at that time was Ammu Krishnaswami who had previously occupied a top position in the Commonwealth Secretariat. Ammu was a friend of Lotika Sarkar, Professor of Law at Delhi University and also a member of the Committee on the Status of Women in India from the beginning. I found in Ammu a delightful friend. Leela Dube at that time was a Fellow at Mysore University. She constituted an organizing committee for the conference in which I

With P.N. Haksar at the conference on 'Women and the Household in Asia', 1985. (Photo by ISI staff photographer)

was also a member. The idea was to share the responsibilities among a group of people. In practice, however, the responsibilities were not equally shared. Perhaps it is not easy when the work to be managed is huge and complex. In discharging my share of the responsibilities, I cannot forget the help received from A. Damodaran of the Administrative Section.

The participants in the conference were mainly Asians. There were some Americans and Europeans who were studying or specializing in Asian countries, but they did not receive any financial support from the conference. The number of papers was huge. It was not easy to have them typed, cyclostyled and ready for distribution on time. There were five sub-themes. I was the coordinator of one of them. The papers in my sub-theme came out as Volume 5 under the title, *Finding the Household – Conceptual and Methodological Issues*. Some younger participants were happy getting their papers published as it had not happened earlier. Though the conference was for five days, in my sub-theme the deliberations were finished in three days. This enabled the members of my group to attend the other sessions in a relaxed manner. I also tried to include papers from the North East which at that time had not entered the arena of women's studies. The last session of my sub-theme was chaired by my neighbour and friend Mene who is a Naga woman. Although Mene is a homemaker, she did

At the conference on 'Women and the Household in Asia', 1985.
(*Left to right*) Oakla Cho, Mene Chandola, K. Saradamoni.
(Photo by ISI staff photographer)

a great job. I did this because I believe that homemakers should also know what is being talked about in such meetings.

In July 1985, the UN World Conference to review and appraise the achievements of the Women's Decade was held in Nairobi, Kenya. Alongside that, an NGO Forum was scheduled from 10 to 19 July, which started five days before the UN conference.

Most of the Indian delegates met in Bombay and flew from there to Nairobi. My younger daughter Anu who was part of a young women's panel at the NGO Forum had left before me. While waiting for my luggage after landing, I met the late Dr Lakshmi Sahgal (for us, the legendary Captain Lakshmi) who was part of Subhash Chandra Bose's brigade. I was amazed at the ease with which she talked Malayalam despite having lived outside Kerala for long. I met her again in Trivandrum more than once. I found her warm and pleasant.

Talking about the UN Conference, like any other country, the

Kenyan authorities too had masked off the poor, the sick, the disabled and the prostitutes away from the conference hall and neighbourhood. The security was tight. I had a letter from the Chief of the Press Trust of India (PTI) in New Delhi. Their man in Nairobi helped to get me the necessary sanctions and accreditation to function as a reporter so that I had access to the UN sessions. I attended the daily press conferences and without fail sent the reports to Delhi. Only when I returned, I came to know that PTI had not used any of my reports.* Perhaps a women's conference was not an important enough event for them. I hold that they missed a golden opportunity to tell the world how the women who gathered in Nairobi perceived the world around them. They had clear views on their rights and suggestions to rectify the wrongs.

Thousands of women from all over the world reached Nairobi to be part of the NGO Forum. They were of all ages. There were women from big cities and unknown villages. They included students, academics, professionals, farmers and artists of all hues. They were activists in different arenas. They wore different dresses, talked different languages and their politics were different too. But I cannot remember these differences resulting in any violent outbursts. In fact, there was a peace tent to discuss and exchange ideas, and spread the message of peace. Many of the panels too discussed the topic of peace. Several participants argued for a total ban on nuclear tests. Women knew how the money spent on war and armaments could be used for education, health, generation of employment and other socially relevant purposes. I attended several panels and participated in some.

The largest number of participants was naturally from Africa. Japan and the US also sent large delegations, and the Indian contingent too was big. There were women from Nepal, Sri Lanka and other Asian countries who were regular participants in our seminars and conferences. There were familiar faces from non-Asian countries too. There was an African-American professor whom I had met in the US, who was researching African healing systems. There was Florence Howe and her group. Two young women all the way from Surinam came to talk to us as they believed that their ancestors were from India.

Our hosts did not stand stiffly, making formal 'welcome' speeches. Instead, they welcomed us through song and dance. They sang about

* See Appendix.

With Leela Dube (*second from right*) and other conference participants in Nairobi, 1985. (Photographer unknown)

the rain and nature. This did not mean they were frivolous. They did everything to make sure that our stay was comfortable, productive, enjoyable and safe. There was a daily Forum newspaper which told us about the events of the day. There were plenty of pamphlets, articles and statements on various issues available at the UN desks and the Forum counters. One I have is titled 'An Alliance with Nature'. 'Women and the Earth's Traditions' was by the Executive Director of the UN Environment Programme. The issues debated at Nairobi included 'Hiring Freeze: What Will it Mean to Women?' and 'Women's Day Panel: Discrimination No Accident'.

We stayed on for some more days and saw some interesting places in Kenya including the famous sanctuary, Maasai Mara. The peaceful coexistence among animals, with no fence or wall to restrict their freedom, was a great lesson. Our intrusion must have been an irritant, but they did not attack us. On the way, we saw the extreme poverty in which many rural Kenyans lived.

During our return journey, my daughter and I had a brief stay in Ethiopia, where Shyamu was working with the Food and Agriculture Organization (FAO). In the UNICEF office, there was a woman I had known while she was in Delhi. At her request, I gave a talk to her

With Dr K. Shyamasundaran Nair (Shyamu), agricultural economist, in Addis Ababa, 1985. (Photo by G. Arunima)

colleagues. We saw parts of the country which appeared very poor and backward. It was predominantly a Christian country, and in terms of the dress and lifestyle of people in these parts, I thought they were still living in the time of Christ.

In July 1986, I went to Heidelberg in Germany to participate in the 9th European Conference on Modern South Asian Studies. It was the 600th anniversary of the University of Heidelberg which was originally a centre of intellectual debates on theology. I had been initiated into the conference by Alice Thorner two years earlier, when it was held at the School of Oriental and African Studies (SOAS), London.

Heidelberg was a quiet, beautiful place. People were friendly. I bought a pair of Birkenstock sandals about which I had heard a lot. A fascinating thing that we witnessed was the arrival there of around a hundred people from the US. They were not tourists. They had come to Heidelberg because it was their ancestral home. They brought a huge doll which they themselves had made as a gift to their roots. Compared to Delhi, all these places looked small. We could not escape running into the same set of people over and over again in one street, the next lane or in the market.

In August the same year, I participated in the World Congress

In Heidelberg with Alice Thorner (*far right*), 1986.
(Photographer unknown)

of Sociology which was held in Delhi itself. Soon after, I helped as a representative of the ISI to organize a subsequent seminar along with UNESCO-INSTRAW and the Nehru Memorial Museum and Library where it was held. This World Congress brought Vida Tomsic from Yugoslavia who had not been able to make it to India in 1982 when I organized the ISI's Golden Jubilee symposium. Mme. Tomsic gifted me a pretty flower vase made of glass. With the INSTRAW Chief, we three had an enjoyable time.

My first trip to China, a fortnight visit, happened on 30 August that same year. It was as part of an ICSSR-sponsored delegation. The main purpose was to participate in the Indo-China seminar on Planning and Socio-Economic Development in Beijing, where I read a paper titled 'Human Resource Development: Changing Characteristics of Women's Participation in the Labour Market'.

It was a very enjoyable trip. Though it was the post-Mao period, the place had not moved on from that era. From early morning, people lined up in long queues outside Mao's mausoleum. Mao jackets were widely worn. I bought three of them, two for my daughters and one for Gopi. The place was full of bicycles. At that time, China perhaps had just a dozen cars to transport foreign visitors who came for official

With Professor Wei Fung Chiang (*fourth from left*) and the Indian delegation to China, 1986. (Photographer unknown)

purposes. Like all socialist countries, they had rows of simple houses for the people. However, I was greatly impressed by the road from the airport to the place where we stayed; it was an old palace. There was a long-term vision behind it.

Another thing that struck me was the feeling of safety the place evoked. As I was the only woman in our team, I always got a single room. The day after we reached, very early in the morning, I went out for a walk. My stroll led me to a big park where women and men, young and old, were engaged in the Chinese martial art, Tai chi, in groups. The country at that time did not have huge hotels or resorts to accommodate guests. Most probably, China in those days was not a prominent tourist destination.

Back home, we were used to 'Chinese dishes' in Indian restaurants which were mostly non-vegetarian. To my surprise, the dining area in the place we stayed offered a large variety of vegetarian dishes to choose from. So was the case regarding salads, which included a variety of green leaves. Fruits were also available in plenty. What they lacked, I think, was milk and milk products.

We were taken to places outside the capital. The trains were neat and comfortable. I remember going to a local-level office, something similar to the panchayat in India. The man in charge told us in detail about the population, occupation and all such information that one could get in a handbook. I was impressed by his ability. We also visited a silk factory. The woman in charge there was very comfortable with answering our queries. She showed us around. It was a small factory with a limited number of workers. Young women workers were standing between the looms, having their meal with chopsticks. China at that time kept both wages and the cost of living low.

We were also taken to the foothills of a huge mountain. It was through those ranges that Buddhist monks from India had crossed over to China several hundred years back. There were many not-so-huge statues on the mountains commemorating the trek made by those monks. We saw more than one Buddhist temple in China. People came there to worship with incense sticks and other offerings.

When we were at a picturesque lakeside where nature was at its best in terms of weather and beauty, a slightly elderly Chinese man approached me. He could easily see that I was from India. He had been in Santiniketan during Tagore's time. He wanted to visit there once again and requested my help. That was certainly a most unexpected encounter in China. When I returned, I discussed the matter with Haksar and Nikhil Chakravartty, the two people whom I thought could help. My plan worked, and the Chinese gentleman did come to Santiniketan, though I was not able to meet him. He brought some gifts for me which I received. Later on, I received a letter and some photographs from him.[*] Unfortunately, we have lost touch.[**]

❖

[*] See Appendix.

[**] He passed away on 5 March 2005.

CHAPTER TWELVE

Leaving Delhi Behind

Looking back, it is hard to believe that I managed to shuttle between so many places, attending or organizing seminars and conferences.

Since the Bombay meet, the women's group interested in economic affairs used to gather for discussions at different places. I went to one organized by Kalpagam at the Madras Institute of Development Studies in Chennai in 1984. But the day turned out to be eventful for a totally different reason. While the seminar was on, the news of Prime Minister Indira Gandhi's assassination reached us. The shock was so great that we did not know what to do. Somehow I reached my sister-in-law's house. My friend Madeleine was in Pondicherry at that time, and I was to go there after the meeting. The person to take me there was a young French scholar, Roland Lardinois, whom I had met earlier at the Tamil Nadu Archives. He managed to come around 10 at night and we dared the trip in a car. There was utter silence, but all along the route, lamps were lit and there were pictures of Indira Gandhi with garlands. We were scared, but fortunately, nothing untoward happened. Madeleine had arranged a room for me at the French Cultural Centre in Pondicherry. I saw the funeral of the slain Prime Minister on television in a house nearby. I can think back on that night's drive to Pondicherry only with a shudder.

I stayed in Chennai for a few days before I flew back to Delhi. Normalcy had not been resumed in the capital. Fortunately, there was a friend on the flight and he arranged my safe passage home. In the areas where I lived and worked, there were no overt eruptions of violence. But the whole atmosphere was tense. We had a Sikh driver at ISI. I was told that he was given protection by a professor at JNU. In and around the place we stayed, there were not many Sikhs. Gopi had a young Sikh colleague in the United News of India (UNI). He was under the safe custody of his colleagues. There were similar stories in many places.

Devaki Jain had earlier in 1975 come up with the idea of creating a women's think tank. However, there were not many takers for that idea. Instead, a get-together of educated women, employed and otherwise, took shape. Some unemployed mothers came with their daughters. If both were employed, they came from their workplace. Though the details have escaped my memory, we met regularly for quite some time. It certainly created an atmosphere where women irrespective of age, caste or class could mix freely, share their experiences, clarify doubts and meet like-minded people. I enjoyed those evenings. Devaki stopped coming after some time; however, the meetings continued. They were held in the Sardar Patel Vidyalaya headed by Vibha Parthasarathy. I wish there were similar gatherings in more places.

Another major event I was part of was the biannual National Conference of the Indian Association of Women's Studies (IAWS) held at the Punjab University in Chandigarh from 1–4 October 1986. A new Executive Committee of the IAWS was elected after its Trivandrum Conference in 1984. Jyotibehn from SNDT, Bombay, Leela Dube, Kalpagam from Madras, Susheela Kaushik from Delhi University, Lucy Jacob, a professor from Jaipur and I were elected to form the new Executive Committee (EC). One day I had a surprise telephone call from the election officer who was a professor at JNU. She gave me the news that I had been elected from two constituencies and suggested that I could choose to give up one.

Jyotibehn was chosen to be the president; I became the treasurer; and the secretaryship was thrust upon Lucy. I say 'thrust upon' because she had just retired, and her family in Kerala was pressing her to return home. She acceded to our request and continued in Jaipur for two more years. She must have either continued to stay in her university accommodation or rented a place outside. We both belonged to the old school, and were very thrifty in handling public funds. She did not keep a secretary to help her; all she had was part-time help to go to the post office and do other small jobs. Most of the EC meetings were held in ISI, where accommodation and food were cheaper than any place outside.

As a member of the EC of the IAWS and treasurer, I had organizational responsibility at Chandigarh. Besides, along with a young history professor Tanika Sarkar, I coordinated the sub-theme,

'Women and Agrarian Struggles' at the conference. I was also a panelist in the plenary session on 'Development Alternatives: Women's Perspectives'. I regret that we did not manage to bring out the papers presented on our sub-theme as a volume. It was at Chandigarh that I met Ajitha from Kerala for the first time. A spontaneous and warm bonding that began there has continued over the years.

During these years, Gopi's health was showing some changes. Despite a very demanding political and professional life even before coming to Delhi, he was both physically and mentally fit. He developed some kind of skin ailment. While holidaying in Kerala we contacted Dr Sarojini, Shyamu's wife, who was a skin specialist. Gentle and soft-spoken, she suggested an ointment and some medicine. Allopathy did not have any effective medicine for the disease, which was diagnosed as psoriasis. We turned to ayurveda, and he was treated at Trivandrum and Coimbatore. The ayurvedic treatment continued even after we returned to Delhi. My brother sent bottles of medicines sometimes through railway passengers he did not know. Looking back, I am thankful to all those people who obliged.

By this time, our daughters had grown up. Asha, a Science Talent scholar, took an MS degree in Chemistry from IIT Delhi. She then took a break, worked with the *Manushi* journal for some time and was engaged in feminist activities. She did not want to continue with chemistry. At that time, she read an article by an eminent neuroscientist at Kamaraj University, Madurai. She wrote him a letter and the gentleman met her in Delhi. He made arrangements for her participation in a study project he was conducting along with German scientists. The study involved bats. Asha enjoyed participating in the Indo–German Workshop on Neurophysiology. In early 1984, she went to the US to do a PhD in Neurobiology.

Anu did an MA in History from JNU, Delhi. One day, when I was about to leave the office for lunch, Gopi telephoned and asked me to buy some sweets on the way back home. I bought some delicacies without knowing what the urgency was. Anu had got a Fellowship to do an MPhil in Cambridge, England. She continued there after the MPhil and did her PhD too from Cambridge.

Before Anu left for England, I undertook a trip to Badrinath along with my friend Indira and her elder daughter. The taxi which was arranged for the trip took us via Haridwar and Lakshman Jhula. On the first day, we stayed overnight in Haridwar at a guest house run by the Sivananda Ashram. There, we met a Malayali woman who had joined the ashram.

I went to those places again after fifteen years, and I saw that by then, the government had done sufficient havoc. To raise income from pilgrims and tourists, more rest houses and pucca roads were constructed. But my mind still retains that early morning in 1986, when the chants from the temple reverberated in the air and entered our ears with a soothing touch as our car descended the mountains. The women from the mountain villages were already collecting firewood and fodder from the jungles. I was not surprised when I heard of the great tragedy that took place at Kedarnath a few years ago, as I had heard of the destruction caused to those fragile mountains in the intervening period. In the name of development, successive governments contributed their share to this.

With both the daughters gone, Gopi and I had a new life together, different from what it was for nearly thirty-five years. But we coped with it. Gopi's health took a new turn. Signs of Parkinson's disease were detected. It started with his seeing double lines while typing. I took him to the Lady Hardinge Hospital where we knew a woman ophthalmologist. When I went to collect the results the next day, I found that the doctor had already shown it to her senior and was perturbed. 'Tip of the iceberg', she whispered. I did not understand what she meant. She referred his case to the All India Institute of Medical Sciences (AIIMS).

I took Gopi to the Neurology Department at AIIMS. He was not admitted there but had to go for regular check-ups. I soon learned how a neurology patient was examined. However, the doctor's observation, 'Mr Nair, for your age you are doing well,' irked me. I was not very happy with the attention he received. I remembered the days when I had been a patient there. It was only after a young doctor in Ernakulam, my brother's friend, gave a letter to AIIMS recommending a CAT scan that it was done. Unsteadiness was a visible sign of Parkinson's disease. It affected Gopi's movements and his mobility was seriously restricted. He loved driving, and it was painful for him to give it up. He was a patient listener, but never a non-stop talker. Even for such a person, it was not easy to accept the fact of a declining ability to speak. The same was true in the case of losing the ability to write or type.

After Gopi's retirement, I started taking the car to the office. There were days when I worked from home. We did this because we did not have domestic help from Kerala after the children finished their school years. After some time, I found a Malayali woman, Karthyayani, to help me with cooking and other odd chores. Over the years, we became very close. I have written her story elsewhere.

Despite the complex demands of my official life, my mind was always searching for things that would ease Gopi's situation. Once, I hit upon the efficacy of yoga as therapy. My daughters had done a yoga course at the Bharatiya Vidya Bhavan. I went to find out whether the guru who had taught them would come home for lessons. He answered that it is more beautiful to do it with a group; and it was true. At that time, the yoga school, Kaivalyadham from Lonavala, used to come twice a year to Delhi. They offered free classes at two places, India Gate and the Rose Gardens near IIT, Delhi. We joined the latter as it was closer to our home and because it was a quiet, beautiful place. We also chose the early morning class. We were in the small group meant for those with health problems. I was there because I could not leave Gopi alone. He was enthusiastic and liked it. He practised

Working at home with Gopi, 1980s. (Photo by G. Asha)

what he learnt even after we came back to Kerala. In those days, we also went for long walks. The Deer Park behind Green Park was our favourite spot for walks.

Soon after the Chandigarh conference, Vandana Shiva, who was a participant there, invited me to a conference in Nepal. As I had never been to Nepal, I was rather keen on going. Though Gopi had visited the Himalayan country, I bought a ticket for him too, and all arrangements were made for our travel. But I changed my decision at the last minute as I was not confident to leave Gopi alone in the hotel room.

In the meantime, I was getting involved in seminars and workshops on a wide range of topics. The Delhi Science Forum used to organize activities and programmes on topics such as health and drugs policy, health education, environment and so on, which I found interesting. 'Jawaharlal and India's Quest for Secular Identity', organized by the Nehru Memorial Museum and Library, was stimulating. I heard the Vice Chairman of the German Democratic Republic at a meeting of the Indo-GDR Friendship. He spoke on 'Disarmament, Development and Peace' – words that seem to have almost disappeared from our vocabulary. At a conference held in the prestigious Vigyan Bhavan, discussions took place on the topic, 'Indian Ocean, a Zone of Peace'. Many countries had sent delegates. Perin and Romesh Chandra who had spent a lifetime working for the peace movement, were the stars at this meet. A two-day conference titled 'Trends in Agrarian Economy and Tasks on the Agrarian Front' was perhaps the last of such events I attended before I left Delhi. It was organized by the Communist Party of India at their headquarters.

I went on a trip to Hissar in Haryana, along with Gopi. It was for a North Western Regional Seminar on 'Land Reforms: Achievements, Problems and Prospects', organized by the Sociology Department of Haryana Agricultural University. Our friend Naqvi persuaded us to make the trip. There, I met a group of young students from the North East. I wondered what they could learn from Haryana which was so different in topography, climate and cropping pattern from their region.

Gopi and I went to Jaipur for a holiday soon after. His patience and cooperation deserved such a holiday, I thought. My friend Lucy Jacob was there, and she booked us into a room on the ground floor of the university guesthouse. We went by tourist bus and returned by train.

Jaipur turned out to be really the Pink City we have heard so much about. At that time, I did not know that Rajasthan was the largest state in India. The turbans worn by the men, the beautiful skirts of the women and the exquisite handicrafts one saw in the emporiums and other shops offered us a glimpse of the great diversity of the state. We went to see the Amber Fort and Palace. The route that led us there, the fort and its entrance, transported us to the grandeur of a past dating back centuries.

Before I retired, we also made a trip to Kulu-Manali. The trip happened at the insistence of a colleague of mine, H.C. Sharma, who hailed from Mandi in the state of Himachal Pradesh. He made arrangements for our stay through a friend. This was not our first trip to the Himalayas. Once earlier, we had driven all the way to the Garhwal side in our car. Gopi was the one who drove most of the time. We were going to visit a journalist comrade who had spent several years in an East European country. An interesting memory from that trip is how various nieces and nephews paid their respects to our friend by touching his feet. The comrade relished it. Another time, Gopi and I had also gone to Dehradun and Mussoorie, when my nephew Ramakrishnan was studying at the Defence Academy.

On all these earlier occasions, Gopi's health had been in excellent form. But the situation was different this time. However, we enjoyed the memorable bus ride along unfamiliar routes. We loved walking around in the Manali area. We walked up to the Hidimba Devi temple. We took a taxi and went to the Rohtang Pass, as well as the house and property of Devika Rani and her husband Svetoslav Roerich.

We went there one more, this time with Asha. While returning, we participated in my friend Hukum Chand's son's marriage feast. As part of their custom, I was gifted a sari, and Asha and Gopi received dress material. As Mandi was once ruled by a king, there were the ruins of a palace on a cliff. We also saw many small temples dedicated to goddesses.

All this while, the heap of data that came out of the fieldwork on women and paddy cultivation was weighing heavily on my mind. True, a few papers had come out. But the delay in the final report was bothering me. I received a letter from my friend Seetha Radhakrishnan, who was a Director at the ICSSR, insisting that I write the report. This encouraged me to finalize the report. Subsequently, it was published as a book titled *Filling the Rice Bowl: Women in Paddy Cultivation* in 1991 by Sangam Books. I was relieved. It is a story of lives filled with hardship, misery, struggles, despair, small joys and hope. For the generations of today and tomorrow, I hope the study will be an inspiration to understand how paddy cultivation and agriculture kept communities and cultures together in addition to their economic contribution to society.

My activities, acquaintances and friends went on increasing. How it happened is inexplicable. I cannot remember every person I interacted with. Still, a few profiles remain ingrained in my memory which I wish to record.

Mira Shiva was trained as a medical doctor. But she never became a 'practising' doctor examining and treating patients at a hospital. Instead, she chose to become a health activist. Her concerns ranged over a wide array of issues such as the health of human beings, the environment, nature, medicines, food safety and quality, and so on. It was quite by chance that I came to know her. One day, a woman came to see me in my office declaring that she was from an NGO dealing with community health and related issues. Her organization was planning to undertake a study and she wanted me to help her select a sample from the total list of people or households she had brought with her. She was Purabi Pande who was working with Mira Shiva. Their office was not far from the ISI campus. Purabi and I became friends, and we met on several occasions. We had common concerns. I started participating in many activities organized by them. Mira and Purabi participated in a workshop on 'Popular Economics' that I organized in ISI in early 1989. I knew Mira's sister, Vandana Shiva, scientist-turned-activist, who became a vociferous supporter of the protection of nature, the environment and organic farming. I met both sisters in Trivandrum when they were here independently to participate in seminars or other functions.

Another person I surely wish to remember is Shafeeq Naqvi. When I knew him first, he was a freelancing intellectual. I came to know that after taking a postgraduate degree in Economics, he had been the secretary of the Communist Party of India (at that time undivided) in Uttar Pradesh for fifteen years. He then joined the Indian Statistical Institute in Calcutta. After retirement, he was with the Gokhale Institute in Pune for some time. I understood that later he was with the Communist Party of India (Marxist). I don't think it mattered to him whether my husband or I were communists or which wing of the party we were close to. He used to visit us and have long chats on various topics. At that time, he was living alone in Delhi. He was married to Hameeda, an expert on medieval Indian history. They had no children, and she was away in Pakistan with her relatives. He took great efforts to bring her back and finally succeeded. I remember having very tasty food in their house. Naqvi was full of energy and dragged me to many of his initiatives. One was the Joshi–Adhikari Institute of Social Sciences, for which we conducted several meetings at different places. Many were in the office of the People's Publishing House which published my first book, quite far from my home and office. His background, experience and genial nature gave him access to many people and homes. His brother was an Economics professor at the Delhi School of Economics. Naqvi Saheb died after we left Delhi.

Kamal Nayan Kabra was another person I befriended during my Delhi days. He was an Economics professor at the Indian Institute of Public Administration (IIPA). He was also a member of Naqvi's circle. I was a participant in many programmes conducted by the IIPA, the Institute of Economic Growth(IEG) and the Delhi School of Economics. At IEG, I came to know Dr P.C. Joshi, another Economics professor. When I think of him, a memory that comes to mind is a remark he made at an interactive discussion we had organized in ISI. It was organized to familiarize a select group of social scientists with the methodology used in the study on women and paddy cultivation, as well as some early observations on the data. Joshi remarked that our reporting was journalistic and passionate. As these were oft-heard remarks in those days, his comment was not unusual and did not result in any ill feeling.

In this context, I must also remember one of my colleagues, a renowned mathematician, K.R. Parthasarathy. He attended almost all the seminars or discussions I organized. He also used to report some of these to his wife. As they lived on the campus, she too was a friend of mine. The last name I would like to mention here is that of Baran Ray. When I knew him, he was associated with the peace movement and was on the editorial committee of their publications. His sudden death was a big blow.

Unlike many of our friends, we did not have to move residence too often. However, the owner of the last house we had rented wanted us to move after a few years of our stay. He sent us a notice, and we replied that we would quit as soon as we found a suitable place.

The last house we rented in Delhi was conveniently located. Today, many of the places I am describing have been swallowed up by Delhi's development process. In those days, I used to walk to South Extension through the open space behind Hauz Khas cutting through small villages that resembled oases. One of them was Gautam Nagar through which we could reach Yusuf Sarai, an important shopping street adjacent to AIIMS. Alliance Française, where I used to go to study French, was at walking distance from here, and I did not have to fear being run over by vehicles.

We decided to join a cooperative housing society. The initiative for the society was taken by a senior journalist, Upendra Bajpai, who was concerned about the housing problem of journalists. Did we have the money? Certainly not enough to buy a house or get one constructed. But for this cooperative effort, there was no single downright payment. To join the society, I took a loan from my provident fund. It was to buy our car that we had taken a bank loan for the first time. I had learned from my mother, who was a proud woman, not to seek monetary help from relatives or friends. I had some savings in the post office recurring deposit scheme and a small-scale chit fund, particularly one in Kerala which was run by people known to us. All these helped us to pay the instalments on time without much difficulty.

The flat in Press Enclave, further south of Hauz Khas, became our home, and we were among the first to move there in 1977. Friends suggested that we rent out the house for some time so that the loan instalments could be paid off easily. Moreover, Gopi at that time became eligible for government accommodation in Pandara Road as a journalist, but we decided to let it go. As for me, I had decided that I would not ask for ISI accommodation. Foolish, perhaps, but we were that.

Around that time, we also got a house built in Trivandrum. Vally had settled in Trivandrum, while our brother bought a plot in Ernakulam and got a nice house constructed there. All this time, Amma continued to live in our home in Kollam where we grew up. This was the home that we returned to from wherever we went. She took great care of the property and the house. One by one, her family members and almost all her aides met with their natural end. Her younger brother, who was her staunch supporter, retired and left for his wife's place where he lived thereafter. My brother would have been happy to have her at his place. But I sensed that Amma was in no mood to move to such a far-off place as Ernakulam. She suggested to me several times to have a house in Trivandrum. Each time I visited the city, I looked for a house or plot close to Vally's. Many friends helped me in looking for a house or land, but nothing satisfied my requirements. At last, a man from Kollam known to us asked me whether I wanted to buy a plot from his wife's property which they were planning to dispose of. He was an engineer, and I asked him whether he would construct the house for us. He agreed. I told him my requirements. Gopi sent a few suggestions. The plan for a small house took shape. Again, money became a matter of concern. Amma in the meantime decided that we would sell the Kollam house and property. Some people suggested that we could divide the compound into small plots and earn a big amount. But we chose to sell the whole property to a girls' high school – Vimala Hridayam – with whom we shared a fence and which we had seen coming up before our eyes. Amma gave me a share of the money. The price of land at that time was much lower than what it is today. So I had some money left even after buying the plot. While building the house in Trivandrum, besides my savings, my brother also came to my aid. Above all, it was Amma's intense belief that I would come back that made this possible. It was destiny.

Press Enclave had an advantage: adjacent to our flat was a large District Park. It was in the making then, and different plants and shrubs were planted in specified areas. We enjoyed taking Zippy for long walks in that park. Within the park and near Press Enclave was a Muslim cemetery. Across the main road, in front of Press Enclave, lived a number of Muslim families. The men there were engaged in skilled work like carpentry and related jobs. There were also potters whose products attracted most of the passers-by, who could not help but stop and admire them.

When we moved in, there were shacks close to the fence on the side of the park. They were occupied by Rajasthani construction workers who had temporarily come to Delhi. They had come with their families. There were women, men and children in those shacks. The parents went to work leaving the children with the elderly among them. At night, they would sing and cook, and the women, in addition, would repair quilts. Those were not days when interstate migration of young boys happened as today. The workers whom we could see from our windows were short-term migrants who came from a joint family, and perhaps had some amount of farming or other occupation back at home. Thanks to Mother Dairy, which supplied milk at affordable prices, these people had tea with milk before going out for work.

The house we chose had an open space in front and at the back: a pathway separated our block of flats from the next. In those days, Delhi did not have buildings which rose high to the sky. The night we moved in, I saw distant lights almost like the ones we see from beaches when boats and ships move along the horizon that is far, far away. That was the open area, which today has been eaten up by our development agenda. All those dreams began shattering before we left Delhi. The District Park began to be encroached from the left and the right. In course of time, schools, hospitals, hotels, malls, residential buildings and the District Court scrambled for land and won.

Before all this happened, we had to bid goodbye to something precious in a tiny resting place near us. The youngest member of our family, dear Zippy, died in 1982. Covered in one of my white saris we laid him to rest along with a few of his toys. That was a sad day.

Our second daughter, from a very young age, had developed a skill in making up and telling stories. Over time, the number of characters increased with each story. I feel sad that they were not recorded. She had this ability for a long time. I even imagined a great raconteur emerging from within her. I console myself with the thought that one has to give up some things when the demands of life become overwhelming. Yet it was a loss that has left a beautiful memory. She was also trained in Carnatic vocal music. She had a taste for that and continued her training for several years. Sankara Sarma, from whom she learned music, was a committed teacher and our families were very close. I believe that one day, when the pressures of life are eased to some extent, she will start singing again.

I have touched upon the Indian Railways many a time. I think it is quite natural as our life's journey was closely linked to the railways. It was an essential part of our life and it exposed us to the wonders of this great country. Both Gopi and I loved travelling. Our children have inherited that love. They started at a much younger age than me. The rail route, initially, was via the tunnel in the Western Ghats to Egmore and then by the GT Express even when they were young. Those were days when engines ran on coal. Besides the driver, there used to be firemen whose job was to shovel coal as and when needed.

People carried heavy luggage which usually included coconuts, jackfruits, dried fish and other unique products of Kerala. After reaching Egmore, getting them over to the Central Station was a problem. There were occasions when even with tickets booked sufficiently in advance, one had to negotiate or quarrel with those who had occupied our seats. With heavy luggage and children, such situations were not easy to handle, but people managed. N.S. Nair, Gopi's sister Ammu's husband, was an employee of the Railways in Madras. Sometimes, we stayed with them for a day or two before proceeding to Delhi. Nair would be at the station to see us off. His wit and mannerisms amused the children. Later, his children Shyam and Prem too joined the send-off party.

Once the train moved out of the station we would wait for familiar landmarks. We had favourite stations, those which served excellent coffee, special *vada* and other delicacies. I was afraid of stations where the snake charmers showed snakes at the windows. We knew when the train entered a new state. River Krishna at Vijayawada attracted us. The station was a favourite not only because of the fruits and the variety of eatables, but also for the long halt which gave us time to 'stretch our leg'. There was a good view of the Eastern Ghats from there. Those days, there were stations where the train halted only to refill the water tanks. I have already mentioned the difference I felt while entering Madras leaving behind the Western Ghats. Going further up, the landmass increased. Unlike densely populated Kerala, these areas were sparsely inhabited. People could be spotted only during the farming seasons. Just one or two passengers got off the train at such stations. They would walk away silently.

Earlier, Kerala had much more land under paddy cultivation. Coconut trees and plantains could be seen everywhere. All these were known to us from childhood. While going towards the north, crops changed according to the season. We saw orange plants looking almost dried up at times and heavy with fruits at others. Farms extending several acres where mustard was in full bloom were a heavenly sight.

There were certain stations that were special to us. Nagpur was one such: a hectic junction, always busy with passengers and porters. Loading and unloading of goods from the train was a common sight. The station was also where we got fresh, cool drinking water. We would take our earthen pitcher to fill water when the train stopped. A sort of queue would be formed. Those were not days when drinking water was sold in plastic bottles. Nagpur was near Gandhiji's Wardha Ashram.

There were stations where young beautiful women would come to sell their handicrafts. The most enchanting point was when we reached the Andhra–Madras border around dusk. The cattle returning home after the day's grazing were indeed a sight to watch. In the background were casuarina trees in plenty. The animals walked one behind the other with a discipline we may not see among schoolchildren walking to class after morning assembly, or even among adults. I used to watch them till the last animal was out of sight. I continued staring at the horizon as if responding to a call from the invisible. For a long time, after a train journey, when I closed my eyes, the sights on the way – the trees, crops, hills, rivers and lakes – lingered before me.

Over the years, many new trains were introduced. One of the earliest was a direct train from Kollam to Ernakulam. This enabled a passenger who boarded at Trivandrum to reach Ernakulam without taking a bus at Kollam as was the practice earlier. Initially, when the Kollam–Mavelikkara line was completed, Gopi and I went on the inaugural trip and returned in a car with some friends. Laying a new railway line through midland Kerala was not easy. It was a thickly populated area and widely cultivated. The land was uneven. Even after that line which touched all the important towns in the area was completed, the long-distance travellers had problems. They had to get off at Ernakulam South station and get to another station to board a north-bound train. The train from there would first go to Madras Central before proceeding north. Slowly, all these hurdles were resolved.

When the Trivandrum–Delhi Kerala Express was started, some friends of ours on the Railway Board told us that it was a gift to us and that it would result in a loss to the railways. This did not turn out to be true. From the very first day, the train was always more than full. The intercity train along the sea coast connecting Trivandrum and Ernakulam was followed by the Rajdhani Express from Trivandrum to New Delhi. Today, there are plenty of trains connecting Kanyakumari, the southern tip of the country, to practically all the states.

No doubt these are achievements, but there is a flip side as well. These are fast and superfast trains. In all of them, there are air-conditioned coaches whose glass windows cannot be opened. This has left us unable to enjoy the beautiful sights or the breeze. This means we cannot watch and enjoy the greatness, diversity and beauty of the country. Many of our favourite stations have got downgraded and their names have been forgotten. I can remember the old-fashioned steel tiffin carriers with hot lunch served along with a sweet, *papad* and banana leaf. Food now is mostly served in unhealthy foil containers. It is also uninviting and polluting. Earlier, the coaches and toilets were cleaned before the empty train arrived on the platform and they were cleaned at intervals on the way. If you were a regular traveller, you became acquainted with some of the staff, such as the bearers from the pantry car; the superintendent who ensured your well-being and safety; and the assistants who distributed blankets, sheets and pillows. The employees and we, the travellers, thought that the train was our property. We did not think of the acres of land acquired mostly from farmers for the purpose. What happened to them? These questions did not bother us at that time.

Of late, we hear about cases of violence, especially atrocities on women, that take place in trains. Bathroom doors often cannot be properly closed. Despite several incidents of crimes occurring in running trains, the doors often remain left open even on long-distance trains.

Indian Railways, perhaps the largest public sector undertaking in the country, had endowed to its workforce, from the lowest to the highest, a sense of pride and commitment to contribute their best. In recent decades, things have changed. The lower-level workers no longer have security in their jobs. New recruits are taken on contract or vacancies are not filled. The changes brought about by automation, privatization and for other reasons are linked to the economic and political policies adopted by the central government.

We should not forget the days when people not only walked to schools and offices but traversed long distances, cutting across land, water and hills, all on foot, probably without footwear. This was to a large extent a healthy practice.

❖

CHAPTER THIRTEEN

Finally to Kerala

During our long stay in Delhi, we used to come to Kerala often. Initially, we made a trip once in two years. I got a travel allowance for these journeys and the children could spend their summer holidays with their grandmothers. From the time I went to France, this pattern changed. We started sending the children every year to spend their vacations in Kerala. They travelled with the maid who was staying with us. Apart from these, Gopi and I have independently made trips for either work-related matters or family functions.

We had never thought of settling down in Delhi. There was a time when most Keralites working in other states of India returned 'home' on retirement. This mostly used to happen when there was a joint family and inherited property to welcome them. Slowly, things began to change. Joint family ties began to wither away. The same happened to property. Many retiring parents began to choose to remain in the place they worked and lived in till then. In the case of Delhi, the Delhi Development Authority (DDA) was introducing many housing schemes. Further, employment generation in Kerala was almost static, and parents felt that they would have to trek back to 'settle' their children. All this prompted them not to return 'home' after retirement.

In our case, Amma never asked me to come back to Kerala, but she genuinely believed that we would. As said earlier, over the years, Amma's network of supporters and helpers had disappeared in one way or another. Deep within me there was a desire to give her a place where she would feel comfortable without hurting her pride and self-respect. I think the small house we built in Trivandrum gave her that. From the end of the 1970s, it was to this house that we came to spend our holidays. When the house was being given a name, I asked Amma whether I could call it Attupuram, the name of our ancestral matrilineal house. She said 'no' without any doubt. So I called it

Tiruvatira, after the star under which I was born. Amma approved it. Above all, Amma loved Gopi like a son and got along well with him. His illness saddened her. She looked after him with great care when he was undergoing treatment in Trivandrum. Her knowledge of ayurveda helped a lot. Her theory was that he had neglected his health and body in his younger days. I did not argue with her.

Amma had green fingers. When she came to Trivandrum, she brought along with her saplings of many plants and trees which she had preserved, from the Kollam compound. These included neem, *konna*, different kinds of crotons, flowering plants and creepers like jasmine. The small compound of our house was turned into a garden by the time we came. The mango tree which she planted gives us plenty of fruit even today. They are delicious, whether used raw or ripe.

I retired from the ISI in April 1988. But it took nearly a year for us to move to Kerala. I had a few engagements which had to be completed. Then there was the tedious job of packing. Gopi's health did not permit him to offer any physical help, but he was always supportive. Each time we moved house earlier, we used to give away certain things. But this time, there were many things we certainly wished to take with us. I booked a lorry which had a permit for interstate transit. We brought our car, the small refrigerator and other household items in that vehicle. Friends like Thankam Unnikrishnan and Savitri Goel who lived in Press Enclave helped by arranging for people to assist us.

Over the years, I had accumulated papers and books both in the office and at home. I donated some books to a library and a young friend agreed to store a few of the books I had in the office. I have mentioned the articles I wrote in Malayalam before coming to Delhi. There I wrote in English too. Gopi's friend Chittaranjan was the person who encouraged me in that.

Before we left Delhi, Gopi and I revisited some of the familiar places and took long walks. We went to the Deer Park in Green Park, the Qutb Minar and its extended surroundings. We had lunch at Kwality in Connaught Place. We viewed many slides on the projector I had brought from Hong Kong. We went for the release of a book which included one of my articles at the India International Centre. Gopi met many friends there. That was a happy evening.

Our return journey to Kerala was by the Kerala Express. Today,

I shudder when I think of the number of train travels we made after Gopi's health deteriorated. In the late 1980s we came to Kerala twice, to attend the marriages of two of our nieces: Gopi's brother's daughter and my brother's daughter. He always cooperated. But there were many things beyond his control. His movements were unsteady. Using the toilet and eating food on a fast-moving train are not easy even for normally healthy people.

My visits to Kerala, mainly to Trivandrum, had acquainted me with many people even before my retirement. I received a Senior Fellowship from the ICSSR and got the chance to engage in research once more, this time affiliated with the Institute of Management in Government (IMG), quite near my home. Padma Ramachandran, whom I had known in Delhi, was the Director of the Institute at that time. The topic I chose for research was matriliny in Kerala. In a way, it was a continuation of my earlier studies which enquired into the status of women. I was given a room in IMG and I became acquainted with the staff of the Institute.

The home front could not be left unattended. There was Amma who was 89, and Gopi who could not do anything on his own. We had one or two women helpers. There was also a man, Appu, who had some difficulty in hearing but he was very intelligent, a Jack of all trades and ever-ready to help. He became a right-hand man to Amma. But someone more responsible was needed at home when I went out. A unit of the Self Employed Women's Association (SEWA) which had been set up in Trivandrum by then came to our aid.

With more and more youngsters leaving their homes and often the state in search of jobs, there was an urgent need for people, particularly women, to help look after the elderly and attend to other chores at home. This was understood by Nalini Nayak, an interesting young woman I had come to know during my earlier visits to Kerala, who set up a SEWA unit in Trivandrum. The organization trained women, mainly from nearby rural areas, to serve the sick and the elderly in their homes. Amma at that time could manage with her usual domestic helpers. She was able to look after the kitchen as well. But in Gopi's case, he needed more assistance. I made him do exercises including some yoga, massaged his body with oil and helped him in taking a bath. The SEWA woman's presence was important as I had to go out for various things. Fortunately, I got a woman with whom I was able to establish good relations. Vasantha was caring and stayed with me for long.

In addition, I got a young woman to type some of my letters, go to the post office, and keep a record of the correspondence and other material. At that time I had a good typewriter. I also got a man to read the Malayalam newspapers to Gopi. I did not want Gopi to strain his eyes though his sight was in good shape. I also did not want him to remain inside the house all day. While the man read the newspapers, Gopi could sit outside on the veranda for some time in the forenoon. He could watch the plants, trees, butterflies, birds and squirrels running up and down the mango tree. He could enjoy the breeze. However, I asked that man to read only casual news items and not the important or serious pieces. I read those to Gopi myself when it was convenient for both of us. I found both these persons through a friend of my brother. Years later, when I was looking for somebody who could render such services for a friend's sister who was in a worse situation, I just could not get anyone. There were plenty of unemployed women and men in Kerala. But none of them seemed willing to take up such work.

My plans for a retired life were very different from what it turned out to be. My life at home and the office was demanding. Under that circumstance, I got almost no time to read the books I wanted to read – the books we bought, those which we received as gifts and those I inherited from my father. I was never a fast reader like Gopi and our children. So reading books other than the ones related to my academic pursuits was a priority I had placed on myself. Something else I wanted to do was brush up on my French. I also planned to revive my love for stitching which had been a passion in my younger days. This had to occupy a backseat when I became professionally busy. Sketching and needlework were my other interests. In my school days, I had done well in drawing and needlework, which included embroidery, crochet and related works.

However, none of this happened. Instead, I got drowned in a whirlpool. I have spent nearly thirty years in Kerala since my return. All these years, except for the last three, have been hectic. In addition to looking after the family and being engaged in research, I went to give talks, participate in or inaugurate college unions, seminars or conferences organized by different groups in places in and around Trivandrum as well as more distant locations.

Speaking at economist K.N. Raj's eightieth birthday celebration. (*Sitting, left to right*) Laurie Baker, K.N. Raj, x, K.P. Kannan. (Photographer unknown)

I continued to be a member of the ICSSR Governing Council and went to Delhi to attend its meetings. I can narrate here only certain incidents which are personally significant to me.

As my life and work were intimately linked to Gopi's health, we have to see how we managed after returning to Kerala. Despite having friends who knew established doctors and hospitals, we did not know that the Sree Chitra Tirunal (SCT) hospital, which was well known for the treatment of heart diseases and had a neurology department as well, had been set up while we were away in Delhi. A doctor who lived nearby referred Gopi to that hospital. At the SCT, there were a bunch of welcoming young doctors. They showed concern and did not put us off. They looked at the records and suggested that Gopi be admitted. He managed to take a bath by himself, go to the toilet and take food without anything untoward happening. The doctors were pleased and referred him to the physiotherapy division of the nearby Medical College after prescribing some medicines.

The Medical College too had wonderful staff. When I took Gopi there, a senior doctor examined him and we were sent to a physiotherapist, a caring person. I continued to take Gopi for physiotherapy for quite some time, besides the exercises he did at home. The car we had brought from Delhi proved to be of great help. In those days, Trivandrum had far fewer cars than today and driving was easy.

Life kept throwing challenges at us. At a time when I did not even have a telephone, I got a call on my neighbour's phone saying that my brother was hospitalized. It was a cardiac problem. As I could not leave Gopi, we went together by train to Ernakulam. My brother was very upset to see us and told me that I should not have undertaken the long journey with Chettan whose health needed more care. I knew he meant it. He was always a very energetic person, engaged in many things and always ready to help others. Our daughters remember how, when they came to Kerala for holidays, Ammavan used to drive them from Ernakulam to Kollam to their grandmother's house. Once, he took a young American economist who was visiting ISI and his wife on a long drive through a beautiful section of the Western Ghats. Almost all our friends were his friends as well. When he was discharged from the hospital, I suggested that he come to Trivandrum and have a check-up at the SCT. He agreed. At the end of the thorough check-up there, he had to have a valve replaced.

My brother worked hard to get Amma what is currently called a 'family' pension. For this, he had to quote a judgment in the case of another person who had died several years ago. It was a small amount and it came to the bank. Amma had lost the ability to understand what it was, though I tried to tell her. Before returning to Ernakulam, my brother went to the bank and made me the nominee of the savings account after Amma's death. He also made arrangements for a telephone connection to our house.

Regrading Gopi's ailments, I was also in correspondence with a doctor in England. Quite unexpectedly, I got an invitation to attend a conference in Amsterdam in relation to my study on internal female labour migration. I consulted a leading physician in Trivandrum, Dr Pai, about taking Gopi along. His reply was positive. I could trust him as he was well-known for his gentle, patient and caring ways while dealing with patients. At that time, our younger daughter was doing research in Cambridge, England, and I thought of leaving Gopi there when I went to attend the conference. All the arrangements including his tickets were made. But that trip did not take place. My brother died.

It was late evening when the telephone rang at our neighbour's house. I called Vally and Chandrettan to inform them. Words fail me when I think of the situation. There was no question of my not going, but taking Amma and Gopi along was a challenge. Rajamma, who had been with our family from our Delhi days, was with us. She was from Trivandrum, but I could not send her to her house as it was getting dark. Besides, she wanted to come as she knew my brother and his family. Two of my nephews also wanted to come with us.

I called a taxi. It was already dark by the time we left. Looking back, it was a daring act on my part to make that night trip with Amma and Gopi. Naturally, it was quite late at night when we reached my brother's house. I have no words to describe what went through our minds when we saw the dead body of my brother placed on the floor. All I can say is that most people get a certain strength when faced with such calamities.

We stayed there for sixteen days till the rituals after the cremation were over. My brother's death was a shock and a big loss which could never be replaced. Nobody talked about it. The silence was painful. It was equally sad that he was not there to see his first grandchild. Gopi and I went to see the newborn, a boy who was named Gautam.

I have said earlier that Kerala dragged me in directions I had not thought of. Among the many programmes I attended, I remember one particular discussion at All India Radio, Trivandrum, soon after I arrived. A.K. Ramakrishnan from M.G. University, Kottayam was a participant in it. Those were days when I used to drive around, and on the way home, I dropped him off as he wanted to see a friend. Within weeks, his wife Elizabeth came to meet me with a friend. They were part of a young women's group and persuaded me to participate in something they were organizing. From then, I associated with several of their activities for long. In 1995, we attended the biannual conference of the Indian Association of Women's Studies in Jaipur together. My young friends were very inspired and formed the Kerala Association for Women's Studies and Action, a registered body. However, I never heard of it again.

Another friend through whom I became involved in social activities was Pushpita John. I came to know her and became very close to her after my return to Kerala. We perhaps had met first at the National Conference of Women's Studies held in Trivandrum in 1984. She had retired as a Professor of Education at Kerala University. Our friend Sarmaji had set up Lenin Balavadi, intended as an innovative pre-primary school to help kids enter the world of learning through plays and songs rather than burdened with 'learning by heart and reproducing'. When I metPushpita, she was in charge of the Balavadi along with my classmate Srikantan Nair's wife Leelavati.

Pushpita was concerned about the issues of women. We went together for many programmes and she enrolled me in the University Women's Association of which she was a part. This was an international body and Trivandrum was a segment of the Indian chapter. I was invited by the Association to talk about women and the new economic policy. One face I remember from that meeting is that of Lakshmi Menon who arrived punctually and occupied one of those shabby metal chairs. She sat through and talked to me when I finished. Though a college degree was the only requirement needed to become a member of the Association and Trivandrum had plenty of women graduates from different strata, the membership at that time was mainly from the middle class. I continued in the Association mainly for Pushpita and became the Vice-President. After some time I resigned. I came to know a large number of women, young and old, through the University Women's Association.

One fall-out of my participation was that my presentation prompted the woman manager of a nearby branch of the State Bank to invite me to speak at a function she organized. It was to examine the status and career graph of women officers of the bank. I came to know that there are many women who refuse to write the necessary examinations for promotion. Transfers would lead to their inability to look after the home. For women, mostly, the family comes first.

Pushpita was unmarried and stayed in a house not very far from ours. Her friend Subhadramma was also nearby. I used to visit Pushpita often. The women in her residents' association used to have a monthly get-together, with a discussion on current issues and lunch. I remember being invited to talk to them once. Pushpita always had health problems, but she moved around not yielding to them. One day, we set out for a seminar at a slightly faraway locale. Before the function was over she started feeling unwell, and we returned. Early the next morning, her sister called to say that Pushpita was no more. It took me a very long time to get over the loss of a genuine soul.

We gradually settled down in our Trivandrum home and

neighbourhood. The compound of our house in Trivandrum was about one-tenth of what we had in Kollam. Our residence comes under the postal zone of Kaudiar. The residential area, which is not an enclosed colony, is called Sri Vilas Lane. The main entrance to Sri Vilas Lane is from a road along which buses from the city centre and further south plied to many places, near and far. That relatively narrow entrance reaches up to another road almost parallel to the main road mentioned above. Earlier, there might not have been more than a dozen families living in the area. Even when we bought the land in the mid-1970s, there were big compounds in which relatively small, old houses stood among trees.

We came to know many interesting people in and around the neighbourhood. When we moved in, not far from our house was a family where a mother lived with her daughters and son. They had cows and used to sell milk to the neighbours. After the woman who looked after the business died, the others built separate houses. In the course of time, more 'outsiders' started buying small pieces of land to build houses. However, it is only in the last decade or so that the large compounds and perhaps the old owners virtually became invisible or vanished.

On the E sub-lane where our house stood, there were a few small houses built and rented out by the owner of the land. In one of those rented houses was a middle-aged couple with three sons and a daughter. They did not belong to Trivandrum. They were most probably here for their children's education. My brother had known a relative of the mother. They were friendly and easy to communicate with. Over time, we became very close. On the side, across the main Sri Vilas Lane, was a retired librarian and his wife, a teacher. On C lane, there was Dr Kurup who had retired as Director of Statistics, Kerala, whom we had known in Kollam when he used to work there. As Amma used to stay here off and on, she made friends with some of the women and families around.

Our friend Sarmaji often visited Gopi. His house was within walking distance; he used to walk along a side road to reach our house. As he was known to many, some people on our lane came to know that Gopi was staying here. This brought a number of visitors to our home. One day, two retired government officers came to visit Gopi – Natarajan and Raghavan Pillai. Both were active in the Non-

Gazetted Officers' Union and knew many top-level communists. Soon after, some women teachers came to see me. Raghavan Pillai's wife Bhavani Amma was among them, and we became friends. She was from Ambalapuzha near Alleppey and had come to Trivandrum after marriage. She taught in the nearby government primary school from where she had retired as the headmistress by the time we met. I found her interesting, and together, we participated in many activities. She never hesitated to come with me to meetings organized by groups of which I was a member. She was not a homebound person and enjoyed going out. She was well-read and an organizer. She was part of a retired women teachers' group and introduced me to some of them. Together, we visited another resident of Sri Vilas Lane, a woman who had retired as an army doctor and was now living alone. As years went by, she developed age-related anxiety. The purpose of our visit was to give her support. Bhavani Amma later became the president of the women's wing of the Sri Vilas Lane residents' association.

Two other interesting people I met were Dr Lalitha and her husband Rama Iyer, known as Swamy. They were Bhavani Amma's neighbours, though I do not remember if that's how I came to know them. Lalitha was a medical doctor, a gynaecologist and a surgeon, who took her work very seriously. She was working at the Government Hospital for Women and Children in Thycaud. I used to see her driving out early in the morning. She was a lover of music and played the *veena*. Swamy had taken voluntary retirement, mainly to look after his aged father. The couple had a large circle of friends and were involved in cultural activities. Swamy was one of the founders and long-term treasurer of Margi, a private cultural organization dedicated to the promotion of traditional art forms, mainly Koodiyattam and Kathakali. Lalitha was with Swamy in all the activities of Margi. She lent me support whenever I needed it. They loved trees, plants and animals. They had dogs and birds as pets. We have spent hours, drinking excellent coffee and discussing all kinds of issues including arts, literature and medicine. Sadly, both of them have passed away. It is heartbreaking to see the empty house and the locked gate while walking along the road. Their dog used to stay there alone, fed and looked after by neighbours. After a couple of years, he too died. Recently the house was sold, and very soon, a commercial establishment is expected to come up there.

Indira Ramakrishna Pillai, not from the neighbourhood, is

another person I came to know on my return to Kerala. I must have met her when I came to the National Conference on Women's Studies. She was the state-level president of the All India Women's Conference. Indira is warm person, and we became close. I participated in many programmes she organized.

On one of the early days, I attended a function organized to mark Women's Day in Kollam. It was quite unusual as there was a procession too. I was invited to the function by two men who dropped in unexpectedly. One of them was Sebastian, now a good friend. It was the first time that we met. The function was organized by the other man and his group. At Kollam, I met a bright young woman, Kochu Rani, who was leading the function. Another group in nearby Kundara heard about this and they invited me to the 8 March meet at their place the same day. A number of ordinary women gathered at a roadside *pantal*. It was quite late at night when I returned. The men who came to invite me picked me up and brought me back.

Yet another cordial friendship began from a similar unexpected visit. One forenoon, soon after I reached my room in IMG, I had two visitors. One was Dr Bhaskaran Nair from the Political Science Department of the University of Kerala. I had friends in the Economics and Sociology departments, but none at that time in Political Science. Bhaskaran Nair was pleasant and had an easy way of talking. He had earlier worked in the North East. We became friends and regularly kept in touch over the telephone, talking about all that both of us enjoyed. I was a regular invitee to many programmes he organized. I remember visiting him once when he had a major accident and was hospitalized. He came back to near-normalcy and went on to hold a position in the Higher Education Council. Despite some physical disabilities, he was coming to the office. One day, he felt uneasy, was hospitalized again and passed away. Sadly, I did not come to know about his death.

The second visitor that day was Ram Mohan, a research scholar from the Centre for Development Studies. I think he was doing his PhD there. He was independently bringing out a Malayalam quarterly called *Kerala Patanangal*, and he wanted me to be on the editorial board. I agreed.

IMG had a large hall where seminars, discussions and debates took place. The smaller ones were used for classes and training conducted by members of the staff or invited speakers. As I was affiliated with IMG, I used to participate in some of these. One day, as I was leaving the hall after a discussion, a young woman approached me. She wanted to interview me for Doordarshan. That was the only television channel in Kerala at that time.

Once, IMG organized a programme in Mitraniketan, an NGO located in a rural suburb of the city. Kerala at the time did not have many NGOs. There was a widespread belief that they took foreign funds which was anathema in a place where left ideology and beliefs had strong roots. However, Mitraniketan had been functioning for a long time. Among their many programmes, there was one which encouraged foreigners to come and learn more about Kerala, its people and their life. These were not regular tourists. They stayed either in Mitraniketan itself or in homes in the neighbourhood. Some of us, academics, social activists and civil servants, were called to talk to them and answer their questions. Two of them even came to see me at my house. One of them thought that her ancestors were from Andhra but she had no other clue.

Some years later I was called to participate in a similar programme in Kochi. The invitation came from Professor Sukumaran Nair, Head of the Department of Economics at Cochin University. The difference was that the group I had to interact with here consisted of students from an American university with whom they had a tie-up. As Kochi was quite far from my place, they arranged for my overnight stay. This continued for quite some time. I enjoyed it.

When I came from Delhi, I had wished to start a group to discuss 'current affairs'. But this did not turn out to be easy. I had no institutional backing. An affiliation was not as helpful as institutional support would have been. However, something did turn out in my favour. I met an IAS officer, T.N. Jayachandran, who was my junior at the University College, though I did not remember that. We established a good rapport. I came to know that he too was toying with the idea of a similar group and knew others who wished to be part of one. We met and discussed the matter several times. Most of the time, it was in his house. Kerala Watch was formed out of our shared passion. The original members included, apart from the two of us, M.N. Prasad, former Chief of the Railway Board, and B.R.P. Bhaskar from Kollam. The latter, my brother's classmate, was passionate about journalism, and he had worked in many of the leading newspapers in different parts of India before returning to Kerala. Our families were close, and they too had moved to Trivandrum.

New members began to join our group. We met and discussed various issues. We followed a pattern where one person would introduce the topic, and a couple of invitees from the fields of politics, academics or social work would respond. This was followed by an interactive session with the audience. We discussed a wide range of topics, such as coalition politics in Kerala, the press and the people, preschool education, health, decentralized planning, the budget and road safety. Most of the time, we met in a room in Trivandrum Hotel, one of the oldest lodge-cum-restaurants in the city. It was conveniently located. This public interest forum lasted effectively for more than ten years.

Another of my ideas was to have a women's group which would meet regularly in the Coffee House. It was not to just have coffee but to establish our right to occupy public spaces. There were to be a minimum number of women, and we were to respond to the issues raised by one or more participants. No group as such was formed, but a few of us met occasionally for a few months. There were Uma Devi and Manu Bhaskar from the Economics and Sociology departments respectively of Kerala University, whom I had known for long. Sometimes Bulu Roy Choudhury, a political activist married to a Malayali comrade joined us. I had known her in Delhi. Instead of coffee, we had lunch and by the time it was over, there was no time or enthusiasm to assert our rights. Yet it was fun!

Within months of our coming back, I had to make a trip to Bombay. In a way, the trip turned out to be an adventure. I was going to a workshop titled 'Visibility of Women in Statistics and Indicators: Changing Perspectives' at SNDT University, supported by UN-INSTRAW. I could not leave Gopi and go, so we went together. However, something unexpected happened. A *bandh* or *hartal* stopped all movement of vehicles in Bombay. Somehow, we managed to reach Gopi's youngest cousin Sasi's house, and he arranged for my reaching the venue. I had a paper to present. After the workshop, I went with Maithreyi Krishnaraj who was working at the SNDT Women's Studies Department. Her husband Krishnaraj, editor of the *Economic and Political Weekly*, took me to Sasi's house. Gopi was looked after well.

We stayed for some more days with another cousin Tampi, and then returned.

Another similar adventure was a trip to Madras, again with Gopi. Vasanthi Devi, whom I had met in Madurai, invited me to the inauguration of a Centre for Women's Studies that she was planning to set up with another young researcher at the Madras Institute of Development Studies. How she got my neighbour's telephone number or why she invited me, I do not know. The other person they had invited from Kerala was Justice V.R. Krishna Iyer. They called me so many times that I had to agree. I went with Gopi, and we stayed with his sister. When I reached there, I found out that the Justice Krishna Iyer had not come. The only person I remember meeting, besides Vasanthi and her friend, is Jayanthi Natarajan who later became a minister in the Congress government at the centre. While looking through my old papers, I was pleasantly surprised to find an eighteen-page typed article which I read out there, titled 'World into Which Our Daughters Are to be Born'. This was translated and included in my first Malayalam book. I do not know what happened to that project. Years later I met Vasanthi again when I went to attend a three-day workshop on 'Survival and Sovereignty' in Tirunelveli. She was then the Vice-Chancellor of the university that hosted the function.

In the midst of all this hectic activity, I was trying to make sense of the project on matriliny. I had no set ideas on how to approach the problem. Gender, kinship and land ownership were linked. I avidly read articles, books and reports. I started frequenting the libraries in Trivandrum. One was the University Library which had come up after my student days. The Public Library and the British Council Library also became my haunts. The Sree Chitra Tirunal Library at Vanchiyoor amazed me as it was a treasure-house for those looking for old documents and journals. I took notes and photocopied what I thought was useful. But my thoughts and activity could not be confined to the walls of libraries.

Many of us would have experienced unforeseen encounters which become lasting bonds. The wish to study a few matrilineal joint families led me to a particular family in Trivandrum, Elankath. I had heard an interesting story about this family. It was said that their ancestral roots were at Clappana, further north of Kollam on the banks of Ashtamudi Lake, and that the matrilineal joint family was set up at Neyyoor, presently in Tamil Nadu, by a young woman who went from Clappana. I had met Dr K.N. Pillai from that family during my fieldwork days. One day, I went to meet him and told him about my intention. He told me frankly that he was not the right person, but his brother Ramakrishna Pillai who lived in Neyyoor would be able to help me. He gave me the address of his brother.

I promptly wrote to Ramakrishna Pillai and he responded quickly. I could see that he thought I was a young research student. I clarified that I was not, and without much delay went to see him. He had told me clearly how to reach his home. I did not get the material to do the kind of study I had in mind, but Ramakrishna Pillai became my Ammavan, and I became a member of that family, which consisted of his daughter Rudramma, her husband and their two children. I was shown thick files of their partition deeds, and the list of their family members who are spread all over the world. They had a family temple. Family members from various places contributed to its maintenance and to the festivals. They also had a library. I think it was here that I met a young woman who happened to be the elder sister of one of my sisters-in-law. I was gradually introduced to immediate neighbours. I was taken to the house of their ancestor, Dewan Nanu Pillai. I also went to see the Mandaikadu temple which attracts large numbers of pilgrims from Kerala even now for its annual festival.

I enjoyed going to R.P. Ammavan's house. The route and the rural setting retained an old-world charm that Trivandrum was slowly losing. I was invited to Rudramma's children's marriages. I cannot remember the number of times I have gone to that house. Once or twice, I stayed there overnight. R.P. Ammavan was a dissident voice in a family of successful politicians and professionals. He was a Gandhian who was engaged in Gandhian constructive work. He too came to my house once or twice. One day, he brought the manuscript of his autobiography. It was then that I came to know that Parivrajika Rajamma who ran the Vinoba Kendra at Vithura near Trivandrum was his classmate. He was keen that I read the manuscript before he got it printed. Unfortunately, that did not happen. He fell ill and died. I regret that I could not return the manuscript to him. After some days, a relative came and took it from me. It is a pity that his version of history was lost to us. That was an acquaintance I cherished.

As said earlier, I used to take Gopi out for long walks in Trivandrum though the city did not have many parks, open spaces or safe footpaths. We used to leave home very early in the morning. I cannot remember whether he used a walking stick at that time. He would walk by my side. It was different from walking in a park but, fortunately, there were not many vehicles on the road. These early morning walks also helped me to make some interesting observations. Private tuitions had become essential for students. At a house not far from ours, a man whom I never spotted outside would be taking classes from 5 am or even earlier. Several batches of children came to him before school hours. Some years later the tuition master caught hold of me and told me that he had stopped the classes and was moving back to his ancestral home. By that time, Gopi was no more. I went inside and talked to him for a while. I realized that I had never seen him outside before because he had some physical difficulties. He told me he had watched us walking along that way. It was nice of him.

During those years, I also saw that people in Kerala had difficulty dealing with ailments, physical or mental. Not many of Gopi's old friends or acquaintances came to see him. Only Sarmaji and a few other close friends came regularly. What many of them found difficult was that he could not freely answer their questions. When we had come to Kollam some years earlier in connection with a wedding, the women in the locality openly expressed their sorrow and shock by exclaiming, 'What a man he used to be!' They were simple and their words were genuine. I never thought of 'hiding' Gopi, though his failing health was painful for me. I took him to the wedding of the daughter of the renowned music composer Devarajan. He had come home to invite us. There were plenty of people from all walks of life at the event, many of whom knew Gopi. Another function we attended together was Sarmaji's son's wedding. There too a large number of people were present – among them writers, journalists, politicians and many from the field of art and cinema. I found Gopi a seat. Somebody I knew after coming to Trivandrum called me aside and virtually scolded me for taking him there. For several months after that I did not talk to him even if we met on the road. At last, we made up. His wife and I remained friends throughout.

That man's remark reflected the societal attitude. Earlier, many parents tried to hide their children if they were in some way not 'normal'. This attitude has undergone a big change in recent times.

Government and voluntary organizations have been instrumental in bringing about many changes, even in the vocabulary used to refer to them. Words like 'deaf' and 'dumb' are not as commonly used these days as earlier.

Besides following all that the doctors advised, such as medicines, exercise and physiotherapy, I continued taking Gopi for walks. On days that we could not go out, we walked in the open space within the compound of the house. I read his favourite Malayalam poetry line by line and made him repeat the verses. He copied the lines I wrote on the top line of a four-line notebook. I devised inventive methods like

With Gopi looking at a lily in the garden, 1991.
(Photo by G. Asha)

playing with balls made of paper to tackle his various disabilities.

Perhaps deep within me, I hoped that he would make some improvement, however minor. What did he think of his ailment? His memory and intellectual faculties were sharp. We never talked of the disease or of death. We had dreams of doing many things together after retirement: travel, reading and writing . . . nothing materialized. Quietly, one night, he vanished into eternity. A part of me went with him, I felt. I lived on. Months later, a close family friend told me, 'People are saying you neglected Gopi.' It was not a pleasant remark. However, it did not affect me.

Amma did not fully understand what had happened. The domestic help and the SEWA woman were with us. People came to express their condolences. Slowly, I came out of mourning and began to go out.

Asha came up with a plan. She assured me that she would take care of Amma so that I could go to England to be with Anu for a month. I went by Sri Lankan Airways. The flight from Trivandrum to Colombo was short. As there was quite some time left before the flight to Heathrow, we were taken to a hotel for dinner and rest. I got a comfortable room.

At Heathrow, Anu was waiting, and we went to Cambridge by train. I had a letter from IMG and the Cambridge University Library gave me access to their collections. The receptionist, the library staff and the students who did part-time work were welcoming and helpful. The multistoreyed library was huge. We could take books from any shelf and find a comfortable space to read anywhere in the library. The next day, we would find the books neatly stacked in their place, something that impressed me. I also enjoyed the sprawling campus and the River Cam where boating was a special activity. Anu took me out to see places. There were several concessions for senior citizens arranged by the tourism department. I also made some trips on my own. One of them was to a beautiful place on the seashore of Wales.

On the way back from England, we had a halt at Colombo, this time a longer one. There, I came to see a batch of about thirty young women being sent to other countries as domestic servants. They met at that hotel and had a buffet lunch. This was before the migration of workers became a huge global phenomenon.

When I was away in England, nothing untoward happened at home. Until we shifted to Trivandrum, it was Amma who used to look

Reading to Amma, early 1990s. (Photo by G. Asha)

after the affairs of the house. She watched and cared for her plants and trees. Gradually, she stopped being occupied with these and was mostly restricted to her room. Sometimes, she came out and sat on the veranda. I always let Amma know when I went out and assured her that I was back when I returned. One day, I asked her whether she liked me. She immediately said 'very much', using a more endearing Tamil word *peruthu*, and added, 'You look after me so well.' Amma had done so much for us. I don't think I could ever return the love and care she gave us. True, she never expected much.

After returning from England, I had to go to Delhi for a meeting. I was also planning to stop in Bombay and visit my youngest sister-in-law's husband Bhasi who was undergoing treatment for cancer. While I was in Delhi, I came to know that Vally had a stroke and was hospitalized. I did go to Bombay, reaching there quite late at night. I found Bhasi waiting for me. The next morning, by the time I got up he too was up, and together we went for a walk. That was the last time I saw Bhasi who was a friendly, cheerful person.

I got back to Trivandrum by noon and went to see Vally in the hospital the same afternoon. I saw that the stroke was not severe. She recognized me and could answer my questions. She could move her hands and legs. Once discharged, she wanted to come see Amma. She had by then sold the house nearer our house, where the children grew up. She stayed with us for a month or so before going to her son's place. I used to help her walk on the veranda and make her do some light exercises. There was a visible improvement in her health, but her confidence to move around on her own was gone. Even after she left, we used to speak over the telephone regularly, and whenever I could make it, I went to spend time with her. I was keen to have her with us once again at least for a few days.

Before my trip to Delhi and Vally's stroke, Amma had shown some discomfort one day. That day, Vally had come to our home during lunchtime. After eating, Amma was sitting on a chair near the window in her room. Both Vally and I felt that something was not right with her. We slowly helped her to her bed. Within minutes, she told us, 'I am all right.'

Amma was getting weaker. I spoke about her health to my friend Dr Lalitha. We decided that she should not be taken to any hospital. I bought a few things to be used in an emergency at the doctor's suggestion. I sensed that the inevitable was not far away and so informed her extended family members. Many of them came. In a day or two, early in the morning, I played a devotional song that Amma loved on the tape recorder. It was over, and Amma breathed her last. I telephoned Vally. Vasantha and I bathed her body and changed her into the fresh white handloom *mundu*, *raukka* and *neryathu* that she always wore. *Vibhuti* and sandal paste were applied on her forehead and we placed the body on a fresh plantain leaf. I informed my sister-in-law in Kochi, and relatives and friends in Kollam and Trivandrum. The rituals before and after the cremation were done according to Amma's beliefs. I offered the *bali* at home for fifteen days and on the sixteenth day, when the death pollution was over, all of us had a bath.

The next day the priest from the Thiruvallam temple, a place considered sacred for last rituals, came home and conducted a puja. He had given a list of things to be bought. Apart from paddy, rice, banana fruit, coconuts, new towels, camphor and incense sticks, there were flowers, banana leaves and many other things to be arranged. I was surprised to find that tucked inside the busy Chalai market there were places where one could find each of these. The lit oil lamps, flowers, incense, *darbha* and the rest created an ethereal atmosphere. Vally's eldest son and I performed the rites that the priest asked us to do. It was mostly about saluting the deceased. The process was to release the *atma* from the corpse or *jada*. I had fasted from the morning and broke it after the rites were over. The priest was sent off with gifts including clothes and money.

We had not conducted similar rituals when Gopi died. Instead, at the suggestion of my young friend Valsalakumari who was the Secretary of the State Social Welfare Department, I got a wheelchair for a resident of the Care Home run by the Department. It was ordered from Kanpur. The physically challenged recipient could operate it by himself. My friend Purabi Pande was here at that time, and together, we went to present it to him. We also watched him operating it. Care Home at that time was housed in a single-storeyed building in a big compound with trees, very near the beach. The elderly women and men who stayed there did not have anyone at home to take care of them. Some had children. Perhaps, they did not have the means to look after the parent or the parent did not want to be with them. I started going there often. I became part of the Friends of the Care Home which had some responsibility in running the place. On the whole, the residents got along well with each other, though there were one or two who were quarrelsome. Others would come and catch hold of me to tell their stories each time I went there. Often, special lunches were sponsored by people in connection with death anniversaries, birthdays and similar occasions. They also had annual day celebrations and competitions. One of the events for women was coconut grating. I have not forgotten the competitive spirit shown by the women. They also had games followed by a sumptuous lunch. Later, I came to know that the inmates were shifted to another locale where they did not have the open space which they had enjoyed till then.

Another place I was associated with was the Mahila Mandiram in Pujapura in Trivandrum. The place was established in 1920. The founder was a school inspector, K. Chinnama. In her work-related travels across the state, she noticed the beginning of the disintegration of matrilineal joint families. Women, particularly those from poorer families, were the main victims of its consequences. The sensitive school inspector decided that women who lost the security of the family should not be left on the streets. Thus the Mahila Mandiram was founded. I used to go there often and arrange lunch or tea and snacks for the residents. Today, they have a high school as well. Young women receive training in many fields including weaving and computing.

A little after Amma's death, our family had to face another loss. Vally had overcome the minor stroke, but she never recovered fully. She was generally restricted to the home. We were not meeting regularly. One day, her eldest son called me and said that Vally was slightly unwell and suggested that I go to their house. I drove there and reached soon. Anu was holidaying with me. She and my domestic help Rajamma too came with me. It was decided to admit Vally to the hospital. She was being treated by a doctor who was also a relative. When I asked her whether I should go with her to the hospital, her reply was, 'If it is convenient for you.' That was our dear Vally. I went, saw the doctor examine her and spent some more time with her before coming back. I used to go to the hospital most days, and she was happy to see me.

One day, I had to go to Kanyakumari with Uma Devi to participate in a programme for four days. As I felt uneasy, I did not stay till the last day and returned early. However, it was getting dark as I was nearing Trivandrum, so I came home straight without first going to the hospital. Vally died the night of 19 May 1996. I lost my eldest sister, loving and gentle Vally.

Though I had lived in Delhi for long, Vally had never visited me there. We had discussed planning a trip more than once. Our plan was to first go together to Calcutta and visit Kalighat and Belur, then come to Delhi and visit Delhi, Agra and the surroundings, and then return to Kerala. Vally was close to the Sarada Ashram and was genuinely interested in visiting these places. She had a sensitive mind. I remember how she once sent me a letter from a place near Bangalore. Her son Unni was the railway station master there. She described the surrounding scenery in detail, including the tiny birds and pretty wildflowers. Our plan remained a dream that never came true.

Amma's and Vally's deaths brought a loneliness which I cannot describe. I felt all alone. The house suddenly became frighteningly silent. I did not want to read or write. I wanted to go somewhere. Where to? I thought of Thrissur where I could read in the Sahitya

Akademi library. My niece Maya arranged for my stay there with the parents of a friend. When my friend Seetha heard about this, she said that I could stay with her at Guruvayur, just an hour's bus drive away from Thrissur. However, on the first day itself, I went to see the family who had agreed to put me up in Thrissur. It was an extremely warm and happy meeting. Maya's friend's father was keen to meet me when he heard that I had been in Delhi. His niece was married to a senior journalist there. Strangely, her younger sister Subhadra was my friend for long, but I had never heard about this uncle before.

We talked for long on various issues. He told me stories of women in his family, which have gone unrecorded. Several generations of women in his family had received higher education. Some had even gone to Ceylon. They taught there and helped to set up educational institutions. On returning, a couple of them went to teach in Benaras. I am not sure that even Subhadra knew this. I have heard about such women from other families as well. Some of them did not marry. No doubt, some women in Kerala enjoyed more freedom than is known today. At some point, all this had a setback. Back in Trivandrum, I told Subhadra about my meeting her uncle. When she called me a few days later to say that he had passed away, I was shocked. It was a sad day for me.

❖

CHAPTER FOURTEEN

A New Routine

Let me remember with warmth some new acquaintances I made soon after we moved to Trivandrum. One was M.M. Thomas, a well-known theologist who most probably was the organizer of the Christian Study Centre for Cultural and Social Change affiliated with Kerala University. I remember attending some of their discussions. Though MMT left Trivandrum after some time, we kept in touch. Between 1990 and 1992, he became the Governor of Nagaland. I have with me a greeting card he sent me from there. He had a strong sense of justice and commitment to the downtrodden. His brother M.M. Cherian, a communist, was known to Gopi.

P.N. Nanoo, a retired income tax officer, was another person I got acquainted with soon after I returned to Kerala. In Delhi, my tax payments used to be looked after by the office. I could not expect that arrangement to continue after retirement. Besides, I also had a fellowship from ICSSR. It was during my search for someone to help me in this matter that I came across Nanoo. Like me, he too had worked outside the state for a sufficiently long period. He had not formally set up a consultancy, but used to help people. We easily established a rapport. Our common concerns went beyond income tax. After some time, he moved to a house slightly further away. Still, we kept in touch and used to meet sometimes. I attended the weddings of his sons. Then came a time when our telephone calls became fewer in number. One day, a call came from the family to inform me of his death. I have not got over the shock and a sense of guilt for not having contacted him. There is a very important event for which I am thankful to Nanoo, which he might not have known. The owners of the place he had rented for income tax-related work, I casually came to know, were Muslims who spoke a sort of Hindustani at home. Suddenly, Jamila came to my mind. A man from there brought her to my house.

With old friend Jameela. (Photo by G. Arunima)

She was living with a brother and his family. We met several times and enjoyed talking about our school days. Just the two of us spent an Onam together. Her younger sister and husband were in the US with their daughter and family. Jameela was keen to visit them but did not get a visa for that. I attended the weddings of her brother's children. Her brother-in-law Azeem Bhai, President of the University College Alumni Senior Citizen's Association, and family are dear friends. While writing this, my memory goes back to the days when Jameela's grandmother waited at my aunt's house, the railway quarters offered to her husband who was a station master. Jameela's father, who was a railway guard, would pick her up from my aunt's house and take her to his home.

Another encounter I still cherish followed an invitation from the Bishop Dr Paulose Mar Paulose Trust. The bishop's first death anniversary was being organized at Thrissur. I presented a paper, 'Women in the Coming Century', to a packed hall. The Memorial Lecture was given by Asghar Ali Engineer, Chairman of the Centre for the Study of Society and Secularism, Mumbai. On his return, he began to send me his publication, *The Secular Perspectives*. I never met him again. I often thought of writing to him, but it did not happen. Years later, I was shocked to hear that he met with a sudden death.

On one of those days, I had quite an unexpected meeting with Fatima Meer – an academic, activist and writer from South Africa. My friend Manu was in a tight spot as she was organizing a conference on

'Women and Society' and the chief guest was unable to make it. It so happened that the film festival was taking place in Trivandrum. I had read in the newspapers that Fatima Meer was here in connection with the film *Making of the Mahatma*, based on her book. We telephoned her, and she readily agreed to our request to inaugurate the conference. Still, to be on the safe side, I went to the place where she was chairing a discussion. As I had feared, she was booked by a friend for a TV programme just before our function. I went with them and managed to bring her to our venue. Manu had kept lunch for us. Fatima inaugurated the function and spent some time with us answering our questions. She was amiable and spoke with the warmth of an old friend. We were sure that we would meet again. Sadly, that also was not to happen.

Around the same period, I came to know many collectives of socially active young women. One was the Forum of Christian Women for Women's Rights. There was the Medical Mission Sisters – a collective of women who wore a sari and went around caring for the needy. One sister I came across everywhere was Sr Annie Punnoose. She rode a moped. Fearlessness and warmth were her strong points. The last time I saw her was just days before she left us for her heavenly abode. There was also the Jumaati Young Women's Collective. Young Nuzrath from the collective often contacted me. They invited many of us from all religions to their office at Palayam for interesting discussions and tasty food. My acquaintance was not limited to women's collectives. I also got involved in the struggles of the fisherfolk fighting to sustain a dwindling livelihood.

As a student, I had an uneasy relationship with Economics, the subject I chose to study. Years later, as an employed woman, I started asking myself why the material on development economics came from places like Sussex and the Netherlands. I learnt from the *Monthly Review* that the Center for Popular Economics (CPE) in the US organizes two institutes – what we may call summer schools – to discuss the domestic as well as the global economy. I was curious and keen to attend the CPE endeavour. At last, I managed it in 1997 with financial support from Mme. Mariam Chamberlain of the National Council for Research on Women, USA. I chose to attend the one where the global economy was to be discussed.

The CPE did not have a permanent place or staff though they had been coordinating the programme for twenty years. A core group of three or four was behind the whole show. The those who took classes or led discussions came from colleges in Massachusetts or elsewhere in the US. The participants included women and men, young and old, students and those who worked in various capacities of community-level activities. The programme took place from 3 to 9 August 1997. The Amherst campus was vast and beautiful. Arrangements for our stay were also good. A huge hall was our dining area. There were plenty of fruits and other food items.

The Director of CPE, Ms Lisa Nelson, inaugurated the institute. Presentations followed. The next day onwards, the sessions started at 8.30 am. On the first day, I attended the workshop on 'The Growing Divide' organized by Marc Bayard of the group, United for a Fair Economy. I was impressed by the young man's grasp of and commitment to what he was telling us. As there were concurrent workshops and classes, one had to choose which ones to attend. My class was on 'The Kerala Model: Can Economic and Social Development be Distinguished?' Not many attended. It was not their fault if they thought that a woman in a sari would not have much to say. Some told me later that they missed my class. The few who came had good comments.

From day one, an African-American woman befriended me. The first thing she told me was that the white teachers and students were pretending that they don't understand my accent. Whether it was true or not, I was not bothered. Anyway, we were together during the breaks and talked a lot. She always wore a cap. She told me that she was a Muslim and did not want to reveal it by wearing a veil. She introduced me to another African-American woman from Boston who was associated with a radio station and interviewed me for it.

I stayed on for some more time and met friends. In Chicago, I had an interactive session with an activist group called India Alert. The topic was 'Indian Women after Fifty Years of Freedom'. It was past midnight when it was over.

While returning, I stopped at Gina and Pankaj's place in Toronto, and also at Croydon to be with Tyrrell and his family. The news of Princess Diana's death came while I was in Canada. When at Croydon, I watched the funeral procession and heard the BBC's running commentary on television.

All this while, I was struggling with the material I had collected for my work on matriliny and was upset that its completion was being delayed. Finally, I managed to finish it and sent it to Sage Publishing House who had published some of my earlier works. Sage published it in 1999, under the title *Matriliny Transformed: Family, Law and Ideology in 20th Century Travancore*. I do not think it was the best that I could have come up with. But under the circumstances my life went through, I could do only that much.

I had been writing in Malayalam for nearly half a century, yet did not have a Malayalam book. So I put together twenty of my articles beginning with one published in the University College magazine, and sent them to D.C. Kizhakemuri, the founder of the D.C. publishing and distributing company in Kottayam. He promptly acknowledged my letter and agreed to publish the book. Though he did not live to see the book, it also came out in 1999. It has a long introduction by my daughter Anu.

These years helped me to get to know many new faces. Meena, a young mother of two children, was running a library with her husband at Ponkunnam in the high ranges. She was also bringing out a little magazine called *Pennu,* the colloquial word for woman in Malayalam. I used to write occasionally in it. She once invited me to her place. The library was celebrating its annual day. The entire locality was involved in the celebration. Sports and art competitions were held; there were film screenings, classes, training for job seekers and interactions with medical doctors. I was to chair a session where issues around women and society were discussed. I was extremely pleased by the event and the ambience it created. We still keep in touch.

I took an early morning train to Kottayam where Meena's friends were waiting for me. Once the function was over, Meena and her husband took me to my old classmate Radha's house in the middle of a forest of rubber trees. The next morning, after breakfast, Radha and her husband took me to Kottayam. I took a bus from there to Chengannur, where Amma's youngest sister lived. She was the only surviving one of Mattemma's twelve children. She made a quick lunch for me and insisted that I reach home before it was dark. I stayed with her for some more time, took the train and reached early enough. Neither the train nor the place was as unsafe as it later turned out to be.

The intellectual atmosphere of those years and the concerns which permeated even ordinary people cannot be forgotten. The university departments, the Ayillyath Kuttiari Gopalan Nambiar (AKG) Centre, the Centre for Development Studies and many others were constantly organizing seminars or workshops. They were not always restricted to what is called development. We discussed language and literature, tradition and modernity. Democratic decentralization was a topic widely discussed. The discussions on decentralization, Panchayati Raj and other topics were not confined to academic gatherings. They sent new messages of democratic rights to the people in general. I was drawn into many of them. I also attended conferences outside the state during this period. These travels never tired or bored me.

As said earlier, Kerala did not have too many non-governmental organizations. There were women's wings of all the political parties. In different parts of Kerala, small women's groups were formed to discuss and deal with their immediate problems and wider issues. In Kozhikode, Ajitha started Anweshi. Initially, violence against women was their main focus. In Trivandrum, Sakhi, initiated by Aleyamma Vijayan, developed into a women's resource centre. Stree Vedi, an independent women's collective, effectively intervened in many socio-political issues with special emphasis on justice for women.

Around this time, a young woman named Hema got in touch with me from Palghat. Her friends from the Revolutionary Feminist Movement came to meet me. They persuaded me to inaugurate their first state conference in Kottayam. Their slogan was: 'Discard the Chains – Let Women's Anger be Unleashed as Powerful Revolutionary Strength'. Another invitation from Kottayam was to participate in a gender sensitization workshop for students, both girls and boys, for four days. The organizers were Christians, and the participants came from relatively less affluent backgrounds. The workshop was held in a rural setting, away from the noise and bustle of the city.

There were also some other individuals, organizations or trusts with whom I came to be associated. How they spotted me remains a mystery. One face I remember is that of Girish Kumar from north Kerala, convenor of the state-level Anti-Capital Punishment Committee. He was also fighting against post-mortems in private hospitals. I was all for non-violence, but I was not sure whether the death sentence should be abolished. He came home many times and I went to many of the programmes he organized in Trivandrum. I have since lost touch with him. P.K. Sasidharan of the Department of Philosophy at Kalady University, while initiating a discussion forum called *Kerala Chintakal*

(Kerala Thoughts), sent me some write-ups. I am genuinely concerned about Kerala but I was not sure whether there was something that could be called *Kerala Chintakal*. Yet we keep in touch and interact on various issues. The Gandhi Smaraka Nidhi and Vakkam Maulavi Foundation Trust drew me into their activities, which I happily attended. Saraswathi Bai and Nanukkuttan Nair of the former, and N.A. Karim of the latter, were friends with whom I interacted frequently. Another group that befriended me and met me often to discuss socio-political issues was the Socialist Unity Centre of India (SUCI).

My travels were becoming quite frequent. That the house was locked up often disturbed me. The idea of constructing a small flat upstairs came to me. While we were away in Delhi, a minor revolution ushered in by Laurie Baker had taken place in Kerala architecture. Traditional architecture in Kerala was certainly simple. What Baker introduced was an environmentally friendly and elegant building style. I came to know a young couple, Sajan and Shailaja, who were his mentees and followers of his style. They willingly agreed to my request to construct a Baker-model house above the single-storeyed house that existed. They did a good job and became a part of my family.

My first tenant was a young woman known to me. Since then, I have had young and not-so-young tenants. There was a young Fulbright Scholar from the US. Her parents and sister came to visit her and had no problem staying with her. There were two young Chinese women who were on their first visit to India.

Towards the end of the 1990s, Anu was on sabbatical for a year at Kyoto University in Japan. She was keen that I visit her. It was also a country I had read about as a child. I finally made the trip to the Land of the Rising Sun. As I hoped that I would be able to attend a conference in Iceland or Norway, I stayed in Japan for less than a fortnight and returned after stopping in Singapore for a few days to be with my niece Maya. Though my stay in Japan was brief, I saw quite a lot.

Anu planned everything like a super tour operator. The country impressed me very much. We toured a lot in and around Kyoto. One could see Buddhist monasteries everywhere. We had entry only to some of them. Some were located on the top of hills. I was amazed to see relatively old women climbing all the steps to pray or meditate. We took a bullet train and went to a faraway locale, where we saw for the first time a temple which was not on the top of a cliff, but on the ground. There was a big tank and we walked into the temple directly from the steps of the tank. It reminded me of a temple we had visited in Kasergode in north Kerala. We also visited the Hiroshima Peace Memorial Museum.

It was the time when the cherry trees were in bloom. We went to the cherry blossom festival. It was different from the flower shows we have where potted plants are brought and exhibited in one place. What impressed me was that women in large numbers, both old and young, walked together along the avenues where the plants stood. There was open space for them to rest, relax and breathe in the beauty which nature offered.

Another interesting experience was the tea ceremony, which we attended more than once.

The discipline and punctuality that prevailed everywhere in Japan impressed me. Buses come to their stops and leave exactly on time. When the train stops at a particular station, there is no commotion; nobody tries to enter before the last passenger gets out.

The twenty-first century began with interesting and unexpected events. Earlier, in 1995, a women's march had been conceived and conducted by a women's group in Quebec, Canada. It was mainly against poverty. Fifteen thousand people greeted the 850 women who marched for ten days to win demands related to economic justice. This was followed by a call for a World Women's March. Women's groups in Trivandrum decided to hold it on 26 October 2000. There was a seminar in the morning where issues related to globalization and women were discussed. Just as it got over, two women came up to me and asked whether I had studied at St Joseph's Convent in Kollam. Of course, I replied. They wanted to know if I remembered Lily Stephen. How could I forget one of my best childhood friends? I don't think that Leela, Lily's sister, knew what a surprise she had brought me that day. She was a retired teacher and headmistress, and was living in Trivandrum.

Early the next morning, I called Leela and we talked at length. Even after decades, there was no problem in revisiting our childhood. Lily had her college education in Trichy in Tamil Nadu, and then joined the Sisters of the Cross of Chavanod Order. She became a teacher and retired as the headmistress of a girls' high school in Munnar in the Western Ghats.

Quite unexpectedly, one day, Leela asked me whether I was interested in going to Munnar to participate in the celebration in honour of the fiftieth anniversary of Lily becoming a nun. I readily agreed. Leela and I went to Kochi by train. There, we were joined by her brother and sister-in-law who came from Hyderabad. The four of us went by car from Kochi. That route was new to me. The scenic beauty along the way captured my soul. Another nun who had joined the Order on the same day as Lily was also being honoured. What I noticed in the convent was that most of the sisters were young. Except for Lily and her companion, the others wore saris. We were warmly welcomed by them. The celebration was grand, serene and solemn. Nuns and priests came from various places. The hall was decorated abundantly with flowers. They were not bought from florists but were nature's bounty. I presented Lily with a rosary. Did she recognize me?

I went to Munnar once again in 2006. This time, my daughter Asha and I went together in a taxi. The purpose was to see the *neela kurinji* flowers which grow wild in nearby hills and bloom only once in twelve years. On the first day, we stayed in a tourist lodge. On the second day, we moved to the convent. The sisters were as welcoming as before. Lily took great care of us. The nuns were amused at the attention she showed even about the food served to the driver.

With Lily Stephen, Munnar, 2006. (Photo by G. Asha)

As we were more relaxed then, she began to talk about my brother and sisters. She also brought out many old photos, some of them in albums and many loose ones. I was surprised to see my old photos. But we did not talk much about the old days. Meeting Lily after so many years, and in a totally different circumstance and place, remains fresh in my memory.

I continued to be engaged in research programmes. A demographer and researcher on migration, Irudaya Rajan, was a friend and he used to call me for many of his programmes at the Centre for Development Studies (CDS). While working on old age, he suggested that I join him and kept aside an amount of money for the project. I did some fieldwork in a place not far from Trivandrum and published the findings as a paper. Again, a surprise awaited me. Carla Risseeuw, a well-known Dutch anthropologist whom I had known earlier, was here. She suggested that the papers from the study could be presented at the panel she was planning in the forthcoming European Conference on Modern South Asian Studies to be hosted by Leiden University.

I had gone to Amsterdam many times, but never to Leiden. The sprawling campus was peaceful. Only bicycles were allowed inside. Our accommodation was within walking distance. A stream flowed through the campus. There was a bridge for those who did not wish to walk through the water. The conference went well. I attended a number of sessions which I found interesting. One or two were on Sri Lanka which was a conflict zone at that time. It was there that I met Silvia Dintino, a friendly and helpful young Italian Indologist who was a friend of Madeleine.

In Paris, I did not stay with Madeleine as she was expecting her nephew. I stayed with Marie Louise, but the three of us met every day for lunch. Madeleine and I often went to her flat and spent time talking. The day before I left for India, we were together till quite late at night. Madeleine came all the way to Marie's flat just to make sure that I had no problem with the metro.

That evening, she narrated a very sweet story, the love story of her parents. It was the early years of the twentieth century when the people in France were mainly peasants. Her father, a young boy, saw a young girl most probably from a nearby village, and liked her. Those were not times when young girls and boys moved around freely. Soon after, he joined the army and left home. He didn't forget the girl. He sent her a letter, but no reply came. When he came home on short leave, he went up to her house and stood outside for a long time. He dared not knock. Actually, the girl was not there. She had gone to another village where a branch of their family had moved. However, the young man was determined and remained persistent. Finally, he married the girl. They had a glorious married life and celebrated the golden anniversary of their wedding. They lived for a few more years, and then both died one after the other. Madeleine believed that her maternal grandmother, who had a small business selling firewood, was never considerate to her father. After she stopped talking, I felt I had watched a movie. I had asked Madeleine several times to write the story of her life. She refused and asked me to write mine instead. That was the last evening we spent together. We were very relaxed too. She was very frail but climbed all the steps to leave me at Marie's.

Within a few years, Marie and then Madeleine left us for the unknown world. Madeleine had retained something of the peasant-world goodness in her, despite leading an intense intellectual life in highly urbanized settings. I have not forgotten the first time I met her. A friendship that lasted for more than sixty years came to an end with her passing away.

I was to make one more long-distance journey, this time to Latin America. Some years earlier a young friend of mine, Gargi Chakravartty, had called me from Delhi and suggested that I become the President of the National Federation of Indian Women (NFIW). My immediate response was that I should not be identified with the Communist Party of India (CPI). She assured me that their presidents were never members of the CPI. She gave examples like the veteran freedom fighter Aruna Asaf Ali. I became the first woman from South India to hold the position of President of NFIW, from 2004 to 2008. I agreed because of my friend's persuasion, and also because I had known and respected many of their senior leaders. I shouldered this responsibility as well as I could, and attended most of their programmes in venues like Delhi, Pondicherry, Hyderabad and Palghat.

It was as the President of NFIW that I went to Latin America. I was a delegate to the International Congress of Democratic Women held in Venezuela in April 2007. There were a few others from India, but since we were coming from different parts of the country, we could not travel together. I loved that first trip to Latin America, especially at the time Hugo Chavez was the President of Venezuela. As compared to Nairobi, this conference had a smaller crowd, but it was as versatile as the former with delegates coming from far and near. A young Russian woman whom I had met at Leiden spotted me. The delegates wanted to meet and support each other, exchange views and, above all, be part of a large extended family. The host country received technical and other support from Cuba. A medical team from Cuba was there all through the conference.

We had many sessions where various urgent issues facing the world were discussed. My memory is that they were not always in the same venue. I participated in several of them. One of my papers was titled 'The Negative Impact of Globalization on Women'. The warmth and eagerness to exchange addresses or emails prevailed throughout.

One day, President Chavez talked to us. He was friendly, even jolly. He told us how the hard life of his mother and sisters helped him get rid of his machismo, and how it converted him into a champion of women's liberation. Some senior women, particularly from other Latin American countries, responded in the same tone, expressing affection and hope for that revolutionary son of the continent.

I was slightly apprehensive about the food I would get there. To my surprise, we were served excellent rice which came from the Far East, well cooked with dishes made of tapioca, raw bananas and similar familiar items.

We stayed a few more days and saw a little more of the country. I went alone to a museum where for the first time I saw installations and fell in love with that art form. At the Caribbean beach, I saw coconut trees, but not as tall as the ones in Kerala. We were surprised and delighted to find ripe mangoes falling right in front of us before realizing that there were mango trees around.

Groups of women engaged in making very attractive handicrafts were a soothing sight in many places. We saw the poor as well as the ultra-rich, hidden behind high walls. It is a tragedy that Chavez left much before fulfilling his dreams and ours too.

Let me stop here and say something about my travels for the love of it, without any conference tagged on. I have travelled or gone on holidays with my daughters, sometimes with both or sometimes with one of them, to different parts of India and Kerala. One of the most impressive was the Char Dham trip (Yamunotri, Gangotri, Kedarnath and Badrinath) in the Himalayas. The places have become more of a tourist attraction than pilgrim spots. Earlier, pilgrims came either walking or riding on the back of a mule with a young boy to guide the route. Most of them did not have much money. They sought solitude and inner peace and of course Bhagvat *darshan*. Today the pilgrim-cum-tourists want their vehicles to reach the top. To cater to their needs, newer and broader roads, shopping centres, eateries and even helipads have been constructed. They have conquered and destroyed the serene mountains.

Most of my trips in Karnataka were with Asha. They include trips to Mookambika temple, Gokarn, Udupi, Moodabidri, Dharmasthala and Mangalore along the coast. Later we also visited Shravanabelagola, Belur and Halebidu. Each one of them took me to the grandeur of an awe-inspiring ancient world. They were not sites for careless passers-by. These are places that demand fresh reading and serious thinking from our side. Unfortunately, in a fast-moving life, this is not possible for everybody. I was rather tired when we went to Hampi and so I could not reach every corner of that ancient empire. Still, my mind traversed through the times of the Vijayanagara empire.

When I go to spend time with Anu in Delhi, she makes it a point that we go on a short holiday. Often it would be to the Himalayas. Kasauli in Himachal Pradesh and Ramgarh in Uttarakhand, both gave us moments filled with mesmerizing scenic beauty and peace. In Chail near Kasauli, we climbed up several steps to see the world's highest cricket ground. To me and perhaps many others, the first place that the word Rajasthan triggers in my mind would be Jaipur or Udaipur. One may be familiar with Pushkar and the Thar Desert. We may also remember their colourful costumes, songs, dance and handicrafts. But the one place that amazed me beyond words was Ramgarh in Rajasthan.

I had not heard about Ramgarh, Shekhawati before. While going to the place where we were to stay, I realized that we are in an abandoned settlement with monuments and North Indian-style *haveli*s, temples and other gigantic structures huddled together. It was the settlement of a highly successful merchant community. The young owner of the place we stayed at had done a remarkable job restoring his *haveli*.

My travels for professional purposes had not ended. Early one morning, a telephone came from distant Mussoorie. The caller, Saroj Arora, was from the Lal Bahadur Shastri National Academy of Administration. Their Centre for Rural Studies was organizing a workshop mainly to discuss contract farming and tenancy reforms. She insisted that I should not decline her request. Another trip was to Allahabad where my old friend Kalpagam called me to be part of a seminar on Rural Women and Development in her Institute. This enabled me to see Anand Bhawan, the ancestral home of Jawaharlal Nehru. We went sightseeing and saw the River Ganga. In connection with the biennial conference of the Indian Association of Women's Studies, I had gone to places like Pune and Hyderabad. But Bhubaneswar and Wardha turned out to be my dream locations. In the first, I stayed for some days after the conference. Besides the Puri Jagannath temple famous for the Rath Yatra and Konark, I saw quite a bit of rural Orissa as well. Wardha was a place I had known since my childhood. Still, it took several decades before I was able to walk around the Gandhi Ashram and its surroundings.

Through this period, I produced two books in Malayalam. One was a collection of twenty articles on globalization, and its impact on different countries and situations. They were translations of English articles published in the bi-monthly *Dollars and Sense* from the US. The name given to the book is *Maarunna Lokam, Maattunnathar?* (Changing World, Who Makes the Changes?). The other work was a collection of short biographies of twelve women, some dead, from different countries, engaged in totally different occupations. I chose those women who taught me that women's honour and safety depend on their self-confidence, complete faith in their stand and fearlessness more than law and policing. The title given to this book is *Ivar Vazhikaattikal* (Here Are the Guides or They Show the Way). One of the women included in this is a Japanese woman who even at a very advanced age was at the forefront of struggles against nuclear wars and advocated peace. Most of what I found about her life was in the Japanese language. By sheer luck, I got in touch with a Japanese woman artist who helped me with the translation. Nakano is today a member of the family.

The Kerala I left in the early 60s was different in many ways from the Kerala to which I returned by the late 80s of the last century. One field that had undergone great transformation was education. In those thirty years, many more schools and colleges had come up in the state. Uniforms and school bags identifying the schools had become common. So too school buses. Private schools and colleges made their presence felt in a big way. The entry of educational institutions even into the remote parts of the state enabled large numbers of girls and young women to have access to education. This period also saw education becoming more expensive. I am not certain whether these schools with many more facilities have raised the children's curiosity and thirst for knowledge more than in our times.

Over time, educated middle-class parents have come to believe that only the medical and engineering, particularly IT, branches of professional courses can ensure higher earnings and status for their children. The kind of pressure which children today face during the school years, especially with special coaching classes to pass the entrance examinations, was thankfully unknown in our times. The expense one has to incur for all this is very high. The result is that many talented students from relatively poor families cannot aspire to reach higher levels in most professions.

Many, including girls, took to jobs within and out of the state. This included the nurses whose lives I have recounted earlier. It was the gradual birth of the much-spoken-about non-resident Keralites or diaspora. Unemployment did not decrease despite the outflow of both highly educated and less educated to other states and countries.

Another big change was the introduction of tap water for which the consumers had to pay. This development happened mainly in the municipal areas where people earlier had depended on wells, ponds and streams for water. Electricity connection also became widespread during these years.

A neo-rich class was emerging through this period. Suddenly, everything changed. Big shopping complexes and malls which were not even heard of earlier made their presence in a big way. Another visible change was the emergence of builders. In a place where the majority had lived in single-storeyed houses, flats have come up distorting the landscape. Construction materials have changed. They have become not only expensive, but also cause environmental damage while depleting natural resources. The respect and concern our ancestors showed for nature, the environment and fellow human beings have largely disappeared.

Another big change that caught my eye was parental anxiety over their daughters' marriages. Weddings have become lavish affairs. Communities among whom dowry was not practised earlier began giving cars and houses as 'gifts' to the bridegrooms. Weddings have shifted to luxurious halls instead of *pantal*s in the home compound. The arrival of caterers has meant the disappearance of the sound and smell of cooking, chopping of vegetables, grating of coconuts and preparing everything from pickles to the final sweet dishes like *payasam*s. Instead of personally inviting a limited number of people – mainly relatives – to the wedding, quite a crowd has begun to be invited. Even the invitation cards reflect the pomp and wealth of the parents. Kerala which upheld simplicity as a virtue is breaking out of that. The extent to which this will go cannot be predicted.

Major changes have taken place on the political front as well. The Communist Party of India split into two in 1964. When Gopi began to report for the *Patriot* and later for the the UNI, he used to cover both parties. Both parties trusted him as well. During those years, I did not see Malayalam newspapers regularly. I was not able to follow the developments in Kerala in minute detail. But I did check on the election results and knew that the left and the Congress alternatively came to power.

It is hard to believe that a quarter of a century has passed since my 'homecoming'. Did I have difficulty adjusting to the place? Perhaps I have had no time to think of it. I will not say that I was forced into a hectic life. There were occasions when I had doubts and questions. Yet, I am thankful to the large number of women and men who accepted me, as I am, in their midst.

Like many thousands of women, I belong to a generation which dreamt of a beautiful new world where equality, fraternity and peace prevail. We had a sense of pride in our Constitution which upholds democracy and secularism. Till a few decades back, we could cling to those dreams even when we witnessed setbacks here and there.

But things are different now. From a time when the word *peace* loomed large across the horizon, large parts of the world have become war zones. Neither India nor Kerala could keep away the onslaught of violence, greed, corruption and all that we considered anti-social. Large sections of the people in our country and elsewhere remain poor and unemployed. Inequality has widened. Speaking of Kerala, the communists and the Congress who dominated the political scene for more than half a century appear to be fatigued. The Bharatiya Janata Party which came to power at the centre in 2014 is trying hard to make inroads into Kerala politics. In the 2016 State Assembly elections, they could win one seat. A serious observer does not see a healthy, contented, caring society emerging, one that is committed to the welfare of all.

For people like me, it is both sad and difficult to adjust to many things that pervade present-day Kerala. Silence over these developments is increasing and it is adversely affecting society in a debilitating way.

Yet I hear murmurs, voices of protest and demands for change, assuring me that I can leave with a smile and hope . . .

❖

Epilogue

In the Prologue, I have mentioned that there was a time when I thought that everybody has a story to tell. My first memories are of childhood, running around the compound watching flowers and butterflies, or floating boats made of paper in the puddles near the house or around the trees. Perhaps these images rush to my mind when I think of my story because such lively activities are rarely a part of the childhood of today's children.

It took a long time to start working on my life story. But once I began to write, I realized that writing one's own history is different from writing a report or a thesis. A narrative like that comes with an idea of the outcome. There would be an outline. Even while collecting the data, one would have an idea, perhaps vague, of what it is going to become. You sit down to give final shape to the data. Everything falls into place easily – the introduction, acknowledgement, chapters, conclusion . . .

An autobiography is different. Even for those who have meticulously written diaries and saved them carefully, it poses difficulties. It may differ from person to person. There may be some who prefer to write their story at a relatively early stage in their life. Some may write only about their professional life or their years in service.

I too have kept diaries off and on. But for various reasons, I did not find them very helpful. The fault is mine. They were not saved in one place. Some could be lost. I started writing this story of mine quite late in my life. I found too many events – personal, social and professional – heaped up in front of me. What to include was a challenging question. My younger days were the easiest. No diary, no notes. All I had with me were notebooks in which I had copied paragraphs from books I read, proverbs and patriotic songs. I also kept a book made of blotting paper, on which the leaves and flowers I collected from different places have found a resting place. Will the readers of this book, including children, be interested to see my collections? My childhood had its charm, innocence and freedom to the extent that was permitted at that time. Words flowed from my mind.

My young adult days ran parallel to our country's freedom struggle. *Charkha*, khadi and new reading material made their way into our lives. However, I was far away from the places where the real action happened. Even now, it remains a mystery how the news of those struggles, fasts and arrests reached us. Those were days when news and information did not flood our lives as today.

It was in the later years that life became serious and demanding in various ways. I realized that 'my story' cannot be an isolated history. My family, friends, neighbours, colleagues and several others were part of my activities and life. To include them and yet keep it 'my' story had its challenges.

In this journey, there are some persons whom I lost touch with and then rediscovered. There are several others with whom I have lost touch and never heard from again, for no fault either of theirs or mine. Still, it continues to bother me. Now that the book is nearly done, I have become aware of the large number of people and events that have not found a place in it. They are not insignificant to me. I tell myself that in this long journey of life, it is inevitable.

Reuniting with Jameela and Lily, whom I had lost touch with after school were unforgettable moments. It was Jameela I rediscovered first. It was through Vally that I was able to get in touch with her. We met many times and spent time talking about many things. After Amma's death, just the two of us had more than one Onam *sadya* at my place. She liked vegetarian food. She loved travelling, but could not manage a trip to the US to visit her sister as she was denied a visa. Jameela was very keen to be with her sister and family for a while. The way in which I rediscovered Lily, already told, reads like a thriller.

There are some moments which I can remember only with a sense of shock. I am yet to get over what happened to Seetha, one among the 'gang of four'. She was living alone in Guruvayur. She was very close to her sisters' children but did not want to be a burden to anyone. We always kept in touch. We used to call each other regularly and talk about all kinds of things. We also laughed a lot. I called her once on her mobile phone late in March 2014. There was no response. I repeated the call after a few days. Again, no response. I got worried. I found out the telephone number of a relative of hers who was in Guruvayur. The worst I expected to hear was that she was hospitalized, but no. She had died in mid-February. I never came to know of her passing away, though a close friend of hers lived nearby and knew me well. She didn't call me then or even later, though she had attended Seetha's funeral. I called Vijayamma and Leela and we talked about our times together.

As my mind wandered, the face of one of my uncles, one of Acchan's many cousins, suddenly came up. He had settled down in Trivandrum after retiring from long service in an important job in Calcutta. Though he did not talk about it, I saw his difficulty in coping with his wife's illness and death. Sometimes he called me many times a day just to ask what he should do. Earlier, I had read two of his articles in Malayalam in a journal. I suggested that he write similar pieces. But he did not try. Sometimes I asked him to water his plants. I don't think he did that either. I have witnessed many similar moments when an individual loses grip over his own life.

An incident that I found difficult to write about was the death of my nephew, my brother's son Ramakrishan, at a very young age and that too in faraway Bali in a motorbike accident. As a naval officer, it was his first trip away from India. Everybody at home was waiting to hear stories of the journey on his return; instead, it was the dead body that came. His parents aged and their hair turned grey overnight. A friend of ours in Delhi who had met him several times said that he should have been a poet. His death was a cruel realization that we have no control over life.

I felt the outpourings of all these persons, events and memories at a moment when I thought I written the last line of my story. They were not hidden somewhere. Life has several layers, I feel. I shall never succeed in penetrating the innermost. Still, there are places and people that haunt me.

I have wished to go once again to certain places I visited. It has not always happened. Australia and South Africa are two countries I was keen to visit. It may not happen. I should not complain. For a girl who grew up in Kollam, I have seen quite a bit of the world.

I have been a relatively healthy person. When I was very young, I used to come down with a fever once a year. That bothered me because

I had to rest at home. A light diet and rest would bring me back to normal life. In the same period, I became a victim of an ailment called *neerilakkam* in Malayalam. All of a sudden, I would start scratching my body. Sometimes I would break out in a sweat and fatigue would put me to sleep. This continued for several years. I even thought that it would be the cause of my death. That has not happened.

Some years ago, I began to feel uncomfortable in my back and went for ayurvedic treatment at a physician's clinic I came to know after returning to Kerala. It was about 10 kilometres from my house and I could easily drive there. A few years later, weight loss embraced me. I was asked to test my blood sugar, cholesterol and some related indicators. An expert in such matters advised me against any rigorous treatment but asked me to be strict with food intake. I have been a vegetarian and with my nature cure background, my food has been generally *satvik*.

After all this, it was detected that I was suffering from a weakening of the backbone. Calcium deficiency was given as the reason. Physiotherapy was suggested. As I do exercises daily anyway, I did not go for that. Asha found out that swimming would help. It was something I had never engaged in. Her persuasion succeeded. I learned to do some exercises standing in water and walking inside the pool. I never swam, the main reason being that I did not manage to use the pool for a sufficiently long stretch of time. The fault was not mine. The public pools in the city began to be closed in the name of renovation.

Then, we began to go to the Museum grounds for a morning walk. People start coming there as early as 4 or 4.30 am. By the time we reached there around 7 am, there would be a huge crowd, women and men, young and old. Some come in groups. It has been five years since I started this. It has certainly helped me. My self-confidence has improved. After walking for some time, mostly taking two rounds, I generally move to the inner circle where there are benches. I sit on one of them around the bandstand and do some exercises. I look at the various trees. Here and there are some palms, but the majority are trees which differ in height, size and shape of leaves, even in their shade of green. The original homes of some of the trees are faraway continents. Many are flowering trees. Many have beautiful flowers that resemble nose-rings or earrings. Some have a captivating fragrance too. To see the morning sun emerge through these leaves and flowers is a glorious sight.

Just like the trees, the people who walk there also captured my interest. I have observed that the average height of women and men in Kerala has increased. Still, there are short people, thin or fat, with faces that are oval or round like the moon. The strangest sight is that except for a handful, the mobile phone has become an extension of the body for a majority. There is no age, sex or class difference in this. Often, while walking, I feel that a group of people is about to overtake me. In reality, it turns out to be one person talking through a device fixed to his/her body.

As I began to grow older, I started thinking that time moves faster than earlier. It may not be scientifically true. It could very well be that my body and mind are slowing down. Asha does not like to see me growing inactive or falling victim to the characteristics associated with old age. She has the story of Frances Crowe, a hundred-year-old woman leading anti-nuclear demonstrations in the US, and Fauja Singh, a hundred-and-twelve-year-old man getting ready for his next marathon. She shows me cartoons and stories from the internet to make me laugh and enjoy. She informs me of signature campaigns, again through the internet, for various causes. Both of us support many of them. These are things I did not know at all even as an adult.

Would I have vegetated if the above things were not there to interest me? I am not sure. I used to be genuinely concerned and interested in things happening around us near and far. I have reacted in one way or another on several occasions. I cannot believe that concern would leave me that easily.

To my daughters, their Amma is still a fifty-five-year-old, ever-active and cheerful.

I have had my share of pain, loss and sorrow. I have known disappointments and have been let down by unexpected quarters. But none of this could erase the spirit in me. I have never been dishonest in my dealings and that means a lot to me. Let the journey continue till it vanishes like the setting sun . . .

Since this was written a few years ago, I have had a major setback in my health. I have lost my independence. Yet I feel a sense of gratitude that I am among the fortunate ones in this country to be able to afford good healthcare. I am also lucky to have my children take care of me

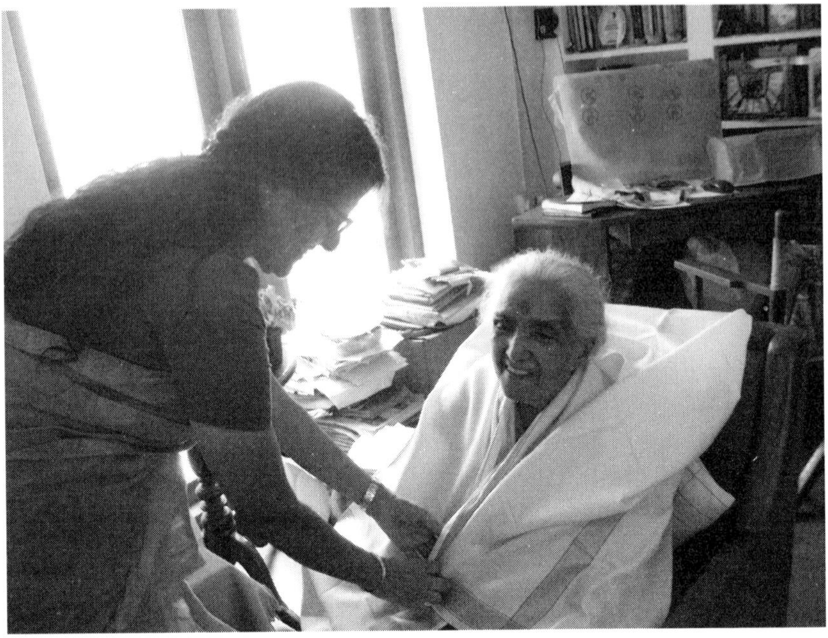

Dr Girija, cardiologist, drapes a *ponnada* during the ninetieth birthday celebrations, 2018. (Photo by G. Asha)

in these times. They even celebrated my ninetieth birthday with great gusto, inviting friends and family for two large parties.

Last, but not least, my doctor of almost three decades, Dr Girija, an eminent cardiologist, has always encouraged me to write and read while taking good care of me physically.

❖

Appendix

Diary entry, 10 September 1968

From economics to writing. Is the distance too long? Perhaps! For me, economics was vital, a medium through which I could serve the country and my people. But it has failed. I am thoroughly disappointed especially after I came to Delhi. Where is the political economy today? Econometricians and mathematical economists and statisticians have come to the forefront. To them, models, equations and high-sounding words are more important. Man does not find a place anywhere in their picture.

This was a perpetual worry for me. It was eating me up, churning my soul. I look around and see many new beautiful things. Many people are prospering. I have improved too.

But the *chapras*is who sleep in the corridors of YB [Yojana Bhavan], the bearer who serves me coffee and the lift bearer who has a constant smile on his handsome face are not changed. They wear the same rough uniform.

Where is the great equality we talk about? Where, where is the equality of opportunity we boast about?

I owe these people a lot. They are the people who threw light on my way, whose respect and smile cheered me out of all despair, whose innocent faces gave me hope and courage.

Life did not smile at them. But they have the greatness to smile at life. What have we done for them? Nothing, should be the honest reply. But I can say 'not much' to satisfy my own conscience.

To them, I owe a lot.

Nairobi Reports, 1985 (via N.V.R. Swamy, PTI)

FROM UN DECADE FOR WOMEN KICC NAIROBI 15.07.85
TO TELEX 312500 PTI INDIA

EX NVR SWAMI, NAIROBI
FROM
SARADAMONI, NAIROBI, JULY 15 (PTI)

THE MAIN PLENARY HALL OF KENYATTA CONFERENCE CENTRE CONSTRUCTED IN 1969 AND WHICH HAD BEEN THE VENUE OF MANY INTERNATIONAL CONFERENCES WITNESSED THE OPENING OF A HISTORIC MEETING - THE WORLD CONFERENCE TO REVIEW AND APPRAISE THE ACHIEVEMENTS OF WOMEN'S DECADE. THE HALL WAS CROWDED BY DELEGATES FROM MORE THAN 140 COUNTRIES, OBSERVERS AND MEMBERS OF THE MEDIA.

IN HIS STATEMENT TO THE CONFERENCE THE UN SECRETARY GENERAL OBSERVED THAT THE GATHERING HAS TO KEEP TWO PURPOSES IN MIND: FIRSTLY TO EVALUATE THAT PROGRESS MADE DURING THE DECADE IN IMPROVING THE SITUATION OF WOMEN AND IN DOING SO, TO IDENTIFY THE OBSTACLES PREVENTING THE FULL REALIZATION OF ITS OBJECTIVES : SECONDLY, ON THE BASIS OF THIS APPRAISAL, TO ESTABLISH PRIORITIES AND STRATEGIES FOR OVERCOMING THESE OBJECTIVES IN A PRACTICAL AND REALISTIC MANNER "IN ADDRESSING THIS IMPORTANT TASK". HE ADDED, "WE HAVE BEFORE US THE OVER-ARCHING CONCEPT OF THE DIGNITY AND WORTH OF THE HUMAN PERSON, WHICH IS ONE OF THE BASIC PRINCIPLES OF THE U.N CHARTER." PRESIDENT ARAP MOI OF KENYA OFFERED A WARM WELCOME TO THE GATHERING AND OFFICIALLY DECLARED THE CONFERENCE OPENED. HE EXPRESSED GREAT HOPES THAT THIS HISTORIC CONFERENCE WOULD RESULT IN SUCCESSFUL OUTCOME. HE ADDED THAT THE WELL BEING OF THE ENTIRE MANKIND DEPENDED UPON THE IMPROVEMENT OF THE POSITION OF WOMEN.

MS. MARGARET KENYATTA WAS LATER UNANIMOUSLY ELECTED PRESIDENT OF THE CONFERENCE. AUDIENCE WELCOMED THIS WITH THUNDEROUS APPLAUSE.

FROM DR. SARADAMONI, NAIROBI, JULY 16 (PTI)

WITH THE INAUGURATION OF THE UN END OF THE DECADE WOMEN CONFERENCE YESTERDAY, NAIROBI HAS BECOME THE POINT TO WHICH THE WHOLE WORLD LOOKS TO. ONE OF KENYA'S PRINCIPAL DAILIES "NATION" BROUGHT OUT A 20 PAGE WOMEN CONFERENCE SUPPLEMENT. BOTH KENYATTA CONFERENCE CENTRE WHERE THE OFFICIAL CONFERENCE IS TAKING PLACE AND THE UNIVERSITY CAMPUS AND HALLS WHERE THE NGOS ARE HOLDING THEIR WORKSHOPS, PANELS AND EXHIBITIONS ARE BUBBLING WITH LIFE AND ACTIVITY. ONE HEARS DISAPPOINTING AND DISTURBING COMMENTS FROM PARTICIPANTS. MANY HEADS OF DELEGATIONS ARE SAID TO BE EITHER FIRST LADIES OF THEIR RESPECTIVE COUNTRIES OR CLOSE RELATIVES OF TOP POLITICIANS AND ADMINISTRATORS.

* * *

FROM DR. SARADAMONI, NAIROBI, JULY 17 (PTI)

IN HER STATEMENT TO THE ASSEMBLY, THE HEAD OF THE INDIAN DELEGATION SMT. MARATHAKAM CHANDRASEKHARAN SAID THAT INDIA HAS, AT ALL TIMES, BEEN AN ACTIVE MEMBER OF THE WORLD COMMUNITY WORKING FOR THE DEVELOPMENT OF WOMEN. SHE REFERRED TO THE NON- ALIGNED CONFERENCE WHICH WAS HELD IN DELHI IN APRIL 1985 AND SAID THAT THAT CONFERENCE REJECTED THE NOTION THAT SUBSTANTIAL IMPROVEMENT IN THE ECONOMIC CONDITION AND SOCIAL STATUS OF WOMEN CAN BE OBTAINED UNDER CONDITIONS OF GROWING RELATIVE INEQUALITY OR ABSOLUTE POVERTY IN THE COUNTRY. THAT CONFERENCE RECOGNISED THAT THE ROLE OF WOMEN IS A DYNAMIC FACTOR AND MUST BE RECOGNISED AS A VALUABLE ASSET. THE STATEMENT FROM THE INDIAN DELEGATE ELABORATED THE LEGAL, EDUCATIONAL AND SOCIAL MEASURES TAKEN IN INDIA SINCE INDEPENDENCE TO IMPROVE THE STATUS OF WOMEN. THE WORK PARTICIPATION RATE FOR WOMEN HAS INCREASED AND IN PROFESSIONS LIKE LAW, MEDICINE, ENGINEERING AND PUBLIC SERVICES WOMEN HAVE AN INCREASINGLY LARGER SHARE. HOWEVER SHE ADDED, " I AM EXTREMELY CONSCIOUS THAT WE HAVE A LONG WAY TO GO." SHE

ADDED THAT DEVELOPMENT IS INTERLINKED WITH ECONOMIC STABILITY. THE INDIAN STATEMENT MADE POIGNANT REFERENCE TO THE REGIONS OF THE WORLD WHERE ADVANCEMENT OF WOMEN IS "IMPOSSIBLE WITHOUT A RADICAL CHANGE IN THEIR POLITICAL AND SOCIAL ENVIRONMENT." THE PROBLEM OF WOMEN AND CHILDREN LIVING UNDER THE APARTHEID REGIME OF SOUTH AFRICA AND NAMIBIA AND THOSE OF PALESTINE WOMEN IN THE ARAB TERRITORY OCCUPIED BY ISRAEL ARE PARTICULARLY ACUTE AND DESERVE URGENT ATTENTION, SHE ADDED. "THIS CONFERENCE IS AN OCCASION TO EXPRESS OUR SOLIDARITY WITH ALL WOMEN AND CHILDREN UNDER APARTHEID AND TO SUPPORT THEIR LEGITIMATE ASPIRATIONS FOR FREEDOM AND HUMAN DIGNITY." THE LEADER OF THE INDIAN DELEGATE MADE SIMILAR PLEA THAT THE PALESTINIAN PEOPLE MUST BE ALLOWED TO RETURN TO THEIR HOMELAND AND DETERMINE THEIR FUTURE BY THEMSELVES. SHE WANTED THE INTERNATIONAL COMMUNITY TO EXERT ALL EFFORTS TO STOP FURTHER UPROOTING OF PALESTINIANS FROM THEIR HEARTHS AND HOMES.

***

FROM DR. SARADAMONI, JULY 17 (PTI)

WOMEN OF THE WORLD WANT PEACE AND THEY REALISE THAT THERE CAN BE EQUALITY AND DEVELOPMENT ONLY IF THERE IS PEACE. THE GOALS OF THE DECADE AS SET BY UN WERE EQUALITY, DEVELOPMENT AND PEACE. MS LETICIA SHAHANI, SECRETARY GENERAL OF THE WORLD CONFERENCE IN HER STATEMENT SAID," THERE IS NO QUESTION THAT PEACE THE THIRD GOAL OF THE DECADE, LOOMS LARGE IN THE MINDS OF PEOPLES THE WORLD OVER, THE LINKAGES OF PEACE TO EQUALITY AND DEVELOPMENT ARE SELF EVIDENT THESE DAYS. -- WORLD PEACE WOULD RELEASE SIGNIFICANT ECONOMIC AND HUMAN RESOURCES, CURRENTLY USED FOR DEFENCE PURPOSES AND SO SORELY NEEDED TO PROMOTE SOCIAL DEVELOPMENT THUS BENEFITTING SOCIETY AS A WHOLE.

***

FROM DR. SARADAMONI, NAIROBI, JULY 18

PEACE SONGS RENDERED THE AIR IN BOTH THE RALLIES. ENGLISH AND SPANISH WORDS COULD BE HEARD TOGETHER. "WE SHALL OVERCOME" IS A FAVOURITE SONG IN THE CAMPUS. To THAT IS ADDED, "WE SHALL MEET AGAIN, WOMEN OF THE WORLD, UNITED AND STRONG WE WILL MEET AGAIN, WE SAY."

DURING THIS TIME, A GROUP OF INDIAN WOMEN WERE BUSY DISTRIBUTING HANDOUTS ON THE BHOPAL TRAGEDY.

THEY PUT UP A BANNER, "WAR DESTROYS BUT MULTINATIONALS TOO" AND WERE BUSY COLLECTING SIGNATURES FROM PARTICIPANTS TO SUPPORT THEIR DEMANDS INCLUDING ASKING UNION CARBIDE TO PAY THE SAME COMPENSATION AS THEY WOULD IN THEIR OWN COUNTRY.

* * *

FROM DR. SARADAMONI, NAIROBI, JULY 24 (PTI)

IN A CROWDED PRESS CONFERENCE, MS. LETICIA SHAHANI, GENERAL SECRETARY OF THE UN END OF THE DECADE WOMEN CONFERENCE GAVE OUT A POSITIVE MESSAGE TO BE CARRIED BY THE MEDIA, IE TO TREAT THE DECADE AS A SYMBOL AND AS A MECHANISM. SHE WAS EMPHATIC WHEN SHE SAID THAT THE IMPORTANCE OF THE DECADE SHOULD NOT BE MINIMISED. IT GAVE NGOS AND INDIVIDUALS GREATER OPPORTUNITY TO FOCUS ON WOMENS ISSUES AND CONDITION AND DRAW THE ATTENTION OF THE WORLD. THE DECADE ALSO CREATED A MECHANISM THROUGH WHICH THE GOVERNMENTS OF MEMBER STATES HAD TO REPORT TO THE UN ABOUT THE CONDITION IN THEIR RESPECTIVE COUNTRIES. MANY NGOS AND INDIVIDUALS HAVE DURING THE TIME UNDERTAKEN INTENSIVE STUDIES AND RESEARCHES THROUGH WHICH WOMENS CONDITION HAVE BEEN HIGHLIGHTED. THIS STEADY AND CONSTANT EVOLUTION OF INFORMATION HAS HELPED RAISE WOMENS ISSUES WHICH REMAINED TILL THE BEGINNING OF THE DECADE WAY DOWN IN THE PRIORITY LIST. SHE SAID THAT WE HAVE TO BE GRATEFUL TO UN FOR DECLARING THE DECADE WHICH BROUGHT THOUSANDS OF WOMEN TO NAIROBI AS MEMBERS OF

THE NGO FORUM AS WELL AS PART OF THE OFFICIAL DELEGATION AND ALSO PART OF THE MEDIA.

DESPITE MS. SHAHANIS POSITIVE APPROACH IN VIEWING THE DECADE SHE DID NOT FORGET THAT THERE IS ANOTHER SIDE TO ALL THE PROGRESS MADE DURING THE TEN YEARS. ALL THE MEMBER STATES AND THEIR GOVERNMENTS HAVE NOT RESPONDED EQUALLY IN IMPLEMENTING THE ACTIONS TO BE TAKEN TO ACHIEVE THE GOALS NAMELY EQUALITY DEVELOPMENT AND PEACE, WHICH OBVIOUSLY INCLUDED EDUCATION HEALTH AND EMPLOYMENT. IN ONE SENTENCE WHAT SHE WANTED TO CONCLUDED WAS 'YES, THERE HAS BEEN PROGRESS, BUT MUCH MORE IS TO BE DONE." AS ONE EXAMPLE SHE REFERRED TO THE PROMISE TO ERADICATE ILLITERACY BY 2000. WHICH IS YET A FAR OFF GOAL.

Excerpt from a letter by Professor Wei Fung Chiang from China, November 1986

浙江省文史研究馆

China, there have been many persons striving to go to India. most of them pretended to be either as good friends of the Indian people or as great scholars familiar with the Indian culture. But in the old days, who would like to go to the oppressed and depressed India? It was I alone, with the deep feelings toward the Indian people, volunteered to go to India and study in Visva Bharati in spite of a great deal of troubles. I was the first Chinese student sent to India by our government, and was the only Chinese ~~disciple~~ student of Gurudeva Tagore in Santiniketan, was the only Chinese disciple of Mahatma Gandhi in Wardha and was the only Chinese schoolmate of Indira Nehru in Visva-Bharati. I had shared the pains and pleasures with the Indian people through the 30s (1933–1939), but I couldn't find any position in the cultural interchanges between India and China. I was forgotten by all until in October 1984, our party leader Mr. Hu Yao-bang general secretary of the Communist Party, introducing my history in India to the people and urged me to do much in the improvement of cultural and friendly relationship between the peoples of India and China.

International Institute organized by the Centre for Popular Economics (CPE) at Amherst, 3–9 August 1997

Three sets of classes, one discussing the US or domestic economy and two others discussing the international economy ran simultaneously for all the days. I attended one of the International Institutes. The CPE has been organizing these for nearly twenty years. They have no building or permanent place of their own. So far, these activities were organized in Amherst as the original organizers who still remain on the staff mainly came from the University of Massachusetts and colleges in the region. However, the total strength of the staff, which is about 50, is drawn from different parts of the USA. They have, besides training in political economy, experience in anti-war and environmental struggles, etc.

The programme was inaugurated on 3 August 1997. Apart from the welcome speech and orientation by Ms Lisa Nelson, the Director of CPE, there were presentations on three important aspects of the economy, viz. downsizing, global development, experiences in cooperative community development and global warming.

From 4 to 8 August, there were regular classes starting from 8.30 am. In my class – the International – there were two teachers, Emily Kawane and Christian Weller, who alternated between them to introduce the aspects of the international economy which were to be covered. There were about sixteen participants in my class, women and men, young and old. There were some students and academics in the whole Institute, but the majority were activists working at different levels in various community activities. This did not create any difficulty in the functioning of the classes which were more or less academic.

On 4 August, there was a special lecture on 'Health Care in America: Why Markets Don't Work', in the evening. It was given by Ms Elain Bernard of the Harvard Trade Union programme. The talk was brilliant and was received well.

On 5, 6 and 7 August, besides the regular classes which lasted from 8.30 am up to lunch and then between 1 to 1.45 pm, there were several concurrent workshops. Though all of them were equally useful and interesting, we had to choose one. On the first day I sat in the workshop on 'The Growing Divide' organized by Marc Bayard of United for a Fair Economy. The unassuming young Marc came fully prepared and showed clear grasp of what he was presenting. In the evening, 7–8 pm, he again talked on 'Teaching Techniques for Popular Economics', but I had to choose another class where 'Gender and the International Economy' was being discussed.

In the concurrent workshops on 6 August, I myself gave a class on 'Kerala Model – Can Economic and Social Development be Distinguished?' There were not too many participants, but those who came showed interest and later some persons told me that they had missed it. I have to believe that my arguments were well taken.

On 7 August, I attended during the concurrent workshop time, the one titled, 'Ask me Anything about the International Economy' by Jerry Epstein, a senior staff member of CPE. Besides me, there was a participant from Senegal who also gave a talk on the economy of her country.

On the whole, the summer and International Institutes were both useful and enjoyable. I found my co-participants, who were mainly activists engaged in community-level development, eager, committed, sensitive to issues and alert. Most of us did not know each other before we arrived in the classroom. But within a week, we felt so close to each other that we began to have a common vision for a new, but different from the one the establishment is projecting, world order.

There might have been minor lacunae in the organization, but the success of the week made them very marginal.

Joyous Impressions of a Visit to Lahore, 2001

My trip to Lahore was to attend the 2nd Transdisciplinary Women's Studies Conference held between 24 and 28 March 2001 by the Institute of Women's Studies, Lahore (IWSL). We were eight from India. A few of us were going to Pakistan for the first time. Some others had gone earlier, once or several times. I went with enthusiasm, without any preconceived ideas or prejudice; but, like most Indians, I too saw Pakistan as a military state unlike our democratic secular nation. But my experience there has left me with many fundamental questions about our democracy and society, including the status of women.

The conference did not have a formal inauguration with VIPs extolling words of wisdom at the audience. It was opened on the lawns of one of the organizers, a well-known artist Salima Hashmi, with songs and dance to the tune of *dholak* beatings and beautiful balloons sent up to reach the bright blue sky. The rest of the five days were spent at the IWSL. The discussions centred around women and society, covering women's studies, the women's movement, the difference between state and people, globalization, WTO, women and livelihood, peace and plans. Among the participants, there were academics – mainly social scientists, literature and theatre persons, artists-painters, poets, dancers and political activists. Most participants were young. I was very impressed by the boldness, conviction and passion which most of them showed. The ambience created encouraged easy interaction among the participants, whether they came from Afghanistan, Bangladesh, Nepal, Sri Lanka, Karachi, Islamabad, Sindh or India. At the end of five days, a new sisterhood was born.

Though my stay in Lahore was short, I must add that the people we met outside the conference hall – at the Lahore fort, the tombs of Jehangir and Noor Jehan, the food street, the Pathan *durwan* at the Liberty shopping complex, the illiterate young man driving the autorickshaw and the early morning walkers in the park – showed us warmth and never treated us as 'enemies' or foreigners.

Some participants visited Taxila, Islamabad and Rawalpindi. Friends of mine in Delhi had warned me against asking for a visa to any place other than Lahore. I wish I had not listened to them!

Glossary

Acchan	father
Aikya Keralam	Unified Kerala
Amma	mother
ammachi plavu	a very old jackfruit tree
Ammavan	uncle, mother's brother
Ammayi	aunt, mother's brother's wife
amrapali	mango grove in Bengali
anchal	postal service of the Princely States of Travancore and Cochin
angadi	marketplace
anna	coin that was in vogue in British India
annan	Tamil for elder brother
arishtam	an ayurvedic medicine in liquid form
ashram	spiritual monastery
atma	a term used for soul in Hindu philosophy
aval	snack made of beaten rice
avarna	one who falls below the *varna* system, traditionally an untouchable
ayah	nanny in Hindi
badam kheer	a sweet Indian dish
Baisakhi	a harvest festival in North India
bali	an offering made to a dead person or one's ancestor
Baul	Bengali tradition of mystic minstrel singing
bhavati	form of respectful address for a woman
chakram	a coin that was in vogue in Kerala
chama	a kind of millet
chappal	a sandal, footwear

charkha	a device used for spinning thread, popularized by Gandhiji as part of the *Swadeshi* movement
Chechi	elder sister
Cheriyamma	wife of father's younger brother or mother's younger sister
Chettan	elder brother
Chettathi	wife of elder brother
chinthakal	thoughts
Chitta	wife of father's younger brother
Chittappan	father's younger brother
choroonu	a Hindu ceremony in Kerala where a newborn child is fed rice for the first time
copra	the dried kernel of coconut without the shell
crorepati	an Indian usage for an ultra-rich person/millionaire
darbha	a grass considered sacred in Hindu rituals
darshan	offering salutations to the deity in a temple
Dewan	the title used by the head of government in the Princely States of Travancore and Kochi
dholak	a percussion instrument hung around the neck and played with both hands
dosa	a South Indian dish – pancake made of rice and *urad dal*
Ekadasi	the eleventh day following full moon, religiously observed by the Hindus of Kerala
Ekanta Darshan	the privilege of offering salutations to the deity in a temple when no one else is present
Ezhava	one of the 'lower' castes in Kerala
ghat	descending steps at a holy riverside, religiously associated with cremation
haveli	a North Indian mansion
homam	a sacred offering made to the fire
illam	abode of a Kerala Brahmin
jada	a dead body/corpse
jamun	a fruit-bearing tree (*Syzygium cumini*)
jubba	upper garment worn by men traditionally in North India
jutka	a cart drawn by a single horse
kadambam	a tropical flowering tree (*Neolamarckia cadamba*)
Karthika	a festival of lights observed in South India
Kathakali	a classical performance art of Kerala
kayal	backwater

khadi	handspun cloth, popularized by Gandhiji as part of the Swadeshi movement
kheer	an Indian sweet dish
kinnanappam	a sweet snack of Kerala
kirtana	a musical composition in Carnatic music
Kochamma	mother's younger sister
kodi neryatu	a new/fresh upper cloth
konna	a flowering tree (*Indian laburnum*)
Koodiyattam	a traditional theatrical performance art of Kerala
kora	unbleached cotton cloth
kottaka	a temporary arrangement to project a movie
kovil	a shrine or a small temple
kuladaivam	family deity
Kumbham	a month of the Malayalam era, from mid-February to mid-March
kuttikal	children
laddu	an Indian sweet
lehyam	an Ayurvedic medicine
Mahanavami	the ninth day of the Navaratri festival
mali	gardener
maya	a Hindu philosophical concept, literally 'illusion'
Medam	a month of the Malayalam Era, from mid-April to mid-May
mishti doi	sweet curd, a Bengali delicacy
mottathala	fully shaven head
mundu	waistcloth of Kerala
murajapam	traditional recitation of the *Veda*s for 56 days
Nair/Nayar	one of the middle castes of Kerala
neela kurinji	a flowering shrub of the Western Ghats that blossoms once in twelve years
neerilakkam	an ailment similar to an allergy
neryathu	a thin garment that women in Kerala used as a wrap around their upper body
neti, neti	Sanskrit expression meaning, 'not this, not this'
Onam	a festival celebrated in Kerala in the month of Chingam (mid-August to mid-September)
oonjal	swing
paisa	a coin that was used in India, a monetary unit

pallamkuzhi	a children's game
pandakasala	warehouse or godown
pantal	temporary ceremonial shelter erected for festivals or functions
papad	thin fried snack made of lentils
paratha	an Indian bread
patanangal	studies
payasam	a sweet dish served at the end of a meal in Kerala
pennu	colloquial word for woman in Malayalam
Peramma	mother's elder sister
peruthu	an expression meaning 'a lot'
ponkala	cooked food offering to a god or goddess
ponnada	a shawl adorned around the shoulders of a person who is being honoured
pucca	Hindi for sturdy, solid or permanent
puja	worship or offering to a god or goddess
pujari	a Hindu priest
pulpaaya	a Kerala mat made of palm leaves or special grass
puri	a deep-fried Indian bread
raja-pramukh	administrative title that was used in India from 1947 to 1956
raukka	upper garment that Kerala women used to wear
razai	quilt
rosogulla	a Bengali sweet
sadhu	a saint
sadya	traditional Kerala feast
salwar-kameez	garments worn by women traditionally in North India
Sanatana dharma	'Eternal order' or 'eternal duty'
Sardarji	a Punjabi Sikh gentleman
sarkar	government
satvik	wholesome, virtuous and balanced
Satyameva Jayate	national motto of India, meaning 'Truth Alone Triumphs'
savarna	one who falls within the *varna* system, traditionally touchable 'upper-caste' communities
seemakonna	a tropical plant in Kerala (*Gliricidea sepium*)
shamiana	a temporary ceremonial shelter erected for festivals or functions

Swadeshi	a movement within the Indian struggle for Independence which emphasized self-reliance and the boycott of foreign goods
sheeveli	a temple ritual in Kerala where the deity is taken around the shrine
Sivaratri	a Hindu festival observed in honour of God Shiva
tali	an auspicious thread that a Hindu bridegroom ties around the bride's neck on the day of the wedding
tairu-sadam	curd-rice
taravad	matrilineal joint family in Kerala
thorthu	a small towel used in Kerala
Tiruvatira	one of the twenty-seven astral signs
vada	a South Indian fried snack
vaidyan	an ayurvedic physician
Valiamma	mother's elder sister
vallam	a small boat
vattal	a dried snack that can be fried and consumed
veera sringhala	a bracelet generally given to the brave
vibhuti	ash, religiously worn by Hindus on the forehead
Vishu	a Hindu harvest festival celebrated in the month of Medam in Kerala
Vrischikam	a month of the Malayalam Era, from mid-November to mid-December

Place Names

Place names were used differently in vernacular languages and English. After Independence, many of the anglicized usages have fallen out of use.

English	*Vernacular*	*Current*
Alleppey	Alappuzha	Alappuzha
Benaras	Varanasi	Kasi or Varanasi
Bombay	Mumbai	Mumbai
Calcutta	Kolkata	Kolkata
Ceylon	Sri Lanka	Sri Lanka
Cochin	Kochi	Kochi
Madras	Chennai	Chennai
Mahe	Mayyazhi	Mahe
Mangalore	Mangalapuram	Mangalapuram
Palghat	Palakkad	Palakkad
Pondicherry	Puducherry	Puducherry
Quilon	Kollam	Kollam
Travancore	Thiruvithamkoor	Thiruvithamkoor
Trichy	Thrissinapalli	Tiruchirapalli
Trivandrum	Thiruvananthapuram	Thiruvananthapuram